THE
EVIL
THAT
MEN DO

STEPHEN G. MICHAUD

WITH ROY HAZELWOOD

ST. MARTIN'S PRESS ☙ NEW YORK

THE
EVIL
THAT
MEN DO

FBI Profiler

Roy Hazelwood's

Journey into the

Minds of Sexual

Predators

Production Editor: David Stanford Burr

Design by Kathryn Parise

Library of Congress Cataloging-in-Publication Data

Michaud, Stephen G.
    The evil that men do : FBI profiler Roy Hazelwood's journey into the minds of sexual predators / by Stephen G. Michaud with Roy Hazelwood.
        p. cm.
    Includes bibliographical references and index.
    ISBN 0-312-19877-9
    1. Sex crimes—United States—Case studies.   2. Sex offenders—United States—Psychology—Case studies.   3. Sex crimes—Investigation—United States—Case studies.   4. Hazelwood, Roy.
I. Hazelwood, Roy.   II. Title.
HV6592.M53   1999
364.15′3′0973—dc21   98-45537
                                                     CIP

First U.S. Edition: February 1999

10 9 8 7 6 5 4 3 2 1

For Louella and Earl

CONTENTS

THE EVIL THAT MEN DO

ONE

"His Influence Is Everywhere"

You could say that Ted Bundy introduced me to Roy Hazelwood.

We first met on a russet Iowa autumn evening in 1984 in the crowded lobby of a Des Moines motel, where next day Roy and I were to address a professional symposium on serial murder.

The FBI man's presence lent the annual gathering considerable cachet. It also guaranteed the symposium's delighted organizers, a local college's criminal justice program, an SRO audience of veteran homicide detectives drawn to dozy Des Moines to hear the world's foremost authority on sexual criminals.

My invitation had come on the strength of *The Only Living Witness*, the biography of Bundy that I'd published the preceding year with my coauthor, Hugh Aynesworth.

Ted was a figure of consuming interest to criminologists, and ours was the definitive treatment of his strange odyssey.

Once a dark legend throughout the West, a roving, phantom killer who murdered, undetected, for years, Bundy finally was convicted and condemned to death in Florida for the Super Bowl Sunday, 1978, bludgeon murders of two Chi Omega sorority sisters. He received a second death sentence for the throat-slash murder of a twelve-year-old Lake City, Florida, child, whose brutalized remains Ted had dumped beneath a derelict hog shed.

But it wasn't the horror of such crimes that made him stand apart in the minds of the police. Rather, it was Ted's extraordinary success. There were no living witnesses, besides Bundy, to any of his murders. Save for a single savage bite mark Bundy left in the buttock of one Chi Omega victim, there also was not a single piece of incontrovertible physical evidence connecting Ted to any crime more serious than shoplifting. One prosecutor called him "the man with no fingerprints."

A onetime law student and young GOP volunteer in the state of Washington, Ted was handsome, witty, and poised, nobody's idea of a deviant killer. But behind what the late psychiatrist Hervey Cleckley, coauthor of *The Three Faces of Eve*, famously termed the sociopath's "mask of sanity," there was a hidden Bundy—the "entity," as Ted first described him to me: a deviant killer who collected and preserved his victim's severed heads on cabinet shelves in his small Seattle apartment.

It was also the "entity" who sought credit for the murders, even as the public Ted indignantly disclaimed them.

In an effort to exploit this split between the public and private Bundy, Hugh and I asked Ted if he would speculate on the type of offender who might have committed the many homicides for which he was a suspect—put himself in the killer's shoes, so to speak.

Bundy, the supreme narcissist, promptly agreed to do so. He had much to tell.

On the audiotapes we later played for the detectives in Des Moines, Ted carefully explained what it was like to be a serial killer.

He said that a killer comes to hunting humans gradually. The appetite builds from a young boy's undifferentiated anger and morbidity of mind to a search for ever more violent pornography, the visual and written material that Ted believed had shaped and focused his fantasy world.

Then comes the window peeping, followed eventually by crudely conceived and unsuccessful assaults. In Ted's case, these gave way, over time, to a sophisticated taste for the chase and its aftermath: the selection of what he called "worthy" victims, pretty and intelligent young daughters and sisters of the middle class, nice girls whom Ted desired to possess, he said, "as one would possess a potted plant, or a Porsche."

No multiple murderer before or since has so vividly communicated the essence of his urge as Ted did on those Death Row tapes, or taught law enforcement more about the ways of a serial killer.

In the end, Hugh and I would learn, the apparent mystery of Ted Bundy was really only a matter of failed perception. The skulls and necrophilia—Bundy revisited some victims in their woodland graves for days—so difficult to reconcile with his attractive public persona were ghoulish but hardly unique examples of how the sexual criminal attempts to create a fantasy that complements his underlying motivations—in Ted's case, a monstrous hatred for women and a consuming, frantic quest for power—and then tries to realize that fantasy.

To the sexual offender, possession is power, and total possession is absolute power.

Roy Hazelwood taught me that.

When I located Hazelwood that night in Des Moines, he was seated alone at a low table, savoring a nonfilter Lucky Strike and a sparkling glass of iced gin, habits he has since reluctantly abandoned. Roy's gaze was obscured by the amber lenses in his aviator frames—a look he'd acquired in Vietnam—and he was bathed in a haze of blue cigarette smoke.

Clustered in knots throughout the lobby were dozens of heavy-limbed middle-aged men, each with a practiced grip on his own cocktail-hour libation. A glance at their weary eyes and wary posture immediately confirmed that here was a room full of cops.

"Roy Hazelwood?" I asked, approaching the celebrated FBI agent.

"Yes." He stubbed out his Lucky. "You must be Michaud."

Hazelwood rose to extend his right hand. We shook.

"Have a seat," he directed. "Care for a drink?"

Roy wore a spiffy dark blue blazer, open-necked white shirt, gray slacks, and carefully polished black loafers, an arresting sartorial contrast to this writer in old chinos and the assembled homicide investigators in their cop mufti, double knits and short sleeves.

The scene is indelible in my mind, and years later the details still play exactly the same way in my memory. It's humid, and the icy cocktail glasses sweat rings through paper napkins onto the damp Formica tabletop. Ecru tufts of stuffing poke up through a hole in the red Naugahyde seat of my chair.

But what turned an otherwise ordinary night into an ineradicable memory was the conversation with Hazelwood. By evening's end I'd already begun an extraordinary journey, a frequently harrowing fourteen-year exploration across the shadowy nether edge of human behavior, the psychic precincts of the sexual criminal.

This book is the record of that trip.

Police departments from around the United States and Canada had paid $145 apiece for their detectives to attend the Des Moines meeting, a bargain ticket given some of the big-dog crime authorities scheduled to lecture.

Besides the meeting's top draw, Hazelwood, speakers included Cook

County, Illinois, state's attorney William J. Kunkle, Jr. Four years earlier, Kunkle had won a death sentence for John Wayne Gacy, the portly bisexual serial killer and Democratic Party operative who strangled or stabbed to death an estimated thirty-three of his sexual partners, young men and boys, throughout the 1970s. Gacy buried more than two dozen of his victims in the crawl space beneath his house in Norwood Park Township, a northwest suburb of Chicago.

Also in Des Moines was Sergeant Dudley Varney of the Los Angles Police Department. Varney was a key investigator during LAPD's Hillside Strangler case of 1977 and 1978, the string of ten (and possibly more) brutal torture-murders for which serial-killing cousins Kenneth Bianchi and Angelo Buono ultimately were caught and imprisoned.

Another of the presenters was Bob Keppel, chief investigator for the Washington State attorney general's office, and probably the world's most experienced serial killer hunter. At the time of the symposium, Keppel was advising various law enforcement agencies in western Washington on the Green River Killer cases, the serial murders of dozens of prostitutes that remain unsolved today.

Hazelwood brought to the Des Moines meeting an altogether different perspective. A member of the Bureau's elite Behavioral Science Unit, based at the FBI Academy at Quantico, Virginia, Roy's domain is the sexual criminal's mental and emotional planes, the deviant mind's hot zones where lust and rage are fused, and deadly fantasies flower.

No one knows this world better than he.

There are more than ten thousand homicides, rapes, suicides, accidental deaths, and miscellaneous acts of mayhem in Hazelwood's casebook. Among them are famous serial murders, savage mass murders, serial rapes, mutilations, explosions, a couple auto-amputations, multiple hangings, eviscerations, bludgeonings, staged deaths and faked rapes, stabbings, shootings, strangulations, garrotings, electrocutions, and a few poisonings.

Roy acquired this vast experience in the process of transforming the subject of sexual crime investigation—once a scorned and degraded facet of police work—into a professional discipline at the FBI.

"His influence is everywhere," says his friend and frequent collaborator, Dr. Park Elliott Dietz, the noted forensic psychiatrist and a heavyweight authority on aberrant criminality in his own right.

"There are very few people who have influenced any area of criminal investigation as profoundly as Roy Hazelwood has sexual crimes. It is an influence that extends to the research community, to victims, to criminals he has brought to justice, to investigators who'd be lost were it not for the guide roads Roy has mapped out for them."

In 1980, Hazelwood was the first BSU agent from the unit's underground office complex at Quantico dispatched to Atlanta to assist authorities with what became the sensational and highly sensitive Atlanta Child Murders case.

Later joined in Atlanta by his colleague, John Douglas, Hazelwood would be the first to tell local lawmen that their serial child killer undoubtedly was an African American male, probably in his twenties. Although it was clear nearly from the outset that more than one killer was stalking Atlanta's black children and youths from 1979 to 1981, the sexual criminal whom Hazelwood and Douglas conjured from the crime scene evidence was Wayne Williams, twenty-three, a black photographer who ultimately was arrested, convicted, and sentenced to life in prison in conjunction with the Child Murders.

Like all BSU agents, Hazelwood also wrote criminal personality profiles, subjective portraits of aberrant UNSUBs (unknown subjects) drawn from the behavioral clues that those offenders inevitably leave at their crime scenes. Depending upon how rich a trove of behavioral clues is available for analysis, Hazelwood can infer an UNSUB's age, sex, race, intelligence, education level, military history, type of work, car, clothing, marital status, sociability, hobbies, possible arrest record, and erotic preferences in his consenting sexual relationships, among other details of his daily life.

One of the first profiles Hazelwood ever wrote was of a predatory UNSUB who in May of 1978 molested and murdered a little boy in St. Joseph, Missouri.

On the afternoon of May 26, 1978, four-year-old Eric Christgen, scion of a prominent St. Joseph family, momentarily was left by his baby-sitter at a downtown St. Joseph playground as the young woman went into a store for a purchase. When she emerged a few minutes later, little blond-haired Eric was missing.

The next afternoon, Eric Christgen was found murdered in a rugged ravine near the foot of nearby river cliffs, about a twenty-minute walk from where he'd disappeared. He'd been sodomized and then asphyxiated.

The local investigation soon faltered, and a request went to the BSU for help on the case. Working with crime scene photos, police and witness reports, and what he knew about the sort of person who abducts, sexually assaults, and then murders little boys, Hazelwood constructed a word picture of the UNSUB.

Roy surmised Eric Christgen's killer was a white male pedophile, aged around fifty. He arrived at these inferences based upon witness accounts and the BSU's voluminous files on similar abduction murders. The offender's race, sex, and sexual orientation were self-evident. His age was a surmise, supported by the witnesses.

Roy also knew from the BSU's past experience with pedophiles that they do not start acting out, suddenly, in middle age. So this UNSUB, he thought, probably had a police record for past deviant acts with children.

Judging from the apparent strength required to scale the thickly overgrown hillside where he'd taken the boy to kill him, the UNSUB also probably was sturdily built.

Hazelwood wrote further that the killer would likely be a loner who had been drinking the day of the slaying. His inhibitions lowered by alcohol, he had snatched Eric Christgen on an impulse. It was a crime of opportunity, with no prior planning.

If employed, the UNSUB would be a laborer of some sort. He was neither stable nor skilled enough to hold down a more demanding position. Most importantly, wrote Hazelwood, if not stopped he certainly would reoffend within a few months.

In Roy's experience, criminal pedophiles, along with sexual sadists, are the only sexual offenders who enjoy the actual commission of their crimes as much as they do fantasizing about them, before and afterward. They are not remorseful for the harm they do, nor do they experience guilt. They never recoil at their excesses. And at no level of consciousness do they ever wish to be caught.

Hazelwood's 1978 profile of Eric Christgen's killer had little initial impact on the investigation. At the time Roy wrote it, the BSU wasn't nearly so well known as it became in the wake of Thomas Harris's spooky novel, *The Silence of the Lambs,* or the ensuing movie, in which Anthony Hopkins won an Oscar for his bloodcurdling portrayal of the flesh-eating Hannibal Lecter. In 1978, the quality and reliability of the BSU's work were largely unknown.

It was also years after Hazelwood completed the profile that Michael Insco, the prosecutor in St. Joseph, finally read it. By then, the Christgen case had taken a surprise turn as well.

Some months after the murder, Melvin Reynolds, a slightly built twenty-five-year-old resident of St. Joseph, confessed during police questioning that he'd abducted, assaulted, and killed Eric Christgen. Reynolds, an unemployed cook, was sentenced to life in prison in 1979.

"We had a person who'd confessed," says Insco, now in private life as a computer-system consultant to law enforcement. "And profiles were something we totally were unfamiliar with. At that time, all I saw was something come across my desk marked 'Psychological Profile.'"

Three years later, a burly itinerant sex killer and convicted pedophile named Charles Ray Hatcher confessed to the crime. Hatcher intimated he was good for as many as sixteen murders over several years. He'd been fifty years old at the time Eric Christgen was killed, just as Roy earlier had conjectured the boy's killer would be.

Faced with the dilemma of two men now having sworn their guilt for the same murder, Insco began reviewing the evidence, including, for the first time, Hazelwood's five-year-old profile. After reading it through, "I realized that Hazelwood had written a description of Hatcher," Insco says. "The profile matched him on something like twenty-one points. And it wasn't just the fact that the profile fit Hatcher so closely. It also described someone far different from the man we'd convicted. It was a very impressive piece of work."

Insco later visited the BSU, where he met personally with Roy.

"I wish that I had gone there much earlier," he says. "If I had known the kind of work they were doing in the BSU I really think it might have saved an innocent man from going to prison. I don't think I would have believed Reynolds."

Charles Hatcher was sentenced to life in prison on October 13, 1983. The next day, after four years behind bars, Melvin Reynolds was released.

On December 7, 1984, Hatcher was found hanged to death from a wire in his cell at the Missouri State Prison in Jefferson City. Cause of death was presumed to be suicide.

Since that first profile, Hazelwood's research projects have taken criminology where it's never been before, from the malignant misogyny of criminal sexual sadists to behavior that often is neither criminal nor violent nor predatory, but nonetheless poses critical challenges to law enforcement.

When I first met him, Roy, with Dr. Dietz and Ann Wolbert Burgess, a researcher at the University of Pennsylvania, recently had published the first and only textbook ever devoted to autoerotic fatalities. These accidental, often bizarre deaths frequently are mistaken by investigators for murders or suicides. Hazelwood has even identified a subset of such cases, *atypical* autoerotic deaths.

Another of his innovations is the "organized-disorganized" aberrant criminal dichotomy, as familiar to homicide investigators today as handcuffs. The dichotomy is a shorthand way for police to quickly ascertain from crime-scene evidence what sort of UNSUB they seek.

If, for example, a killer brings with him the weapons and restraints he requires to commit the crime, and then takes pains to secrete his victim's body, he is demonstrating foresight, and is probably an experienced, mature, coherent criminal—"organized." If, by contrast, the crime scene is chaotic, and reflects no planning nor any particular care taken to get away safely, the offender is apt to be young, inexperienced, or possibly even psychotic—"disorganized."

When it is clearly evident that an UNSUB is organized or disorganized, that knowledge is vitally useful in focusing the critically important early stages of a criminal investigation.

"The disorganized and organized classification of crimes was fantastic, a brainstorm," says Vernon J. Geberth, a retired New York Police Department lieutenant commander and author of the standard police textbook, *Practical Homicide Investigation: Tactics, Procedures and Forensic Techniques.* "For a police officer to be able to define and describe behavior without using clinical terms was just fantastic."

Besides noting his evident style, my first impression of Roy in Des Moines that Monday night was how different he seemed from the other BSU agents Hugh and I had met. Roger Depue, unit chief during the BSU's heyday of the 1980s, once told me that overseeing Hazelwood and his brother profilers was a little like coaching a football team with eleven quarterbacks.

"They were all different, with very strong ideas about what they wanted to do, and how to do it," said Depue.

Intelligent, highly motivated, hardworking, and good company, especially when they've had a few drinks, profilers tend to combine the giant, fragile ego of the brain surgeon with the tireless intensity of genius-level computer programmers.

They can be a strange bunch.

Depue remembers camaraderie in the unit, a sense of specialness that this platoon of psychological commandos—*Psychology Today* called them "mind hunters"—shared. But the fault lines in the unit also ran deep. There are certain present and former BSU agents it is best not to invite to the same function.

Roy, a natural diplomat, remains on cordial relations with all his old buddies. He's centered in a way that many of them are not. He also maintains a healthy perspective on his work.

Roger Depue recalls that Hazelwood was one of the very few BSU agents who could leave profiling's horrors on his desk each night, and then pick up the burden of reconstructing ghastly murders afresh each morning.

As Roy tells it, the key is not to dwell in the overwhelming evil, but to sequester it or defuse it. He employs one of the homicide investigator's trustiest emotional allies in this battle, mocking irreverence.

Some years ago, after listening to Hazelwood lecture at a conference, an older female psychologist approached him.

"How do you cope with all that violence?" she asked.

"I looked her right in the eye and said, 'Masturbation!'" Hazelwood recollects.

She literally staggered.

"I said, 'I'm joking! I'm joking! I'm joking!' I do the same thing you do. I compartmentalize. This is my job, not my life. I have a home and family and a faith in God."

Another common inquiry: Why the fascination with such extreme criminal behavior?

Hazelwood often senses this questioner's implicit assumption that cops and criminals are two sides of a very thin coin, a connection he emphatically rejects.

"I always answer that one with a question of my own," he says.

"'When you go to the zoo, what is your favorite animal to look at?'

"Some people say, 'I like the snakes.' Others say, 'I like the lions.'

"'Why?' I ask.

"'Because they're dangerous.'

"'Well,' I say, 'that's why I study sexual offenders, because they're dangerous.'"

As the cocktail-hour conversation matured into a genial exchange of stories and opinions, my attention wandered repeatedly to a typescript lying on the table between us. It was entitled "An Analysis of Materials Seized from James Mitchell DeBardeleben," and it rested beneath Roy's gleaming Zippo, emblazoned with the insignia of the Fourth Infantry Division, Hazelwood's old unit in Vietnam. Whenever he lit a smoke, Roy returned the lighter to the transcript, like he was checking a poker bet.

I was intrigued.

"DeBardeleben is a fascinating case," Hazelwood finally said, gesturing toward the report. "It ought to be your next book."

The year before, Mike DeBardeleben, then forty-three, was arrested in Knoxville by Secret Service agents who for years had known him only as "the Mall Passer," a rare solo forger who printed his own bills and passed them himself, principally in malls.

Hazelwood told us that although DeBardeleben was as wily a counterfeiter as the Treasury Department ever encountered. His true dimension as a sort of omnicriminal only became clear after Secret Service agents tossed the two miniwarehouses where he'd stashed his printing gear.

Along with DeBardeleben's Multilith press and plates and inks and unfinished examples of his handiwork, the federal agents also found guns and knives, drug paraphernalia, dildos, chains, handcuffs, K-Y jelly, jewelry, women's bloody underwear, and hundreds of photos of women and girls in various states of undress and consciousness, many of them clearly torture victims.

Then there were the audiotape recordings of the torture sessions themselves. These included one tape in which DeBardeleben himself plays the victim. It certainly is among the strangest sexual sessions ever recorded.

"I want you to do it! Do it! Do it!" he screams on the cassette. "Bite it! Bite it!

"Aw! You're bitin' it right now! Oh, the pain's sharp! I love the pain! Bite it harder! Suck it! Bite it! Make the nipple bleed! I hate myself! I hate myself!"

A three-man Secret Service task force—agents Dennis Foos, Greg Mertz, and Mike Stephens—investigated Mike DeBardeleben. They discovered assaults, murders, kidnappings, rapes, bank heists, drug dealing, flimflams, car thefts, and almost every other possible felony in DeBardeleben's background.

Meantime, the agents invited Hazelwood to analyze the materials seized in the two searches, hoping to gain some insight into the criminal incubus they'd captured almost by accident.

Roy's key finding was DeBardeleben's criminal sexual sadism. For such offenders, sex and suffering are one and the same. This perversion, or paraphilia, is surpassingly unusual, even among sexual criminals. But those who harbor it are the most dangerous of all aberrant offenders. They are the great white sharks of deviant crime, marked by their wildly complex fantasy worlds, unequaled criminal cunning, paranoia, insatiable sexual hunger, and enormous capacity for destruction.

Ten years later, I'd retell Mike DeBardeleben's saga in my book *Lethal Shadow*. But even as Roy first related it, somewhere in the double-digit hours of that Monday night in Des Moines, I already was considering ways of shaping a much different story, this one.

It couldn't happen right away: The subject was vast and detailed, and required an extensive commitment of my time and attention. Moreover, with ten years left before retirement from the Bureau, much of Hazelwood's most important work still lay ahead of him. He would publish pioneering studies of serial rapists and sexual sadists, as well as a separate survey of the former wives and girlfriends of sexual sadists.

He'd also lecture extensively in the United States and Europe, and contribute his expertise to the resolution of some of the highest-profile criminal cases of the past fifteen years.

They include the April 9, 1989, turret explosion aboard the USS *Iowa* in which forty-seven sailors were killed; the false accusations of rape and assault made by teenager Tawana Brawley in 1987; and Toronto's so-called Ken and Barbie sexual murders of the early 1990s.

Through all this time, Roy was my frequent and invaluable mentor. And as I developed and discarded outline after outline for this book, he was a constant source of revelation.

I learned from him that sexual criminals are so varied that almost any encompassing statement about them will be inaccurate or misleading. With serial killers, for example, about the only safe generalization is that an inexplicably large percentage of them are name Wayne or Ricky Lee.

Hazelwood commenced my tutorial where all sexual crime begins, in the fantasy world of the offender.

As he explains it, "I teach police officers what I call Hazelwood's Golden Rule of sexual crimes.

"The crimes are fantasies being acted out. The more complex the crime, the more complex the fantasy and the more intelligent the offender. Most people have no trouble connecting intelligence with a complex robbery. But rape-torture is a depraved act, which they cannot remotely relate to. They therefore resist crediting such offenders with intelligence. This is true even of police officers.

"On the other hand, consider an impulsive offender, the type who walks up, strikes a woman over the head, knocks her down, penetrates, ejaculates, and walks off. You'll probably find this guy is of average, or less, intelligence. He'll have little, if any, criminal sophistication.

"He's only got one thing on his mind, as opposed to this other offender who has all this stuff mixed up with what he *calls* sex. That's the guy who's interesting to me."

We spoke of the importance of ritual to many sexual offenders, particularly the more intelligent ones. Ritual, sometimes referred to as "signature," is any behavior that heightens the offender's psychosexual pleasure. It is not connected to the libido's hardwired component, the procreative urge, or to physiology and hormones.

Instead, ritual is a product of the imagination, a matter solely out of the conscious mind, where an estimated 70 percent of the human sex drive is generated. It is highly individualized, offender-specific behavior.

Roy told me about a serial rapist he'd interviewed who was by far the most ritualized offender he'd ever encountered.

A "power reassurance rapist" in Hazelwood's typology, this man was a highly presentable middle-aged westerner with a master's degree in metallurgy and a comfortable income. Successful as he seemed, he was so totally incapable of interacting appropriately with women that rape was the *only* form of sexual intercourse he'd ever experienced.

He told Hazelwood that he would drive 250 miles from his home to a neighborhood where on previous reconnaissance trips he'd already preselected up to six potential victims. Reason: "If for any reason he failed in an attack," says Hazelwood, "while the police were responding to the first victim he could be raping another one safely in her home."

On nights he chose to commit assaults, he'd arrive in the neighborhood, park his van, and pull on what he called his "going-in clothes": coveralls, a ski mask, leather gloves, and oversize sneakers.

He'd enter his intended victim's house via a preselected window using a glass cutter and suction cup to remove the excised glass pane. Next, he would disconnect every possible light-emitting appliance in the residence, and reconnoiter an escape route. Then he would exit, leaving a window or door ajar as he did, and return to his van, where he changed into his "rape clothes": black coveralls, black ski mask, surgical gloves, and undersize sneakers.

As the rapist reapproached the house, he was alert to any hint that he'd awakened his intended victim. If, for example, the window or door he left open was now shut, it was on to the second preselected victim.

Then came the weirdest part of all. The rapist would head for his victim's bedroom and stand over her silently, counting in his mind in one-half increments—one-half, one, one and a half, two . . ."—until he reached ten.

"At that point," says Hazelwood, "he would leap on the victim, squeeze her breasts once or twice, penetrate, ejaculate, and leave. He said the longest he was ever with any victim was a minute and a half."

He explained to Roy that the rape itself was the least enjoyable part of the experience for him. The reason for counting, he went on, was to put the act off as long as possible.

"Why didn't you just turn and walk away?" Hazelwood asked.

"Mr. Hazelwood," he replied, "pardon me, but after all I'd gone through, it would have been a crime *not* to have raped her."

In Hazelwood's experience, white males of European descent predominate among aberrant offenders to an extent unrivaled in any other crime category, save perhaps white-collar crimes.

"Every single sexual deviation is overwhelmingly dominated by white males," he says. "And most sexually related ritualistic crimes are committed by white males."

As a black male juror in Georgia put it after hearing Roy testify about James Ray Ward, a white murder defendant in whose possession was found approximately three thousand dollars' worth of women's lingerie, all neatly packaged in clear plastic, labeled, and indexed:

"What's wrong with you white guys? Can't you just have sex?"

The more complex and sensational the case, the more likely the perpetrator is a male of European descent.

Roy's research has elaborated upon some long-standing assumptions about the antecedents of criminality. The so-called classic triad, for example — bed-wetting, fire starting, and animal abuse — was posited decades ago as predictive of later violent behavior.

In Hazelwood's work among incarcerated serial rapists, he found boyhood bed-wetting among 40 percent of them, cruelty to animals among 19 percent, and fire setting in 24 percent. Significantly more common in their backgrounds were youthful alcohol abuse, 63 percent; stealing and shoplifting, 71 percent; and assaultiveness toward adults, 55 percent.

The same study showed that sexual criminals most apt to become more violent over time — and thus pose the greater challenge to law enforcement — are those given to sexual bondage and anal sex and, curiously, those who transport their victims in a vehicle.

Addressing sexual assaults from the victim's perspective, he's found no statistically significant relationship between the amount of resistance a victim puts up and how much harm is done to her. Fighting back may scare off a rapist, or it might cause him to escalate the violence.

Nor is there any relationship between the presence of a weapon and injury to the victim. Just because a rapist is not carrying a gun or a knife does not make him unwilling to hurt his prey. Just because he is armed does not mean he will use the weapon.

There *was* one statistically significant relationship. Hazelwood found that when a victim resisted, the rapist remained with her twice as long as when there was no resistance.

Roy's conversations with the imprisoned rapists, particularly one long session he spent at Louisiana's Angola Prison with Jon Barry Simonis, the Ski

Mask Rapist, convinced him that women were receiving potentially dangerous advice from so-called rape experts. The upshot was one of his more influential papers: "Rape: The Dangers of Providing Confrontational Advice," published in 1986 in the Bureau's *Law Enforcement Bulletin.*

The search for a narrative thread through such diverse material led me at last to settle on a thematic organization for the book, a chapter by chapter exploration of sexual criminals and their victims, divided according to offender types, their motives, and their modus operandi.

Which left a final decision: Where to begin?

Roy Hazelwood's personal experience with the world of strange and outrageous human behavior antedates even his toilet training.

When he was just six months old his father, Myrle P. "M.P." Reddick, a hustler and itinerant musician, kidnapped Roy from his mother's home in Idaho and took off for California with him.

"For half a year no one knew where I was," says Hazelwood. "My grandmother later told me that M.P. took me into joints where he was playing, and would sit me up on the bar to attract women. Finally, after six months on the road he took me to his mother, who then returned me to my mother. He was a psychopath. There's no doubt about it."

Another possible starting point was 1958, the year a casual girlfriend, vacationing in Nebraska, was found murdered in a barn. There were indications she'd been slain by Charlie Starkweather, the multistate thrill killer who, with his fourteen-year-old girlfriend, Caril Ann Fugate, terrorized the Midwest that summer.

Although Roy's friend isn't included in the list of Starkweather and Fugate's twelve known victims, "I'm almost sure they did it," he says.

The list of such strange events and peculiar interludes in Hazelwood's life is long. However, there was one organizing event, a single experience that became the touchstone for his career.

In the autumn of 1960, Roy arrived at Fort Gordon, Georgia, for his army officer's orientation course. He had been accepted into the Military Police Corps.

There, on a steamy Georgia afternoon in criminal investigation class, Hazelwood experienced his epiphany, a stunning, full-bore psychic collision with this century's prototypical sexual criminal, the first modern aberrant offender and giant mystery to criminology: Harvey Murray Glatman, the Lonely Hearts Killer.

Says Hazelwood: "I could not *believe* Harvey Glatman."

TWO

The Lonely Hearts Killer

H arvey Glatman hit the front page like a comet.

Before the Lonely Hearts Killer slammed to earth along a Los Angeles freeway in 1958—he was caught after an intended victim, bleeding from a gunshot wound to her leg, grabbed his revolver and held him at bay until police rescued her—sexual crimes of the sort Glatman committed were largely unknown.

Such deviant criminality, plus much less sinister behavior, was both curbed and concealed in America at midcentury by a moral climate hostile to sexual extremes or erotic experimentation of almost any sort.

The conservative cultural consensus extended even to what passed for pornography.

"In those days, people appearing in what was called hard-core pornography still wore masks," Hazelwood recalls. "*Playboy* was new. Mickey Spillane's books were considered explicit.

"In the last three or four pages of *I, the Jury*, for example, Spillane describes a man holding a gun on a woman as she slowly unbuttons her blouse. Beads of perspiration run between her breasts. That was the book that high school guys gathered around to read during lunchtime, and those were the particular pages most frequently read."

Such fare may serve to stoke a healthy male libido. But to an offender such as Glatman, a sexual sadist, it lacks the specific connection between sex and violence necessary for his arousal.

Whether he is a low-order, impulsive criminal who uses violent pornography, in Roy's term, *reflectively*, to construct fantasies around what he observes, or is a generally more intelligent, ritualistic offender who absorbs violent pornography *inflectively*, by incorporating it into an existing fantasy, the softer, less violent the material, the less arousing the sadist will find it.

Ritualistic offenders such as Glatman or Bundy shop assiduously for their pornography, which they regard as among their most prized possessions. The photos or videotapes or narrative passages they select and keep are those that most closely complement their fantasies and deviant sexual practices.

For that reason, a careful study of it can provide investigators with important clues to a suspected deviant offender's ritual, the psychosexually driven "signature" behavior that is consistent no matter how much he may vary his MO.

For example, a rapist may alter how he approaches his victims, or even shift his victim class from, say, prostitutes to hitchhikers or runaways hanging around bus stations. They are, after all, victims of convenience.

But like the metallurgist rapist with his clothing changes and counting ceremony, ritual isn't just part of the crime—it is central to the offense.

Similarly, the pornography he purchases, or makes at home, must tap into that fantasy in order for him to become aroused by it.

Aberrant offenders use pornography to validate their deviance as well. The more they see of it, and masturbate to it, the more their behavior is reinforced.

Bundy used pornography that way. He told us that material in which sex and violence were intertwined aided him in creating inner justifications for his crimes. He even persuaded himself the killings were necessary.

Rare as sexual offenses were at the time of Harvey Glatman's final arrest, they commonly went unreported. And even if they were brought to the authorities' attention, successful prosecutions were unusual.

Hazelwood recalls an episode he encountered in 1962 as a young second lieutenant at Fort Rucker, Alabama.

A staff sergeant's wife reported her husband for sexually abusing his two daughters, aged ten and six. The girls' mother had known about the abuse for twelve months before reporting it.

"I couldn't understand why she didn't report it immediately," says Hazelwood. "And no one seemed to know the motivations for his behavior. No one understood it.

"'Why do you think this guy was having sex with his daughters?' I asked one senior investigator.

"'Well, his old lady probably cut him off,' he said.

"I said that even if that was true, it didn't explain why his wife didn't report him at once.

"'Oh, some women are just like that,' an agent from the Criminal Investigation Division told me."

Typical of the time, the case eventually imploded, leaving no record, other than the permanently scarred victims, that the incest ever occurred.

"I remember investigators saying that the sergeant was a 'sick pervert,'" Hazelwood continues.

"I agreed. 'Yeah, of course.' I didn't know anything about this subject. But I wondered how he'd been so successful in covering up. If he was so sick, how was he able to become a staff sergeant? He got up and went to work every day. He belonged to a church.

"I had a thousand questions that didn't compute with 'sick, weird pervert.' When you say sick pervert, you think of stoop shoulders, green teeth, and strange eyes. You think of Henry Lee Lucas. This NCO looked like everyone else!

"His captain said he'd testify on his behalf. The officer told me that the sergeant had been in his command for two years and was an outstanding trooper."

In the end, Roy recalls, it wasn't a quest for justice but practicality that dictated the case's outcome.

"The sergeant's attorney convinced the girl's mother that she'd lose her husband's income and their on-base housing if he was convicted and sent to prison. So she withdrew her charges.

"That case has bothered me for a long time."

At the time, most law enforcement officers, military or civilian, were reluctant to investigate sexual offenses because they lacked the training to do so, lacked support from their superiors, and feared being tainted among their colleagues for working with perverts.

"It was just one of the sadly neglected areas of law enforcement training," says Frank Sass, a retired FBI agent who joined the Bureau in 1948 and later inaugurated what was known as sex crime instruction at Quantico. "We were all so damned naive that we didn't know what we were talking about. We were sadly lacking in knowledge in those days."

A vivid case in point was Harvey Glatman.

Born in Denver in 1928, he was an athletic, musically gifted boy with jug ears, acute acne, a lopsided smirk, and a reported IQ of 130.

Very early in his boyhood Glatman developed an unhealthy attraction to ropes and bindings. His mother once discovered Harvey alone in his bedroom, nude, with one end of a string tied to his penis, and the other attached to the doorknob. Her son wouldn't say what he intended to do with this apparatus.

When he was about twelve, Harvey's parents began to notice angry red marks on his neck, telltale signs that he was experimenting with autoerotic asphyxia.

Known informally today among teenagers as "head rushing" or "scarfing," autoerotic asphyxia involves temporarily diminishing the flow of oxygenated blood to the brain. The resultant cerebral hypoxia, as it is called, can induce a sense of exhilaration—not unlike the giddiness that pilots sometime experience in the thin air at high altitudes—and is believed by many people to enhance sexual sensations. This euphoric state is most commonly achieved by mechanically compressing the carotid artery and/or jugular vein, often by self-hanging.

Glatman as a youth achieved his autoerotic highs by hanging from attic rafters. How a twelve-year-old Coloradan in 1940 would have learned of such practices is unexplained, although it is possible Glatman discovered cerebral hypoxia in failed attempts at suicide.

The family doctor downplayed the seriousness of Harvey's solo-sex habits, predicted he'd outgrow them, and prescribed sedatives for the boy in the meantime.

Harvey's father took a somewhat harsher view of his behavior.

According to a 1950 report done at New York's Sing Sing Penitentiary, where Harvey later served time, Glatman Senior was "hostile and domineering" and drove the boy into "frenzies of fear by continually upbraiding him for masturbation."

The writer noted that Harvey "was told it would drive him crazy and would rot his brain. He was told his pimples resulted from it, and that the pimples revealed his habit to the whole world. He was told that every time the act occurred he lost the equivalent of a pint of blood."

However terrorized the boy must have been by his father's threats, he was not deterred in his dangerous autoeroticism. When Glatman as an adult couldn't find a suitable female victim, he'd dress up in women's clothes and hang himself.

Such behavior turns out to be recurrent among sexual sadists, the most polymorphously perverse of all aberrant criminals.

Glatman's first arrest came just after high school, in Boulder, Colorado. He accosted girls with a toy gun, tied their hands and feet, and then gingerly fondled his victims. He occasionally robbed the girls, but only for insignificant amounts of money that he never spent.

Then he moved to New York and began committing felony robberies as the so-called Phantom Bandit. After doing five years at Sing Sing, where he received intensive psychiatric care, Glatman returned to Colorado, and then moved on to Los Angeles, where his mother set him up in a small television repair business.

When Harvey left Sing Sing, an optimistic prison counselor wrote that "he is beginning to understand himself, and is making great strides in overcoming his neurosis, although a great deal of work remains to be done with him."

Indeed.

Socially isolated in Los Angeles, Glatman began seriously to connect with his paraphilias, primarily sexual bondage and a rope fetish. Searching for images to serve as raw material for his paraphilic fantasies, he found one source that was plentiful even in the straitlaced fifties—detective magazines.

Glatman later told investigators that he collected detective magazines, "sometimes for the words, sometimes for the covers," which in those days invariably portrayed an ample-chested victim, often bound with ligatures and with a gag in her mouth, helpless and horror-struck, cringing under the menacing figure of a male.

Only after Hazelwood and his longtime colleague, Dr. Park Dietz, published a critical study of such periodicals in 1986 did the tone of these cover illustrations change.

Glatman set about making his fantasies real. He posed as a freelance detective-magazine photographer under the names Johnny Glynn and George Williams, and joined a lonely hearts club in pursuit of potential victims. With sure instincts for the vulnerable, and skills at manipulation, he persuaded these women to disrobe for him, as well as to allow him to bind them for his "shoots."

Glatman tied his knots and wrapped his ligatures with painstaking, exquisite care. Judging from the photographic evidence, it must have required considerable time. Only after the intricate work was completed to Glatman's aberrant taste did he then murder his victims.

After he was caught, the Lonely Hearts Killer claimed to have raped his three known murder victims. However, Glatman also disclosed that he was impotent in the absence of bondage.

Hazelwood believes Glatman may have fabricated the rape story as a means of making his behavior more comprehensible to the policemen who interrogated him. In those days, even veteran police officers weren't likely to understand how for some sexual offenders all that is required for sexual gratification is a rope, a camera, and a weapon.

Bob Keppel writes in his book, *Signature Killers*, that Glatman, again like Ted Bundy and many other sexual killers, kept a box full of trophies—photos of the victims and articles of their clothing to help him relive the killings.

Keppel also isolates Glatman's sexual sadism. "Glatman first photographed each victim with a look of innocence on her face," writes Keppel,

> as if she were truly enjoying a modeling session. The next series represented a sadist's view of a sexually terrorized victim with the impending horror of a slow and painful death etched across her face. The final frame depicted the victim's position that Glatman himself had arranged after he strangled her.

After a three-day trial, Harvey Glatman was convicted of murder and sentenced to death. He discouraged his lawyers from filing appeals. "He told me that he couldn't stand the other guys on death row," Pierce Brooks, a legendary Los Angeles police detective who conducted many interviews with Glatman, recalled to me just before his death in the spring of 1998. "He said they were so stupid that he'd rather be executed than spend the rest of his life around them."

Glatman was put to death in the San Quentin gas chamber in August of 1959.

Roy Hazelwood first learned of the Lonely Hearts Killer in military police training about a year later. It was an astonishing experience for the twenty-two-year-old soldier whose knowledge of the world was largely confined to tiny Spring Branch, Texas, where he grew up.

"Glatman just seemed to come out of nowhere," Roy recalls. "I didn't understand anything about him. I wanted to know why he took pictures of the victims. Why did he tie them in various positions and in various stages of undress?

"Glatman seemed so ordinary to me, yet his crimes seemed so sophisticated compared to other criminals of the time. I wondered, Where did he learn these things? Why was he aroused by them?

"Why did he tie a victim's legs entirely, instead of just her ankles? Why put a gag in her mouth when they're out in the desert? These questions were swimming in my head.

"And another important thing that struck me was how very little people seemed then to know about this behavior. All of us in the class asked questions of the instructor.

"Basically, his answers were: 'Well, we don't know those things.'

"That made a hell of an impression on me. I remember thinking, 'Someday I'm going to look into this.'"

Harvey Glatman ever since has served as a touchstone case for Hazelwood. He was the first sexual offender Roy ever encountered, and in many ways remains one of the most complex criminals he's ever studied.

THREE

"I Don't Like Women All That Much"

Harvey Glatman also was Hazelwood's introduction to multiple killers.

An itinerant subtype of these predators—for whom the term "serial killer" was coined in the 1980s by agent Bob Ressler at the BSU—seemed to explode out of nowhere in the 1960s and 1970s, and to spread like a virus. In truth, although serial killers often can seem magically immune to capture, they are no more uniquely modern than any other criminal.

Like all irrational offenders, they sort themselves along a behavioral continuum from the patient, deliberate hunters, such as Bundy, to wild, murderous outlaws, such as the killing team of Juan Chavez and Hector Fernandez, described later in this chapter.

In between, there are startling anomalies, such as Henry Wallace, a thirty-one-year-old African American who confessed in 1996 to sexually assaulting and killing eleven black women in several southern states between 1992 and 1994. Unlike the majority of serial killers, who principally prey on strangers, Wallace raped and murdered women he knew, or worked with in various fast-food restaurants. It was a very poorly thought out MO, which invited Wallace's eventual detection.

"If he elected to become a serial killer, he was going about it in the wrong way," said Bob Ressler, who interviewed Wallace and testified as an expert witness for the defense at Wallace's murder trial.

Another, far better known multiple, or spree, killer added his own, individual twists to the crime in 1997.

Andrew Cunanan, slayer of flamboyant Italian clothing designer Gianni Versace, lived extremely well as a domestic companion to wealthy older gay men—"a gigolo," in his mother's uncompromising description.

He also was a familiar figure in the haute gay worlds of San Diego, Los Angeles, and San Francisco, well remembered by a succession of friends and lovers as vain, charming, highly intelligent, and articulate—a homosexual Ted Bundy.

Cunanan spent lavishly—he reportedly owed Nieman Marcus forty-six thousand dollars at his death—and dealt and consumed (sometimes injecting) a variety of drugs, including cocaine, methamphetamine, and the male hormone testosterone, which can induce rages.

According to several sources, he favored sadomasochistic pornography. One partner characterized Cunanan's sexual habits as "extreme."

Late in 1996, his patron of the moment severed his relationship with the young man, just as two of Cunanan's romantic interests, Jeff Trail, twenty-eight, and David Madson, thirty-three, both of Minneapolis, reportedly were trying to put him in their pasts.

By the following spring, Cunanan appears to have gone broke and was drinking heavily. On April 18, 1997, a friend in San Francisco saw Cunanan for what would prove to be the last time.

"Something had snapped in him," John Semerau told Maureen Orth of *Vanity Fair.* "Now I realize the guy was hunting—he was getting the thrill of the hunt, the thrill of the kill. I saw it in his eyes. I saw it in his body. He had stepped over the edge."

Cunanan flew to Minneapolis from the West Coast in late April 1997. He made no effort to hide the visit. On Tuesday afternoon, April 29, Jeff Trail's body was discovered, wrapped in a carpet, in David Madson's blood-spattered apartment. Trail had been repeatedly struck about the face and head with a hammer, which was found in Madson's apartment.

Saturday morning, May 3, Madson's body was found by fishermen at a lake about one hour's drive north of Minneapolis. He had been shot three times with a .40-caliber weapon; once in the head, once in the eye, and once in the back. His red Jeep Cherokee was missing.

Police later matched the .40-caliber slugs recovered from the Madson crime scene with a box of .40-caliber ammunition discovered in Jeff Trail's apartment.

Roy Hazelwood, who followed Andrew Cunanan's saga in the newspapers, recalls thinking at the time that Cunanan must have been very much concerned at the direction in which his lifestyle was leading him prior to the killings.

"He was physically attractive," Roy observes, "and had traded on his appearance and youthfulness to both validate his self-worth and to enjoy a very high standard of living.

"But then he began to age. His appearance—the essence of his self-esteem—began to fade. He was finding it difficult to attract the rich and appreciative sexual partners he believed he deserved. To make matters worse, their use of him was one of the factors causing him to age, and because of that they no longer desired him as they once had.

"So Andrew Cunanan, I believe, decided to get even. He did so by killing those who represented or symbolized the men who'd ruined and then rejected him."

On May 4, Chicago real estate developer Lee Miglin's sadistically broken body was discovered in his home. Miglin, seventy-five, was bound hand and foot. His body was partially wrapped in plastic, paper, and tape. His face was also taped, except for two airholes at his nose. He had been tortured—several of his ribs were broken—and stabbed. His throat had been cut open with a saw. He had been left under a car in his parking garage across the street from his Chicago town house.

A search of the Miglin residence showed no sign of forced entry. However, as much as ten thousand dollars in cash was missing, as was a collection of the elderly tycoon's expensive suits. Several months later in Miami, Cunanan would pawn a gold coin he apparently stole in the course of murdering and robbing Lee Miglin.

On Tuesday, May 6, David Madson's red Jeep was recovered by Chicago police around the corner from the Miglin house. Discovered inside the vehicle were newspaper clips of the Trail and Madson killings.

Miglin's dark green Lexus also was missing. The car, with Andrew Cunanan behind the wheel, was already in New York City.

Friday night, May 9, the Miglin Lexus was found outside an office at Finns Point National Cemetery in Pennsville, New Jersey. Inside the office, cemetery caretaker William Reese, forty-five, lay dead on the floor in a pool of his blood, a .40-caliber bullet in his head. He had been shot with the same gun that had been used to kill David Madson, and would be used to kill Gianni Versace.

Reese's 1995 Chevy truck was missing, too.

Andrew Cunanan knew his killing spree was a national news story. Several papers devoted long stories to the murder saga, including the *New York Times.* He was about to hit the FBI's Ten Most Wanted List. And he could read and hear how the Bureau was warning certain prominent gays of his acquaintance to mind their personal security.

Cunanan suddenly was famous and powerful, an object of fear, loathing, and national fascination.

Cunanan also had exhibited enough traits of the antisocial personality— lying, substance abuse, promiscuity, disdain for social norms, cruelty, use of aliases, lack of a fixed address—to warrant a curbside opinion that he was a so- ciopath, and a narcissist as well.

He parked Reese's hot pickup, carrying stolen South Carolina plates, in a Miami municipal garage on June 10. Since May 12, he'd been living under an assumed name in a moderately priced residence hotel on the beach. Accord- ing to several witnesses, he joined South Beach Miami's busy gay scene. Ac- cording to the night manager at his hotel, Cunanan came and went in a variety of disguises.

It can never be known if he chose Miami as the perfect setting for his apotheosis, or, more likely, because he knew the city from a previous gig work- ing there for a gay escort service. Cunanan certainly knew he could easily move without calling attention to himself in a district where gayness was the norm.

But Miami also had collateral appeal for a fugitive such as Andrew Cu- nanan. It is a busy international city from which there are a thousand ways to quietly disappear for destinations as handy as the Caribbean, and as remote as Rio.

All you need is money and connections, which could partially explain his choice of Gianni Versace as his final victim.

Cunanan may well have been sending a very specific message to a very spe- cific person, the way kidnappers make their point by sending a victim's family photos or a tape recording or even a body part to emphasize the seriousness of their demands.

Versace was by far the most famous of Cunanan's five known murder vic- tims, but he was the only one with whom Cunanan did not have an intimate relationship, or from whom he did not steal something he needed.

In a theory first advanced by Joe Swickard, a veteran crime reporter at the *Detroit Free Press,* Cunanan's intent behind the brazen Versace murder may been to intimidate one of Cunanan's wealthy acquaintances into fronting the

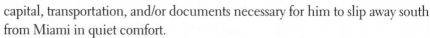

capital, transportation, and/or documents necessary for him to slip away south from Miami in quiet comfort.

Any individual, no matter how rich or well protected, would likely take to heart such a demonstration of daring and lethality.

But the ploy, if that's what it was, failed.

Cunanan did make what has been described as a frantic, unsuccessful telephone appeal to a West Coast acquaintance for help in securing a passport. Whether that call was part of an overall strategy that included Versace's murder.

On July 23, still trapped in Miami and suffering from a stomach wound, Andrew Cunanan was discovered by a caretaker aboard a houseboat, and fired a final, fatal .40-caliber round into his mouth.

It was of course no coincidence that three, perhaps four, of Cunanan's victims were gay or bisexual. Many multiple murders are sexually motivated. Those who commit them also tend to share a pleasure in the physical act of murder. The more they do it, the more they enjoy it.

Lone wolves like Cunanan or Bundy or Wayne Williams foremost are opportunists. They search and wait for the moment they feel is propitious, and then strike. Their horrific depredations may shock and seem uniquely modern, but the main reason for their rise is that opportunity today is abundant.

In the cohesive culture of an older, simpler, slower world, people noticed strangers, watched them and remembered them. A would-be multiple murderer was forced to act with utmost circumspection. The urge to act out certainly existed, as Harvey Glatman's story attests. But the chances to commit anonymous serial murder, and therefore the crime's overall incidence, were limited.

In contemporary society, with its fractured sense of community and hurried pace, a single killer can move quickly from place to place and across police jurisdictions, which habitually do not interact well with one another. In this environment, where strangers are a commonplace, the artful multiple killer — who is not necessarily intelligent, but usually is quick-witted and crafty — becomes a cipher, turns essentially invisible, and thrives.

Ted Bundy taught me that.

Killers at the other end of the spectrum, outright savages such as Richard Ramirez, the Los Angeles Night Stalker, trust more to luck and audacity than cunning. They murder heedlessly and recklessly, and frequently are caught soon after they start.

Ramirez, who indiscriminately stabbed, beat, shot, and mutilated both male and female victims aged six to eighty-four, was at large for little more than a year, during which time he killed at least thirteen victims and assaulted many others.

Chavez and Fernandez killed twelve people in the four months they were loose around Dallas, Texas, in 1995. Bundy, by contrast, murdered thirty women or more in an intermittent killing career that lasted throughout the 1970s.

He was part of the sudden epidemic of serial killers that would provide the Behavioral Science Unit with a mission: The BSU quickly became the world's leading institution devoted to the study of these rare, but highly lethal, pathogens.

Hardly a significant known instance of serial homicide anywhere in the world escaped the BSU's attention. Ramirez. Wayne Williams in Atlanta. Peter Sutcliffe, Great Britain's "Yorkshire Ripper." David ("Son of Sam") Berkowitz in New York City. The Trailside and Zodiac Killers in California. Even the great dissembler, Henry Lee Lucas, the one-eyed, snaggletoothed drifter who claimed to have murdered hundreds of victims from Guyana to Japan (but probably killed no more than three people, including his mother). All were scrutinized in the BSU laboratory.

Few escaped Roy Hazelwood's attention, either.

In 1994, following his retirement, Roy began to consult on serial murder cases as a member of the Academy Group, a Manassas, Virginia, consultancy made up of his old BSU colleagues, plus other former federal agents. Roger Depue, Roy's former boss, founded the Academy Group and served as its first president before leaving to study for the Roman Catholic priesthood. Other agent-members include Dick Ault and Pete Smerick from the BSU, and retired Secret Service agent Ken Baker. The Academy Group's client list ranges from prosecutors and defense attorneys to companies with security problems in need of employee threat assessments, and even television programs, including the popular Fox series *Millennium.*

One of Hazelwood's first assignments after joining the Academy Group was to consider a pivotal, if deceptively simple-sounding, question about a particularly heartbreaking homicide.

The victim was twenty-one-year-old Monica Smith,* last reported alive early on a Friday evening in October 1992. A neighbor in the suburban Birmingham, Alabama, apartment complex where Monica lived with her

*Denotes a pseudonym.

mother saw the young woman heading for her car in the parking lot at about 7:45 P.M.

Mrs. Smith had gone to church that night. Monica's destination was a shopping center approximately one mile away, where she would purchase chocolate yogurt at a Baskin-Robbins outlet.

Hours later, Mrs. Smith returned from church to find her daughter's car, glasses, and yogurt in the apartment complex parking lot.

She ran to her apartment and dialed 911.

Monica's partially clothed body was discovered around noon the next day, Saturday, lying in a roadside ravine about eight miles from her home, plainly visible to passing motorists amid the miscellaneous trash strewn around an illegal dumping site.

About three weeks later, a killer named Jack Harrison Trawick was arrested on a parole violation and subsequently confessed to Monica Smith's murder, which Trawick also described to investigators in some detail.

The question posed to Hazelwood by the Smith family lawyer, who was pursuing a premises liability action against the apartment complex owners, was this: In Roy's expert opinion, would the presence of a guard on duty that night in the complex's deserted security shack have deterred Trawick from murdering Smith, and thus saved her life?

Hazelwood parsed the problem step by step, beginning with a close look at the victim.

Monica Smith, he learned in conversations with her mother and others, was a timid, likable young woman afflicted with a learning disability. She was sweet-tempered, naive, and socially passive, highly unlikely to offer much resistance if confronted by an attacker. Her mother believed her to be a virgin.

Trawick was a white male, forty-five years old, whose criminal history included at least three previous murders he acknowledged at the same time he pleaded guilty to killing Monica Smith. He'd been arrested, as well, for burglaries, impersonating a police officer, kidnapping, placing threatening calls to women, and breaking into one victim's house, where he destroyed her undergarments.

Trawick was highly intelligent, and a diagnosed psychopath. Doctors and counselors described him as a sexual sadist, preoccupied with sex and violence, and a fetishist. In 1982, at his request, Trawick received a so-called chemical castration in the form of the female hormone progestin. The following year he required a mastectomy as a consequence of the drug's side effects.

Trawick spent from 1983 to 1990 in prison.

During his confession, he provided police with sketchy reconstructions of his three earlier homicides, the first of which Trawick said he committed in the early 1970s.

This victim was a prostitute whom he picked up late one afternoon in his Toyota van. Trawick said he choked the woman and stabbed her in the throat. Outside the van, he used to knife to mutilate one of her breasts, as well as her hips "and maybe, even, her stomach." He wasn't certain. He may also have pushed the weapon up his victim's vagina, he said.

Trawick added that he had expended so much energy in throttling the prostitute that he was unable to unbutton her clothing, and had to cut it away from her body with his knife.

However, he did not rape her.

He then drove home and cleaned up the van, noting to his surprise how little blood he found in the vehicle.

In his second murder, for which Trawick did not provide a date, he recalled standing in an isolated aisle of a large department store and observing an employee, a "young lady," walking toward a service area in the back of the store. After checking for surveillance measures and seeing no mirrors, one-way windows, or cameras, he went after her. Trawick cornered the clerk in the otherwise empty service area, strangled her until she passed out, and then cut the woman's throat with his pocketknife.

As in the previous attack, he did not assault his victim sexually.

Before leaving the store, Trawick wiped her blood from himself using clothes from a rack, and removed his bloodstained outer shirt, which he hid. Then he walked out of the store in his T-shirt and threw the knife away.

Victim number three was another "young lady" of about eighteen whom he'd seen from his vehicle as she walked down a street about noon one day in 1992. Trawick said he parked in a garage, caught up with the woman, placed his arm around her, and held his knife to her body.

She didn't struggle, he said, but she did lift up her skirt as they walked together. It apparently was an attempt to attract attention. He forced her to push the garment back down.

When they reached an alley, Trawick continued, he choked the woman until she passed out. When she regained consciousness and began screaming, he stabbed her to death and left. Again, there was no sexual assault.

This time, he got rid of his knife by throwing the weapon away in someone's yard.

Trawick, who lived with his mother and supported himself by doing odd jobs, such as moving furniture, told investigators he enjoyed scaring women, including his ex-wife, who'd divorced him in 1971.

He fashioned a toy gun, Trawick explained, and used it on several occasions to frighten women. "I don't like women all that much," he said at one point.

In one instance, he said, he pulled the gun and growled, "Come here," at a potential victim, but did not give chase when she ran away. In another, he immediately stopped his harassment and drove off when his target went in search of a mall security officer.

He also placed obscene calls for the same reason, but elaborated that the calls were never directed at "people," just "women," an important distinction to him.

According to one published report, Trawick sometimes telephoned women anonymously to tell them their husbands had been injured or killed in car wrecks. He liked to listen to their fright and pain.

Making the calls was "sort of a thrill," he said.

The Smith slaying, Trawick said, began in this way.

He'd had a bad day, and was cruising around the mall in his van when he saw Monica walking to her car. At that point, Trawick insisted, his intent only was to scare her with the gun.

Trawick followed Smith back to the apartment complex and drove into the parking lot past the empty guard shack, pulling up next to Monica in his van as she was walking from her car.

During the police interrogation, one of his questioners tried to bluff Trawick, telling him that a guard had taken down his license plate number that night. Trawick knew better, and at one point later in the questioning even returned to the subject. "I was thinking there wasn't any, there wasn't a guard there," the killer recalled.

Trawick said he showed Smith the barrel of the toy gun. But before he could say anything to her, she put down her purse and the container of yogurt and "was just saying 'you can have anything you want' and she started taking her pants off," he told the police.

Trawick jumped out of the van and pushed Smith into it. He also grabbed her purse from the pavement.

Inside the van, he finished removing her pants and bound her with nylon rope he'd used in moving furniture. He gagged Monica, who was lying on her stomach, with duct tape. Although she made no resistance, he said, he hit her in the back with his fist before covering her with a tarp and driving off.

Altogether, Trawick recalled, he spent approximately ten minutes in the parking lot with Smith, with his engine running and his headlights on. The interior of the van also was periodically illuminated as he got in and out of the vehicle.

No one reported seeing a thing.

According to his statement, Trawick then drove around in a random search for a secluded neighborhood, where he intended to assault Smith. She still made no sound or attempt to escape even though one of her hands came free as they drove. Trawick found that very unusual, he said.

Along the way, he jettisoned his roll of duct tape.

When he found a sufficiently quiet spot, Trawick stopped the van, climbed in back, and strangled Smith, his thumbs pressing down together over her pharynx. "She didn't fight hardly at all," he said.

He also battered her on the head with his hammer and stabbed her beneath her breastbone. He remembered angling his knife blade upward so as to hit her heart.

Trawick later burned the hammer handle and threw the metal head away. He kept the knife, though, and cleaned, polished, and reoiled it.

At the time of his arrest, he said, it was still in his van.

Total time spent in the "secluded neighborhood" was six or seven minutes, according to Trawick. He said he did not rape Smith because "I couldn't." He did insert one finger in her vagina.

He then drove to the roadside dump site. A car came by, and "I didn't have time to, uh, dispose of the body," he told his questioners, "so I just put the tailgate down" and pitched Smith's dead body down into the ravine. He remembered seeing clearly where it came to rest, despite the darkness of the night.

Trawick dumped the contents of Smith's purse, except for her wallet, in a trash barrel. From the wallet, he removed eighty dollars in cash—with which he bought gas that night—plus her driver's license and credit cards. He tossed them, and the wallet, out the van's window on his way home.

Roy noted in his later analysis that Monica Smith was what the BSU calls a "low-risk" victim; that is, she had gone nowhere and done nothing which normally would have placed her at risk of being the victim of a violent offense.

Her murder, however, was a chancy, "high-risk" crime. Trawick had followed Monica to the apartment complex parking lot, where Smith's chances of encountering someone she knew were quite good. Moreover, he spent ten minutes with her there. Also, after killing her, he disposed of her body almost casually, at a site where she very likely would soon be found, and she was.

Even when he had her under his control, Trawick improvised his actions. An organized killer would have brought with him what the BSU calls "weapons of choice." Trawick simply used what was at hand in the van: a knife, a hammer, duct tape, nylon rope, and the tarp.

Trawick clearly put almost no planning into his murders, at least not the final three. That is not to say he hadn't repeatedly fantasized committing them. But the murders themselves were spontaneous, free-form crimes in which Smith and the others were all victims of opportunity.

His motive also clearly was irrational, a generalized and deep-rooted anger toward women. The mutilation of the prostitute and the extreme force he used against the completely passive Monica Smith bespoke an enormous rage.

Trawick's impulsiveness, lack of planning, irrationality, and apparent willingness to take risks suggested strongly that he was a loose cannon, out of control. Anyone who'd ad-lib homicide in the way he did surely wouldn't give much thought to the presence or absence of a guard at the apartment complex that night.

Or would he?

Hazelwood combed carefully through the mass of available evidence, from trial testimony to Trawick's personal correspondence. He read all the depositions and police reports, reviewed photos, studied the autopsy report, and personally visited the shopping center, the apartment complex, the crime scene, and even Trawick's neighborhood.

He examined every jot and tittle of evidence, and extracted from the whole a surprisingly consistent behavior pattern.

First, Roy noted that many of the crimes Trawick committed early in his criminal career—offenses such as obscene telephone calls—involved no physical contact at all with the victim, and therefore posed a minimal risk of arrest for him. Trawick was aware of what could get him into trouble, and what was less likely to.

He apparently remembered these lessons. His various comments to the police suggested that although he seemed to act willy-nilly, in fact he paid close attention to protecting his anonymity.

He had fled when the girl in the mall went in search of a security officer. He carefully searched the department store for security devices before committing his murder there. He coolly escorted his third murder victim down a street and into an alley before killing her.

"Trawick," wrote Hazelwood, "is the type of offender who kills out of anger, but it is a controlled anger. That is to say, he will not engage in behavior which poses an immediate threat to his well-being."

That is why, Roy continued, Trawick took note of the missing guard the night he killed Smith, and proceeded onto the apartment complex premises in pursuit of her for precisely that reason. He even told the police about it.

"Had a guard been present," Roy wrote, "Ms. Smith would not have become a murder victim."

Trawick was convicted of capital murder in criminal court and sentenced to death. Before a civil jury was given a chance to reflect on Roy's analysis, a settlement was reached in the case. Mrs. Smith received an undisclosed sum, which she donated to charity.

In a second premises liability case, Hazelwood again was engaged as an expert, this time by the defense team.

Although the behavioral issues in the case were less nuanced, its reality was far starker. Over the spring and summer of 1995 in Dallas, a paroled killer named Juan Chavez, twenty-seven, paired up with a young accomplice to wantonly and brutally murder twelve people, injure five more, and rob six other victims, principally in and around the Oak Cliff district, south of the Trinity River.

A Dallas police spokesman told the *Dallas Morning News* that Chavez is "the most prolific killer in Dallas County history."

One victim, Kevin Hancock, a security guard at the Indian Ridge Apartments on Mount Ranier Street in Dallas, took two bullets to the neck and was paralyzed.

Hancock sued his erstwhile employers, claiming among other things that a broken front gate at the apartments had allowed Chavez and Fernandez access to the property, and thus to him.

In Hazelwood's opinion, however, so ruthless and rabid were the two killers that no practical security measure would have prevented "Johnny" Chavez and his mentally slow partner, fifteen-year-old Hector "Crazy" Fernandez, from shooting and paralyzing Hancock.

Johnny Chavez, tenth in a family of eighteen brothers and sisters, was born in Fort Wayne, Indiana, and brought to Dallas as an infant by his parents, migrant farm workers.

Greg Davis, the Dallas County assistant district attorney who later prosecuted Chavez, believes ethnic hatred may have underlain the defendant's cold-bloodedness. Although robbery was Chavez's putative reason for many of

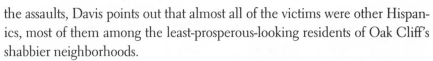

the assaults, Davis points out that almost all of the victims were other Hispanics, most of them among the least-prosperous-looking residents of Oak Cliff's shabbier neighborhoods.

Chavez's killing career actually began ten years earlier, on December 28, 1985, when Johnny, together with his brother Jesse and a friend, Julian Garcia, decided to rob their Oak Cliff neighbor, Vicente Mendoza. Garcia later testified that he wanted the money to finance a trip to Mexico.

They kicked in Mendoza's front door and robbed him at gunpoint. Then, to eliminate him as a witness, Johnny shot Vicente dead in the top of the head. He also shot Mendoza's cousin in the eye.

Chavez was arrested three weeks later in Houston. In 1987, he was tried and convicted for the Mendoza murder and sentenced to fifteen years in prison. He was paroled in 1994.

Back in Dallas, he met Fernandez, who'd recall to jurors that he began hanging out with Johnny "because he was nice to me. He was cool and stuff."

Their homicide spree began the following spring.

At about 8:00 P.M. on an evening in late March, Chavez pulled into an Oak Cliff self-service car wash where twenty-three-year-old Jose Castillo was washing his vehicle in an open-air stall. Then for no reason except, as Davis suggests, "the thrill of killing," Chavez shot Castillo several times.

Two months later, just after midnight on May 20, 1995, Chavez and Fernandez used a 20-gauge shotgun to murder eighteen-year-old Juan Hernandez as he sat at the wheel of his 1983 Buick Regal in a food store parking lot.

They stole the Buick, stripped it, and then torched the vehicle. The burned-out hulk was recovered nearby nine days later.

The two then stole a red pickup truck, again in the same general vicinity, sometime between 8:00 P.M. and midnight on June 23.

At 12:15 P.M. on the twenty-fourth, Chavez and Fernandez came upon two women and a man together in the parking lot of a west Dallas restaurant. They leveled a handgun from the stolen pickup's cab and demanded wallets from all three, who readily complied.

A few minutes later, Chavez and Fernandez rolled into a movie theater parking lot in the northwest part of the city and similarly accosted a young couple walking to their car.

"Give me your wallet," Johnny demanded of twenty-nine-year-old Timothy McKay. Then he gave McKay's companion, Pattie Matherly, to the count of three to surrender her purse.

Forty minutes later, Chavez and Fernandez were back in Oak Cliff, where they discovered Kenneth Shane on the curb outside 610 East Tenth Street. Shane was unloading some possessions from his car. Chavez pointed a handgun at Shane, took his wallet, and shot him once in the chest.

The next spasm of violence began just after midnight on July 2.

The killers approached thirty-nine-year-old Jose Morales as he was placing a call from an outdoor pay phone in a largely Hispanic neighborhood just north of Dallas's Love Field. Chavez shot Morales in the chest and took his wallet, which contained two dollars in cash. Then as Morales lay wounded on the ground, Johnny Chavez shot him a second time in the chest, killing him.

The killers next targeted Susan Ferguson, a uniformed but unarmed forty-one-year-old security guard at a construction site in the area.

Fernandez told investigators Ferguson raised her hands in surrender.

"Do you have any children?" he remembered Johnny asking the woman. "Yes," she replied.

Chavez then shot Ferguson in the face, just below her nose, and ran over her in the stolen Chevrolet Caprice they were driving.

As Ferguson lay dying, Chavez and Fernandez headed once again for southwest Dallas, where they came upon twenty-five-year-old Kevin Hancock as the security guard sat in his car doing paperwork in the Indian Ridge Apartments parking lot.

Hancock warned them off the property, but Chavez was unfazed.

"Let's see both hands, don't fuck with me," he said as he pointed a gun at Hancock, demanding the security guard's 9mm handgun. He also demanded his wallet. When Hancock said he didn't have one, Johnny Chavez shot him twice in the neck.

And still the carnage went on.

At 1:50 A.M., as Francisco Jaimez and his friend, Alberto Guevara, sat together talking in the front yard at 400 East Ninth Street in Oak Cliff, Chavez and Fernandez drove up, produced a gun, and relieved Jaimez of one hundred dollars and Guevara of his wallet. Fernandez shot and wounded them both. Chavez shot and killed a third victim at the scene, twenty-five-year-old Jesus Briseno, who innocently had happened by while the robbery was in progress.

After committing three murders and three other shootings in less than two hours, Chavez and Fernandez next encountered Alfonso Contreras, thirty, and Guadalupe Delgadillo-Pina, twenty-five, who were parked together in a vacant lot at the intersection of Ormsby and Seale Streets, about two miles from where Jaimez, Guevara, and Briseno were shot.

They robbed Contreras of his billfold and two hundred dollars, then shot him with Hancock's gun and ran over Contreras with his own truck.

According to Fernandez's later statements to police, he followed in the Caprice as Chavez drove Delgadillo-Pina in Contreras's truck to the Trinity River bottoms, the river's dark and deserted floodplain. Fernandez said Johnny ordered him to shoot Delgadillo-Pina in the head, after which Chavez ran over her, as well, with Contreras's truck.

That vehicle also was torched.

Two nights later, on the Fourth of July, Johnny and Hector returned to the immediate vicinity of the Indian Ridge Apartments, where they'd shot Kevin Hancock, and committed the double gunshot drive-by murders of thirty-one-year-old Manuel Duran and twenty-seven-year-old Antonio Rios, both tire store employees, as they left work. Chavez also shot and killed fifty-three-year-old Antonio Banda, whose ill fortune it was to be coming around the street corner at just the time of the shootings.

They committed no further crimes in Dallas for eighteen days.

Then at about 1:00 A.M. on July 22, Chavez and Fernandez shot seventeen-year-old Gabriel Yerena in the head, stole his vehicle, and left him lying in the middle of South Randolph Street as they drove away in his car.

Twenty-four hours later, driving a stolen Camaro, Chavez and Fernandez pulled up behind Juan Macias and Manuela Salas on West Canty Street. A shot from the Camaro hit Salas in the arm. After Macias refused to pull over, he took a fatal gunshot to the back of his head. His vehicle careened out of control and struck a house.

Salas jumped out the car, ran to a neighbor's, and called the Dallas police.

A short while later, as officers were securing the scene, Chavez and Fernandez returned in their stolen Camaro. They were ordered to stop and get out. Instead, they dropped the Camaro in reverse, gunned the car, and drove straight back into a fence.

The two fled on foot.

Two weeks later, they were finally arrested. In March of 1996, Johnny Chavez was tried and convicted for the Morales murder and sentenced to death. "Crazy" Fernandez, who testified against Chavez, received ten years' probation.

"Chavez and Fernandez obviously were on a crime spree," Hazelwood observes. "The victims were randomly chosen.

"They were oblivious to risk.

"Chavez had shot Vicente Mendoza at a residence at seven-forty-five in the evening. He also shot Jose Castillo multiple times in front of several witnesses at the car wash at about eight P.M.

"They were impulsive. They'd see a car they wanted, for example, and would just start following that car.

"They lacked criminal sophistication. They committed crimes in front of witnesses, crimes that involved high risks to themselves. They left evidence, expended rounds and fingerprints.

"They were prepared for, and desirous of, killing. When they drove by the apartment complex where Hancock worked, one of them reportedly said, 'Let's get him!' They wanted to kill. It was a thrill for them.

"A working gate at the apartment complex would not have deterred this crime. Remember, they weren't stopped by Hancock, who was armed and uniformed. What's a gate going to do?

"Additional guards also would not have deterred this crime. Cameras would not have deterred this crime. Better lighting would not have deterred this crime.

"Nothing was going to stop those two."

FOUR

The Dead Speak

The world of aberrant crime forcefully reclaimed Hazelwood's attention in 1968, when Roy, by then a Vietnam veteran and a major in
the army, accepted a yearlong fellowship at the Armed Forces Institute of
Pathology, based at Walter Reed Army Hospital in Bethesda, Maryland. The
AFIP was the best-equipped and most advanced facility of its kind anywhere in
the world.

Roy by this time was familiar with the dark side of human nature.

From Fort Rucker he'd been transferred to West Germany, where Hazelwood first served as provost marshal (police chief) of the Fourth Armored
Division's home base at Göppingen. He then was sent to Stuttgart, where he
commanded a stockade.

There are very few jobs less attractive than being a jailer. But for Roy Hazelwood, the yearlong responsibility of managing 150 criminals was a welcome
chance to interact directly with them—to be educated on criminality by criminals.

"I learned a lot running that stockade," he says.

He also demonstrated a natural feel for dealing with felons.

One of Roy's innovations, developed with the help of a psychologist, was to
color-code the facility's interior. Thus, when new arrivals first came to Captain
Hazelwood's prison entrance, they found the walls and floor painted a bleak
gray, underscoring the seriousness of their situation.

To emphasize that in this place their lives no longer were their own, Roy directed that black hands and feet be painted onto the walls and floor. These indicated precisely to the newcomers where they were to position their own hands and feet as they were searched, and then marched through the entrance's outer and inner gates, or sally port.

Inside the lockup, Roy added a Dantean touch. Those in maximum security found their area covered completely with a dark, dull green paint. As the men worked their way up, via good behavior, to the moderate-security wing, they discovered the vile green relieved by a white paint on the upper walls and ceiling. Those well-behaved enough for minimum security enjoyed curtains, rugs, and furniture.

Troublemakers were placed on suicide watch: locked down naked, with no mattress or blanket, under twenty-four-hour guard in a brightly lit cell with only a Bible and their wedding ring to remind them of their higher responsibilities.

After two days of this, Roy would personally visit the inmate, excuse the guard, and speak privately. "I'd tell him that if he'd tell me he was sorry for what he'd done, I'd let him out, and no one would ever know he'd apologized. It worked ninety percent of the time."

If it didn't, Hazelwood shipped the miscreant off to a far less congenial environment, the former Nazi concentration camp at Dachau, then being operated as a special lockup for soldier-inmates with behavior problems throughout the European stockade system.

Although Roy couldn't know it, these one-on-one encounters with the baddest of the bad in his custody were an invaluable prelude to his later confrontations with America's most deviant offenders.

Mentally sparring with a killer is very different from sharing a lemonade on the veranda with your aunt Kate. It is very hard work in which a simple slip of the tongue, or even a mistaken gesture, can cancel days, even weeks, of effort.

There's no cookbook, either.

In Stuttgart, for example, Roy was faced with the problem of a glib and personable inmate whom the prison psychologist had diagnosed as a psychopath.

This prisoner, a persistent reoffender with a long record of incarceration, had voluntarily assisted with overhauling the stockade's archaic office record-keeping system. But in the weeks he worked around Roy's staff, Hazelwood realized that though superficially charming, the inmate was a chronic liar who failed to complete most of the tasks he was given.

Besides enjoying the change of scenery, he also took advantage of the circumstance to ingratiate himself with several members of Roy's staff, while he

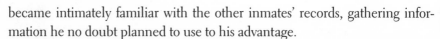

became intimately familiar with the other inmates' records, gathering information he no doubt planned to use to his advantage.

Hazelwood knew he would have to make a countermove before the prisoner had consolidated his relationships and established his own power center inside the prison staff, a potentially dangerous challenge to Roy's authority.

But confrontation, a public showdown, wouldn't work. This was a model prisoner, and Hazelwood could only undercut his own credibility by treating the popular inmate peremptorily. The answer had to be a response in kind—subterfuge replying to stealth.

Consequently, contraband postage stamps were discovered in the prisoner's bunk, a rules violation from which there was no appeal. He was summarily issued a one-way ticket to Dachau.

"You know I didn't steal those stamps," the inmate said indignantly to Roy on his way out the door. "You set me up, didn't you?"

Roy nodded and smiled and wished the man a safe journey. The defeated prisoner paused briefly and smiled back, apparently appreciating the craftiness with which he had been finessed.

Hazelwood's next overseas posting was South Vietnam, where in 1967 he was assigned command of the Fourth MP Company, known at the time as the "Fucked-Up Fourth" for its lack of discipline, low morale, and dismal performance record. At the time Roy took over, seven soldiers in the company were in the stockade for attempting to kill a noncommissioned officer with a hand grenade.

Roy again intuitively recognized that creativity would get him much further than confrontation, an insight also of great value for interviewing violent deviant offenders.

On his first day in charge of his new command, Hazelwood inspected the MPs' living quarters and equipment. "They were pretty awful," he says. "I picked up one soldier's rifle and discovered that it was rusted shut.

"The first sergeant said, 'Sir, here's your chance to establish your authority. Court-martial the soldier.'

"I said, 'No, I think I'll put him on the lead jeep on tomorrow's four A.M. convoy escort—with this weapon.'

"That PFC spent the entire night cleaning his weapon."

By the time Hazelwood moved on, the Fourth was not only squared away, but had become one of the most decorated MP companies in Vietnam.

His next stop was An Khe, home of the First Cavalry Division, where for four months Roy coordinated convoy security for more than 250 miles of the most dangerous roadway in Vietnam.

His last assignment was as "number one papa san" in charge of cleaning up "Sin City," the one-square-mile red-light district in An Khe.

Sin City was notorious throughout that part of Vietnam for its overpriced and diluted booze (known as Saigon tea), diseased hookers, and the frequency of street brawls that broke out among the U.S. Army personnel who were Sin City's most frequent visitors.

Not unlike some western sheriff determined to tame his town's outlaw element, Roy instituted reforms that eliminated most of Sin City's violence, improved the girls' health and hygiene, and regulated liquor prices.

The fighters tailed off dramatically when he forbade officers and enlisted men to mingle in the same establishments.

"In fact," Roy recalls, "we had the brothel owners construct, at their own cost, three separate facilities: one for officers, one for noncommissioned officers, and one for the enlisted men."

He saw to it that price-gouging ricksha operators, who charged exorbitant sums to transport soldiers to and from Sin City, suddenly had an affordable competitor, a regularly scheduled, round-trip minibus service.

Hazelwood also ordered that all prostitutes were to receive weekly physical examinations and be tested for sexually transmitted diseases. Those who were sick were ordered out of their brothels. One violation, and the whorehouse itself was shut down.

Roy further directed that all employers and employees from Sin City's papa sans to their bartenders and the bar girls were to rise at 6:00 A.M. each day and thoroughly police the entire district for trash.

"Everyone took part; it was a true democracy," he says.

In the summer of 1968, his tour complete, Major Hazelwood returned home to confront a major decision. The army offered him a choice: attend Michigan State University to pursue an advanced degree in criminal law enforcement studies, or accept a year's fellowship in forensic medicine at the AFIP.

Hazelwood decided in characteristic fashion.

"I went to the dictionary and looked up 'forensic medicine.' It said, 'medicine as it applies to courts of law.' That sounded fascinating, so I accepted the fellowship."

Roy had seen a tremendous amount of violence in Vietnam, but the AFIP introduced him to a different variety of mayhem—random, pernicious violence and its victims. Assisting in autopsies at the Baltimore medical examiner's office, retrieving floaters (dead bodies) with the harbor patrol, observing the psychiatric intake ward at Walter Reed, and learning forensic anthropology at the Smithsonian Institution, Hazelwood for the first time began to sketch his own mental frame around the borders of extreme and dangerous behavior.

"My professional interest in death and violence really came together at AFIP," he explains. "There was so much violence, and I was confronted daily with its victims. Some of the victims would be expected to encounter violence in their lives. Prostitutes and drug addicts, for example. But many of the other victims I saw were selected randomly to be killed. That point has stayed with me for my entire career."

Another lingering recollection is of black humor and practical jokes in the Baltimore morgue.

Early in his fellowship, one of the assistant MEs called the working day to a close and gestured to Roy that he could find a cold beer in cooler number 6 along the wall. Hazelwood opened the locker. Out rolled a corpse on its shelf, a cold six-pack tucked into the crook of its arm.

Another time, working intently on a dissection, Roy discovered a little slip of paper in the cadaver's mouth.

"Eat at Dino's," it said.

He learned from the experts at the AFIP that if you know how to listen, the dead can tell you a great deal about how they got that way.

Roy met world-class authorities in toxicology, pathology, radiology, odontology, entomology, anthropology, and even geology, all of whom contributed at various times to AFIP evaluations.

A toxicologist, for example, might establish if the victim was drunk or sober or had been poisoned. A pathologist might determine that a bruise or a scrape was a defensive wound, or estimate from how far, and in what direction, a fatal bullet was discharged.

An odontologist might identify the victim via dental records, or identify the killer via bite marks left on the victim's skin. The entomologist could tell from insect larvae associated with the corpse if it was dumped where it was found, and how long ago. If there's soil, clay, or rock associated with the body, a geologist can offer useful knowledge of where it came from, or the settings in which the material is used.

Hazelwood was fascinated by it all, not least because so much of this knowledge was based upon experience and observation. For example, radiologists familiar with injuries characteristic of child abuse know to be alert to so-called spiral fractures of the forearm and lower leg bones if the possible victim is very young or immobile. Reason: Abusers tend to twist a child's arms or legs as they grab them by their wrists or ankles, torquing their bones, which then fracture in a familiar spiral pattern.

Hazelwood personally researched stabbing and cutting wounds at the AFIP, and put together a text-and-photo syllabus for teaching the subject that is still in use in pathology classes around the country. Among the very strange cases covered in the syllabus is that of a man who committed suicide by repeatedly jamming ballpoint pens into the side of his head.

But a more intriguing area of investigation for Roy was personality: Who would do such a thing, and why? Could such a person be described?

Hazelwood wasn't thinking like a clinician. He was thinking like a cop, wondering if a combination of experience and research could yield reliable *behavioral* data to assist investigations, the way the hard sciences produced physical evidence.

One day in conversation with his AFIP mentor, Dr. Charles Stahl, a navy commander and forensic pathologist, Roy mentioned Harvey Glatman, and his own interest in one day conducting a study of autoerotic fatalities.

"Oh, we did one of those," the pathologist replied, and he directed Hazelwood's attention to Stahl's published survey of forty-three autoerotic asphyxial deaths, all white male members of the military, culled from the 1.4 million cases in the AFIP's voluminous files. At the time, Stahl's study was the largest ever published.

Roy's idea was to build on Stahl's beginning by conducting a much broader survey aimed at assisting police departments in the investigation of these strange, often bewildering deaths. He got his chance in 1978, the year he joined the Bureau's Behavioral Science Unit.

FBI assistant director Ken Joseph, then in charge of the FBI Academy, issued instructions that all Academy instructors, including the BSU's mind hunters, were to undertake original research projects. Larry Monroe, then BSU unit chief, called his profilers together to announce the directive.

Agents Bob Ressler and John Douglas were delighted, and relieved, at the news. Since early in the year Ressler and Douglas had been paying informal visits to maximum-security prisons around the country, where they sought out America's most infamous and prolific incarcerated killers. The profilers' objective: to conduct deep interviews with the likes of Edmund Kemper and Sirhan Sirhan, Richard Speck and David Berkowitz.

Suddenly, with Ken Joseph's blessing, Ressler and Douglas could elevate

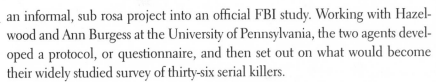

an informal, sub rosa project into an official FBI study. Working with Hazelwood and Ann Burgess at the University of Pennsylvania, the two agents developed a protocol, or questionnaire, and then set out on what would become their widely studied survey of thirty-six serial killers.

Other BSU agents at the meeting with Monroe that day proposed to study subjects ranging from pyromania to suicide to stress. Then came Roy's turn.

"I want to study autoerotic fatalities," the new profiler said.

Silence.

"Huh?" Monroe asked finally.

Undaunted, Hazelwood rose and explained autoerotic fatalities to the group. When he finished, fellow profiler Dick Ault asked whether such a rare phenomenon—approximately fifteen hundred to two thousand such deaths occur in the United States each year—merited the time and resources necessary to study it as thoroughly as Roy proposed.

Clearly not on the basis of mortality alone, Hazelwood conceded.

But there were two good reasons for undertaking the project, he said.

One, more than almost any other type of death, the autoerotic fatality creates a painful emotional resonance among the victim's family and acquaintances. Because most victims keep their solo-sex habit well hidden, such deaths almost always come as a sudden, ugly, and shameful surprise to survivors. When the deceased's private, deviant sexual practices are suddenly made plain in death, there is bewilderment, disgust, denial, guilt, and often considerable anger among those closest to them.

Hazelwood told the group of one instance where a victim's parents litigated his death for two years, insisting their boy had been murdered. In another, a father pressured the local coroner to change his son's death report from "accidental during autoerotic acts" to "accidental due to physical exertion."

Hazelwood's second, more persuasive argument to the group was that his research would provide police departments with the basic information and tools necessary to differentiate autoerotic deaths from homicides or suicides.

As he explained, some police agencies weren't sure what an autoerotic fatality was. For example, Roy once received a telephone call from a local police official inquiring whether he was available to lecture.

Roy said yes, he was, and listed his areas of expertise, including autoerotic fatalities.

The chief considered for a moment.

"Well, I don't think that last one would be very useful for us," he finally said. "We don't have too many traffic deaths down here."

Misreading an accidental autoerotic death can have serious consequences. Among Catholics, for example, an autoerotic death mistaken for a suicide may mean the deceased is denied burial in consecrated ground.

To misidentify an autoerotic death for a suicide can also be expensive: Some life insurance policies refuse to pay in the event of suicide.

Mistaking one for homicide raises a separate set of potential problems. Time, money, and energy are wasted. The victim's family, as well as the community, is subjected to needless stress.

Conversely, if a homicide is successfully staged as an autoerotic death, justice is evaded.

To illustrate his point, Hazelwood told the group of a case that the police at first filed away as an unsolved sexual homicide, but which turned out to be an accidental death due to a dangerous autoeroticism.

The victim was a respectable midwestern businessman and community leader who one day disappeared.

He was not known to have been depressed in any way, and had no apparent motive for vanishing. The police considered kidnapping the likeliest possibility. However, no ransom demand was made.

A few days later, searchers discovered the businessman dead in a secluded woods not far from town. He was partially clothed and elaborately bound, suspended from a tree limb, with his head and shoulders touching the ground. He'd died from exposure.

Nearby was a briefcase containing several well-thumbed erotic magazines. Photos of some members of the deceased's family were superimposed over some of the erotic pictures.

Investigators surmised that something must have gone wrong with the kidnap plot, something that panicked the abductors, who then fled, leaving their captive to die in the forest.

The theory seemed to fit the facts, and the local pathologist agreed.

Cause of death: exposure.

Manner of death: homicide.

Then a member of the police department who'd attended Roy's class at Quantico asked Hazelwood to review the case.

After examining the photos of the death scene and reading the police investigative report, Roy noted that both were consistent in every detail with the characteristic features of an accidental autoerotic fatality.

He explained to the police and the local pathologist how it was possible for the victim to bind *himself*, and then pull on the ropes to induce hypoxia.

Unfortunately, it appeared that the businessman's weight prevented him from also releasing himself. A session of self-arousing sex had cost him his life.

Cause of death: exposure.

Manner of death: accident.

Case closed.

After receiving official Bureau sanction to proceed with his project, Roy began collecting cases for consideration. Altogether, there would be 157 histories included, most of them submitted by U.S. and Canadian police officers who attended classes at Quantico.

From a law enforcement point of view, this approach ensured he'd gather the best possible selection of histories. Students only submitted cases for consultation and discussion at Quantico if they otherwise defied solution, or were so strange that the officer sought enlightenment from experts.

Among the mysteries Roy helped to explain was a college professor discovered dead in full western gear, including chaps, twin .45s in his hip holsters, and a ten-gallon hat on his head. Another victim was found dead in scuba gear. A third was fully attired as a surgeon.

One female victim was dressed as a harem girl.

He was able to show the officers how in each case the individual died of accidental asphyxiation while engaged in dangerous autoerotic acts.

In another consultation, Roy reviewed the death of a black woman, twenty-three, who was found nude in her bathroom, resting on her knees, with her head submerged in the bathtub. Her hands were bound in front of her, and a nine-and-one-half-inch metal bolt, which she had previously inserted within her, lay on the floor beneath her buttocks. A rope was looped around her neck, with the two free ends draped over her right shoulder.

"She is thought to have been engaging in a masochistic fantasy (hence, the bound wrists)," Hazelwood wrote in his analysis, "inducing hypoxia with the neck ligature, when she lost consciousness, falling across the tub and into the water."

The most violent death was also the most horrible. A young man with a roller-skate-strap fetish trussed his wrists and ankles with twenty-eight of them. Then he lowered himself into a garbage can, buttocks first, with his knees drawn up to his chest, intending to sink to the point where the garbage can constricted his chest and induced hypoxia.

His escape mechanism was a roll of wire standing next to the garbage can. As Roy reconstructed the death, the young man failed to appreciate how low his center of gravity would go, making it impossible to tip it over the garbage by grasping the roll of wire.

He died, slowly and painfully, from progressive asphyxiation.

"Neighbors," says Roy, "reported that they thought they heard a dog howling all night. It was this young man."

FIVE ✗

Terminal Sex

I n October 1979, Dr. Park Dietz, then director of forensic psychiatry at the Bridgewater Hospital for the Criminally Insane in Massachusetts, invited Hazelwood to appear within him on a panel to discuss autoerotic fatalities at the annual meeting of the American Academy of Psychiatry and Law.

"I remember Roy as a short guy with peculiar interests," Dr. Dietz says. "I shared those interests, and that's why I liked him."

Dietz, the son of a Camp Hill, Pennsylvania physician, is today as central a figure among forensic psychiatrists as Hazelwood is in law enforcement.

Among the infamous defendants Dietz has evaluated for both prosecution and defense attorneys have been Jeffrey Dahmer, Milwaukee's flesh-eating serial killer; Arthur Shawcross, the upstate New York serial killer; Susan Smith, the North Carolina mother who murdered her two sons; John du Pont; and Betty Broderick of San Diego, whose murder of both her ex-husband and his wife prompted not one, but two made-for-TV movies.

Dietz has also done pioneer studies of stalkers, and worked as a security consultant to celebrities including Michael Jackson and Cher.

He operates the Threat Assessment Group in Newport Beach, California, a consultancy to government and business which focuses on the potential threats posed by disgruntled employees and solutions for dealing with them.

Dr. Dietz's fascination with aberrant minds started even earlier in his life than did Hazelwood's.

"I can trace that interest in odd behavior back at least as far as my boyhood, when I tagged along with my mother when she did volunteer work at the state hospital in Harrisburg, near where we lived," he recalls.

"She'd organize Christmas parties. I'd help with refreshments and decorations and would sometimes dance with the patients."

Dietz says he never seriously doubted that he'd follow his father into medicine, or that his specialty would be psychiatry. However, as his interest in odd behavior deepened, he began to question what sort of light, if any, psychiatry could shed on these subjects.

A premed student at Cornell in the late 1960s, where he studied biology and psychology, Dietz seriously considered bolting for the University of California at Berkeley to take up criminology.

Then one day in the Cornell bookstore he discovered a text, *Forensic Medicine*, by the British physician Keith Simpson. The experience proved an epiphany every bit as profound for him as the discovery of Harvey Glatman had been for Roy Hazelwood.

It changed Park Dietz's life.

"That book was my salvation," he says. "It was full of dead babies and skeletons and bodies in trunks. It made me see that there was a way to do criminology and medicine at the same time, so that my parents would pay for my education and I could do what I wanted to do."

His senior honors thesis at Cornell was on the sociology of deviance. When he later studied medicine at Johns Hopkins University in Baltimore, Dietz worked in the same medical examiner's office Roy Hazelwood had on his AFIP fellowship five years earlier. It was in the Baltimore morgue, coincidentally, that Dietz encountered his own first autoerotic fatality, a young girl who'd hanged herself with her panty hose.

Forensic psychiatry afforded Park Dietz an avenue of access to explore strange behavior, the stranger the better. In an early and memorable case, he interviewed a young schizophrenic who, during a psychotic episode, deliberately had placed his right arm across a train track for the limb to be severed by a passing locomotive. When the psychiatrist wondered *why* the gory self-amputation, the patient said the explanation lay in the Gospel according to Matthew, and quoted to Dietz the applicable verses.

"Whosoever looketh on a woman to lust after her hath committed adultery with her already in his heart.

"And if thy right eye offend thee, pluck it out, and cast it from thee: for it is profitable for thee that one of thy members should perish, and not that thy whole body should be cast into hell.

"And if thy right hand offend thee, cut it off."

Where forensic psychiatry disappointed Dietz was in the way it subordinated scientific inquiry to the narrower, practical needs of the law. "At the time, it wasn't considered a psychiatrist's job to critically assess a police investigation," says Dietz, "or even to get hold of information about it. Certainly we were not to go out and reinvestigate where the police already had been. Nor were we to ask them to go back to check something."

Park Dietz, however, wanted to *investigate* aberrant behavior, not just study or describe it. Instead of a doctor-diagnostician, he wanted to be doctor-detective.

It was Roy Hazelwood, says Dietz, who showed him the way.

"It was when I first started working with Roy on the autoerotic fatalities research project that I got the idea that forensic psychiatrists were probably getting a lot of things wrong by not conducting our own inquiries," he explains. "So I started to do that, and for a while I called it investigative forensic psychiatry."

Dr. Dietz's first major opportunity to apply what he learned from Roy and to demonstrate his new approach to forensic psychiatry came eighteen months after meeting Hazelwood. He was retained by government lawyers to examine and evaluate would-be assassin John W. Hinckley, Jr., who shot and wounded President Ronald Reagan at the Washington Hilton Hotel on March 30, 1981.

Hinckley, twenty-five, became obsessed with Jodie Foster after seeing her play the young prostitute, Iris, opposite Robert De Niro's character, Travis Bickle, in the film *Taxi Driver.* Hinckley began harassing the nineteen-year-old Foster by telephone and mail.

Just as the unstable Bickle eventually became a political assassin, Hinckley decided to kill Reagan in an effort to impress Foster. He'd later call the shooting "the greatest love offering in the history of the world."

Dietz interviewed Hinckley at a number of federal detention centers up and down the eastern seaboard. He was first to uncover Hinckley's motive for the shooting.

But the forensic psychiatrist also discovered one reason why Hinckley chose to shoot at Reagan from such close range, practically guaranteeing that he'd be captured, if not killed himself.

Poor eyesight.

"We went to Colorado to interview Hinckley's parents," Dietz says. "They let us go through his bedroom. I found some shot-up targets the Bureau had missed when they searched the home. They were labeled, so we could see that Hinckley was a lousy shot beyond close range."

Another question was why Hinckley waited to shoot until Reagan was departing the Hilton, rather than when the president was walking in. The crime scene photographs offered no explanation, so Dietz decided to visit the Hilton himself.

"It was clear when we got there that Hinckley didn't have a clear shot when the president was on his way in," he says.

"There was a curve in the brick wall at the Hilton, which limited the amount of time he would have had to aim and shoot. But as the president emerged, Hinckley had more time and stood at closer range."

Hinckley also planned to draw Jodie Foster to him by abducting a planeload of airline passengers, whom he intended to trade for the young movie actress as his hostage. Dietz shed light on those plans with a discovery he made while sorting through Hinckley's personal effects.

In the bottom of Hinckley's suitcase the forensic psychiatrist found a Band-Aid can. Stuck to its bottom was a folded-up note that previous searches had overlooked.

Written on the secreted sheet was a skyjack demand that Hinckley had cribbed almost verbatim from the book *The Fox Is Crazy, Too,* which Dr. Dietz also found in the suitcase.

Besides applying what he learned from Hazelwood to the Hinckley investigation, by 1981 Dietz also was well into his joint research with Roy on dangerous autoeroticism. Dietz had begun his work with a review of the medical literature, which he found disappointing.

"It was largely garbage," Dietz says. "One or two case histories. A couple accounts of people who survived. A hodgepodge of information."

His historical researches took him as far back as A.D. 1000 and a Mayan stone sculpture from that era. On display at the Anthropological Museum in Mexico City, the sculpture depicts a naked man with a rope around his neck. The figure is scarred on his cheeks and forehead. His penis, clearly carved in erection, is partially missing.

Although the sculpture does not prove the Maya had discovered hypoxia, to Dietz it strongly suggested they did. He also points out that the Maya believed the souls of those who hanged themselves went straight to paradise, where they were met by the goddess Ixtab, who is depicted in an extant manuscript in a

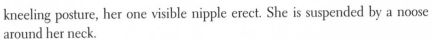

kneeling posture, her one visible nipple erect. She is suspended by a noose around her neck.

Eight centuries later, the Marquis de Sade included an autoerotic hanging scene in his novel *Justine*, probably the best-known treatment of sexual asphyxia in Western literature.

Much more compelling to the scientist in Dietz was an anonymously written pamphlet, *Modern Propensities: Or an Essay on the Art of Strangling*, that he traced to a microfilm collection at Yale. *Propensities*, published in London at the end of the eighteenth-century, describes in detail the deaths of two men due to sexual asphyxia: one a Reverend Parson Manacle (possibly a pseudonym), and the other, Francis Kotzwarra, a Czech musician and minor composer, whose demise is possibly the earliest recorded example of an accidental autoerotic fatality being mistaken for homicide.

On September 2, 1791, Kotzwarra visited a London prostitute named Susannah Hill. After performing what her trial transcript describes only as "several acts of the grossest indecency" with her, Kotzwarra asked Hill to fetch some cord with which he wanted to hang himself.

She obliged, and watched as Kotzwarra accidentally killed himself. Charged with manslaughter, the prostitute saved herself with her seeming honesty and frankness over what had occurred. Hill withheld nothing of the incident, repeating to the judge the same unpleasant details she had related to both a neighbor and a constable.

The court reporter added his own bit of corroborative detail:

> She was neatly dressed in common apparel; and, on her countenance, we could discover nothing that seemed to indicate a rooted depravity; nor was there any thing in her person particularly attractive: from which it may be inferred that the unfortunate—if not lamented—Kotzwarra trusted more to the charms of the *cord* than to those of his fair one.

Dietz's discovery of Kotzwarra's prototypical autoerotic death led the forensic psychiatrist to suggest a title for their book in progress, *Kotzwarraism*. Hazelwood was adamantly opposed.

"I think it was the only thing about which we ever had a true disagreement," Roy recalls. "I was inflexible. The book was going to be called *Autoerotic Fatalities*. Park agreed."

Hazelwood, Dietz, and Ann Burgess from the University of Pennsylvania analyzed 150 deaths in all. Of the seven female victims, four were white. Of the 143 male victims, 139 were white.

The victims' average age at death was twenty-six. Three out of ten, male and female, were married.

The oldest victim was a seventy-seven-year-old man; the youngest was a nine-year-old paperboy found asphyxiated in a deserted stable. Sears catalogs opened to lingerie ads were spread around him on the floor.

According to Hazelwood, children as young as six have died during experimental asphyxia. Some years ago, three California children died in their grade-school washroom as a result of placing their necks in cloth towel dispensers and twisting.

Hazelwood, Dietz, and Burgess also evaluated eighteen nonasphyxial auto-erotic fatalities. Among them, six victims died by electrocution, four suffered heart attacks, three from inhaling an aerosol propellant, two from aspirating vomit, and one from "popping" a volatile nitrate. Another, the midwestern businessman originally believed to have been kidnapped, died of exposure. The eighteenth victim's cause of death was undetermined.

From his extensive interviews with survivors and associates of the victims, Roy discovered how difficult autoerotic practices can be to detect. One father told Hazelwood that he'd noticed a red linear mark on his son's neck. When he asked his son about it, the boy reasonably explained he'd been playing football, and that someone had grabbed his T-shirt from the rear, causing the shirt collar to leave the mark. One month later, his father found him dead, clothed in his mother's lingerie, suspended from a rope in his closet.

"There are no definitive signs of involvement with dangerous autoeroticism," says Hazelwood. "Outside of general, nonspecific indicators such as red eyes or red marks around the neck, there are no clues. I know of nothing that will alert a person to the possibility that someone is participating in this type of activity. To all appearances, they are perfectly normal and healthy people. They certainly are not psychotic.

"Unlike suicides, victims of dangerous autoeroticism rarely are described as depressed, anxious, irritable, or particularly stressed prior to their deaths. To the contrary, the great majority are described as optimistic and future oriented."

Nor does there seem to be a single source, or type of source, from which most people learn about the practice. Besides fictional treatments such as *Justine*, the victims' apparently learn about hypoxia from friends and acquaintances, discover it by accident, read about it in magazines (Larry Flynt's *Hustler* published a widely read article, "Orgasm of Death," in 1981) and newspapers, or encounter it in the cinema, most recently in the movies *And Justice for All* and *In the Realm of the Senses*.

Those attracted to terminal sex, as it has been called, also are willing to fill in their blanks. The 1970 movie *A Man Called Horse*, for example, features the British actor Richard Harris as an itinerant nineteenth-century British noble-man who is subcutaneously skewered and threaded with buckskin cords by a band of Indians. The Indians test Harris's mettle by hoisting him high above the ground by the leather ligatures in a sort of aboriginal crucifixion ceremony.

The scene, reprised in two sequels, is powerful but hardly erotic.

Nonetheless, Hazelwood recalls a *Horse*-inspired autoerotic fatality in which the victim, wearing a horse bit and bridle, pierced his nipples with fish-hooks before hanging himself by the neck.

The props and paraphernalia found at an autoerotic death scene will vary according to the victim's fantasy, and the variations are endless.

Roy cites a case in which a man was found dead, cross-dressed in his wife's lingerie, with a pair of her panties pulled over his head. He had sus-pended a ligature from a garage rafter and tied a thirteen-loop hangman's knot in its free end. Then he climbed on a stool, placed his neck in the noose, and stepped off. His feet did not quite touch the garage floor, so he died from asphyxiation.

The key to understanding his ritual came later, with the discovery among his personal papers of a handwritten fantasy script, describing the military exe-cution of his wife for treason.

As Roy put the evidence together, the victim was enacting this script, stand-ing in as surrogate victim. By donning her lingerie he symbolically became his wife. For the condemned's hood, he used her panties. Stepping off the stool was analogous to the hanging victim's thirteenth and final step before dropping to his or her death.

In another case, a shoe fetishist secured a rope a doorknob, ran the line over the door, and accidentally asphyxiated himself while hanging from it, totally nude, on the opposite side.

"Surrounding him," Roy recalls, "were four full-length mirrors. Attached to them, and the door behind him, were women's high-heeled shoes.

"He had hanged himself surrounded by the shoes. Everywhere he looked he would see himself and his love objects."

Asphyxiation caused by hanging is by far the most common form of acci-dental autoerotic fatality.

"Outside of jails or mental institutions, I've never seen a nude suicide by hanging," says Hazelwood. "So if I find someone hanging nude in their bedroom I'm going to suspect it is an autoerotic fatality."

Among the atypical deaths, one victim was discovered seated on a couch, dressed only in a shirt.

He'd set up a projector and screen to watch an erotic film.

Judging from the plastic bread bag found near his left hand, and the aerosol can he still grasped in his right, the twenty-three-year-old victim apparently had planned to enhance the experience both by asphyxia (the bread bag) and by inhaling the can's fluorocarbon propellant.

Instead, he suffered what the medical examiner believed was a fatal cardiac arrhythmia.

Hazelwood counsels investigators that the autoerotic experimenter, unlike a suicide or murder victim, invariably includes some sort of escape, or self-rescue, mechanism in his or her apparatus. Tempting death may be a partial objective for many of them—achieving it is not.

The safety arrangement need not be elaborate. "It may be nothing more than the victim's ability to stand and relieve the pressure on his neck," says Hazelwood.

Evidence of bondage also is commonly found at autoerotic death scenes. Bondage, although not yet recognized as a distinct paraphilia by the American Psychiatric Association, is in fact integral to such a wide spectrum of aberrant sexual activity, especially criminal behavior, that Hazelwood emphasizes its importance in all his presentations.

Hazelwood and Dietz distinguish between two types: motor bondage (restricted movement of limbs) and sensory bondage (blindfolds, hoods, gags, etc.), and they have devised a method for discriminating sexual bondage from the general use of restraints.

In their opinion, an investigator may confidently conclude sexual bondage is involved when

1. the victim has been bound in a variety of positions, or
2. bindings aren't necessary for restraint (as in the upper arms or calves), or
3. the bindings reflect that time and effort were spent ensuring their neatness and symmetry; for instance, if both wrists are bound identically, or each eye is covered with an exactly two-inch-long piece of white adhesive tape.

Fetishism also is frequently encountered in autoerotic cases, as well as sexual crimes in general. Twelve of the victims in *Autoerotic Fatalities*, for example, practiced some form of fetishism.

Almost any inanimate thing can be a fetish.

"I always caution investigators not to apply their own criteria when searching for materials that someone else might find sexually exciting," Hazelwood says.

For that reason, he asks three questions when assessing whether an object is a possible fetish item.

1. Is there an abnormal amount of the material present?

One hundred fifty roller skate straps were discovered in one victim's possession.

2. Does the material belong where you found it?

There are few everyday reasons for keeping lengths of chromium chain in your bedroom.

3. How much financial investment does the individual have in the item?

A three-thousand-dollar investment in lingerie would be excessive.

On occasion, a fourth question may arise: Why did the victim keep this object hidden?

Dangerous autoeroticism commonly is associated with masochism. Yet Hazelwood has also discovered the habit among sexual criminals.

Harvey Glatman cross-dressed when he hanged himself.

Gerard Schaefer, a serial killer who himself eventually was killed by another inmate at the Florida State Prison, practiced dangerous autoerotic sex in the Florida swamps.

He would cross-dress and suspend himself by the neck from tree limbs. In Roy's opinion, Schaefer was using himself as a prop in the absence of available female victims, whom he also took into the Florida swamps and hanged. He even took photos of these autoerotic sessions. The purpose of the picture taking, Roy believes, was to perfect the manner in which Schaefer hanged himself, as well as his victims, hoping to enhance both experiences for him.

Mike DeBardeleben, an archetypal sexual sadist, created his *Bite it!* audiotape and, according to one of his victims, dressed in a miniskirt, sweater, and high heels while he was with her.

Dangerous autoeroticism seems to exert a potent seductiveness on nominally normal people, too. On at least two occasions after Roy has lectured to professional audiences on dangerous autoerotic practices, audience members have accidentally killed themselves attempting dangerous autoeroticism themselves.

"No one knows why one person acts on aberrant sexual fantasies, and another person does not," says Hazelwood. "What is known is that many people have aberrant fantasies which, if acted out, would be criminal.

"In the case of dangerous autoeroticism, what criminals and noncriminals have in common is that they engage in the same types of solo sexual acts."

In their textbook, Hazelwood, Dietz, and Burgess warn sternly: "Do not attempt any of the autoerotic activities described or depicted in this monograph. . . . There is no reason to believe that these activities are pleasurable to the average person, and there is every reason to believe that they may prove fatal."

SIX ✕

Louella and Earl

Back in the days when he dipped his ducktail in baby oil, favored black shirts with pink lapels, and wheeled around Spring Branch, Texas, in a '49 Mercury, cut low to the ground, looking for girls and/or trouble, few people would have predicted that Robert Roy (he's always been known by his middle name) Hazelwood someday would become a federal agent.

Least of all Roy himself.

"I was very, very fortunate I didn't get into serious trouble," he says of his rowdy youth. "The last thing I ever expected to do was go into law enforcement."

In truth, Roy had no clear notion of the future, or any plan for it. As a boy and as a man, he has always been content for opportunity to find him. The theme of chance, more or less spontaneous decision making is strong through Hazelwood's life.

"The only thing I've always been sure of is what I didn't want to do," he says.

Roy was born in Pocatello, Idaho, on March 4, 1938. He has no early recollections of his outlaw father, or any other member of Merle P. Reddick's family.

The man he called Dad was Earl Hazelwood, a barber and former minor-league first baseman, who married Roy's mother, Louella, in 1941, about three years after she divorced Reddick.

Earl Hazelwood was a contradictory and complex figure who bulks large in his stepson's memory. The two came into almost immediate conflict.

"I look back now," Roy says, "and I can see that it was jealousy over my mother's affections. My mother and I were very close. And I wasn't his natural son."

Earl Hazelwood had a quick temper. Roy recollects a family argument in which it appeared that his stepfather was about to strike his mother. Roy stepped between them.

"He said something like, 'I'll knock the hell out of you!' and my mother grabbed me and put me behind her."

Earl Hazelwood had a secret flaw, too.

"He was sick a lot," says Roy. "He'd come home from work and go straight to bed. On Sundays he was in bed all day. I was told he had a stomach problem. I was twenty-two years old before I realized he was an alcoholic."

In all important ways, however, Roy believes that growing up a Hazelwood was a distinct improvement over the alternative, life with the missing M. P. Reddick. The Hazelwood family even had about them their own whiff of renegade celebrity that Roy savored.

According to his dad's possibly apocryphal account, Hazelwood once was spelled Hazlewood. Shortly after the Civil War, however, a Hazlewood who happened to be a minister made the mistake of delivering a meal to the outlaw Jesse James, and was hanged for his trouble.

The rest of the clan, according to Earl, changed their name to Hazelwood to avoid further disgrace.

Roy's mother, Louella, was a devout, but hardly doctrinaire, Baptist.

"She didn't see anything wrong with having a beer occasionally, or dancing," Roy recollects. "When we'd have the youth fellowship night at our house, my mother would tell us, 'Okay, kids. I'm going to keep Pastor Ken and his wife busy drinking coffee in the kitchen. You go ahead and dance.'"

When her oldest boy later joined another famously dogmatic and occasionally inflexible organization, the FBI, he'd discover ways of bending the rules in ways that would have made Louella smile.

Earl and Louella were married in Minnesota, then moved south in a protracted, multistage migration to his native Texas. They'd travel for a while, then stop so Earl could cut hair and replenish the family finances.

Louella bore Roy's half brother, Jimmy, while the Hazelwoods were stopped in Nebraska. Half sister Earlene debuted in Missouri. Louella's final pregnancy ended in a stillbirth in Kansas.

When they reached Texas, Earl settled his family for a time in a one-bedroom trailer in Houston. When he found steady work, they were able to afford fifteen dollars a month for a so-called shotgun shack—three rooms lined up in a row with a bathroom off to one side—"named for the fact that you can shoot a shotgun from the front door through the back door and not hit anything," Roy explains.

By 1950, his dad was doing well enough at barbering to move the family to a brand-new sixty-dollar-a-month tract house in Spring Branch, then about forty miles outside of Houston.

Roy reached his full adult height, five feet nine inches, early on at Spring Branch High School. A slender youth who bore a faint resemblance to the young Sinatra, he wouldn't weigh more than 141 pounds until he quit smoking forty years later.

He was quick and agile enough to letter in basketball on the ninth-grade team. Under Earl's expert tutelage, he played shortstop through high school.

Outside of recognized sports, however, Roy had little use for socially sanctioned recreation.

On one occasion, he and two school pals headed north to Bedias, his dad's hometown, ostensibly to hunt deer on some acreage Earl owned there. The real objective was to drink beer.

The three friends lost their way and strayed onto a neighbor's property. Soon enough a pack of dogs chased Roy and his pals into a tree. Behind the dogs came the deputies.

"You're trespassing, boys," said one officer.

The teenagers were handcuffed and driven away in cruisers, red lights flashing and siren wailing, to the nearest town of any size, Huntsville, where the tipsy trespassers were brought before a magistrate.

"How do you plead, guilty or not?" the judge asked gruffly.

Before Roy had a chance to answer, down came the gavel.

"Guilty," said the judge. "That'll be a twenty-five-dollar fine."

Roy did not have that much money, which meant calling his dad.

Earl Hazelwood drove up from Spring Branch and dealt with the situation adroitly. Resisting a fatherly impulse to lecture his stepson, Earl paid Roy's fine and drove home with his grateful stepson. No record was ever made of the incident.

Another time, Roy unwisely stopped for a meal at a hamburger drive-in located within a rival high school's home turf.

"I was with the love of my young life, Charla West," he recalls. "I had some words with this guy, who grabbed me and cut me under my right arm with a switchblade. I still have the scar."

Overmatched in hostile territory, Roy slyly rescued himself by means of a ruse. "I grabbed some of my blood and smeared it all over the front of my shirt. Then I bent over, fell to the ground and started moaning. It worked. He thought he'd really killed me and took off.

Meanwhile, Charla vomited all over his front seat.

By this time, Earl Hazelwood was operating two seven-chair barbershops in Spring Branch. As a result the mortgage was paid and there always was food on the Hazelwood family table, but only because Louella managed the home economy, says her son.

"One time my dad won something like a hundred thousand dollars in a poker game. Then he took it to Las Vegas and lost it all in three days. On another occasion, my mother went home to North Dakota for a visit. While she was gone, he gave me her car and bought new Fords for each of them. When she got home she raised hell with him. He had to return the Fords and take back her car."

In retrospect, Roy believes Earl Hazelwood was manic-depressive—or bipolar, in modern psychiatric parlance—swinging between exultant highs and troughs of despond.

"My dad chased rainbows. He was constantly making deals, selling this and buying that. I'd come home night after night to find him sitting up in the living room, bent over, an ashtray full of cigarette butts next to him. He was thinking of ways to make money!"

Man and boy finally did stumble toward common ground, growing closer as Roy matured from aimless adolescence into adulthood, a process Earl did much to abet. If he wasn't much of a role model, Earl Hazelwood nevertheless provided Roy with frank and sensible advice.

When Roy graduated from high school and announced he planned to buy a '57 Chevy, his Dad asked him, "Where do you want to live?"

"What do you mean?" Roy asked.

"You're eighteen, a man now," Earl said. "You have thirty days to find yourself a place to live and get a job."

He let that prospect sink in for a moment, then suggested an alternative. If Roy would forget about the car and consider heading for college, Earl said, he'd help finance Roy's education.

School had scant allure for Roy, but the prospect of manual labor was even less appealing.

"Uh, college sounds pretty good," he said.

It was Dad, as well, who urged Roy to join the ROTC at Sam Houston State, and to remain with it even though Roy hated the ROTC.

"You can certainly drop it if you want," Earl said, but he then reminded Roy he'd surely be drafted into the army the moment he graduated. "You'll be the one who's going to be peeling potatoes instead of giving the order for them to be peeled," Earl advised.

Roy heeded what he was told, and entered the military police as a second lieutenant after college. True to his nature, he didn't choose the MPs out of any particular interest in law enforcement or intention of making them his career. Rather, Roy perceived that among his alternatives—infantry, cavalry, engineers, and the rest—MPs were the least likely soldiers to sweat and get dirty.

Earl was satisfied.

Then in 1962, Roy was sent to Oxford, Mississippi, to help protect James Meredith, the first black student to enroll at the University of Mississippi.

"My dad almost disowned me over that," he recalls. "He was a racist. When I told him I had orders to go to Ole Miss, he said, 'Resign your commission.' I told him I couldn't. I'd taken an oath to uphold the Constitution of the United States."

Time and Earl's advancing ill health eventually resolved all conflicts between them. In 1975, as his dad lay dying a painful death from emphysema in a Houston hospital, Roy spent two weeks with him. To the end, Earl remained in charge of their relationship.

"Go on back home," he announced to Roy from his hospital bed one day. "You were here when it counted. You don't need to come back for my funeral."

Not long thereafter, Earl expired in Louella's arms.

SEVEN ✖

Organized and
Disorganized

Roy's best-known contribution to criminology—the organized-disorganized criminal behavior dichotomy—first occurred to him one day while he was taking a shower.

He had been contemplating James Odom and James Lawson, Jr., a pair of convicted rapists who'd met as inmates at a state mental institution in California. While locked up together, the pair had shared their fantasies; Odom described to Lawson his dreams of rape, and Lawson confided to Odom his violent imaginings of female evisceration and mutilation.

"We'd fantasized so much that at times I didn't know what was real," Odom later said.

Upon their release, the two hooked up in South Carolina and went hunting victims together. They abducted at gunpoint a twenty-five-year-old convenience store clerk and drove the woman to an isolated location. Odom raped the victim in the backseat of a Ford belonging to Lawson's father. Then Lawson cut her throat with a knife the clerk had sold him earlier, and savagely mutilated her dead body with it.

"I wanted to cut her body so she would not look like a person, and destroy her so she would not exist," Lawson said in his subsequent confession. "I began to cut on her body. I remember cutting her breasts off. After this, all I remember is that I kept cutting on her body."

Odom and Lawson put scant effort into concealing what they'd done. Their victim was soon discovered, the car was easy to trace, and within days they were arrested for the clerk's murder.

As Hazelwood pondered this crime, he couldn't get over how haphazard and sloppy the killers had been. "I said to myself, 'Gosh, this was really not well planned, not well thought out. These guys were really kinda disorganized.'

"And I compared them to Ed Kemper. He was *really* organized. Kemper put a lot of time and effort into his crimes."

Edmund Emil Kemper III occupies an extralarge niche in the BSU's early history with aberrant criminals. Not only was the six-foot nine-inch, three-hundred-pound necrophile a highly intelligent and well-spoken serial killer, an ideal subject for interview, but Kemper also had a sadistic wit.

He was serving seven life sentences in California's Vacaville State Prison when Bob Ressler, pursuing his serial-killer study, paid Ed Kemper a call. It was their third meeting.

After spending several hours together with Kemper, talking murder and dismemberment in a locked cell adjacent to death row, Ressler buzzed for a guard. None came. He buzzed again, and a third time. After fifteen minutes of waiting, still no guard.

The agent tried not to betray his nervousness, but Kemper saw his chance.

"If I went apeshit in here, you'd be in a lot of trouble, wouldn't you?" he toyed with Ressler. "I could screw your head off and place it on the table to greet the guard."

As Ressler disconsolately imagined how easily such a scene might play out, he gamely warned Kemper of the trouble he'd be in for committing such a crime.

"What would they do, cut off my TV privileges?" the killer replied with a smirk.

Inwardly berating himself for the stupidity of allowing such a situation in the first place, Ressler continued to keep Kemper talking, trying out every interrogation and hostage-negotiation trick he'd ever been taught—plus some he made up as he went along—hoping someone, soon, would happen by to rescue him.

Finally, a guard appeared to escort the homicidal giant back to his cell.

"You know I was just kidding, don't you?" Kemper said on his way out the door.

"Sure," Ressler answered.

Kemper was every bit as depraved as James Lawson. At age fourteen, he murdered his grandparents, and he spent seven years at the maximum-security

California state hospital at Atascadero (where Odom and Lawson later met) before being paroled to his mother's custody in 1969.

Over the succeeding nine years he killed eight more people: six young women he picked up hitchhiking, plus his mother and one of her female friends.

All were dissected or decapitated or sexually assaulted after death. He cut leg meat from two of his victims into a macaroni casserole he prepared and ate.

Kemper bludgeoned his mother with a hammer as she slept. He sawed off her head, had sex with her corpse, and carved out her larynx and shoved it down the garbage disposal. Afterward, he propped her severed head on the mantel for dart practice.

Hence Bob Ressler's informed unease when Kemper threatened to "screw your head off."

But Ed Kemper had more than one dimension to him.

What distinguished him from a James Lawson, Hazelwood recognized, was organization. Patience and planning and attention to detail were the reasons Kemper was able to commit serial kidnap-murders for so long without being identified. Ed Kemper thought through his every move, and even rehearsed his crimes.

He would pick up a girl, try a personality on her, and then release her unharmed and unaware of his intentions. He experimented for months with different approaches, perfecting what Hazelwood calls the killer's "service personality," the image he projects to mask his true intentions.

Highly disciplined and a perfectionist, Kemper learned to be conversational, unthreatening, to project a mild, even attractive, persona with which he would smoothly transact the critical first phase of his assaults, the approach.

Afterward, despite the ghastliness of his postmortem behavior, he never left messy crime scenes or in any way called unnecessary attention to himself. Kemper wasn't caught until he called California police from Colorado, confessed what he'd done by telephone, and then waited in his car to be arrested.

This, Hazelwood recognized, was the antithesis of James Lawson's and James Odom's *disorganized* behavior. Ed Kemper was *organized*.

Pursuing the distinction further, Hazelwood realized that what he'd really captured with his dichotomy was the broad difference between crazy (psychotic) behavior, and irrational yet sane (psychopathic, or antisocial) behavior.

In time, the insight led to a practical and handy way for homicide investigators to quickly categorize their UNSUBs into three major classes: organized, disorganized, and mixed offenders.

Hazelwood unveiled his organized and disorganized analytical framework in an article entitled "The Lust Murderer," published under his name and John Douglas's in the April 1980 FBI *Law Enforcement Bulletin*. It was the first professional article Roy wrote as an FBI agent. Since then, "The Lust Murderer" has been the most frequently reprinted of all BSU papers.

The title comes from an old catch-all clinical term for homicide committed during passion. Hazelwood and Douglas appropriated *lust murder* for any killing that involves mutilation and/or removal of the victim's sexual parts. In either sense, the term today has fallen largely into disuse.

Hazelwood used it to describe the Odom-Lawson slaying, because "there really isn't another term that captures what those men did to that woman," he explains.

He describes the organized offender as indifferent to his fellow humans, irresponsible, and self-centered—the classic psychopath. He is manipulative, deliberate, and full of guile, outwardly amiable for as long as it suits his objectives.

If the organized offender is a crafty wolf, then the disorganized offender is more like a wild dog.

He has few, if any, social skills. Typically, he is a loner and manifestly so. He may not wash or shave for days, or change his clothing or comb his hair. He feels rejected, and for the most part is incapable of forming normal relationships with other people of either sex. He lacks the organized offender's craftiness, and commits his crimes on impulse, in a frenzy, with little planning or preparation.

His spontaneous fury may be sparked by anger or passion, drugs or alcohol. He may also be mentally retarded or psychotic, or may simply lack experience or maturity.

Unlike the organized offender, who preys for the most part on strangers, the disorganized offender may kill a friend, relative, acquaintance, or neighbor, indifferent at that moment to his risk of capture.

He also will score lower on standardized intelligence tests, although here Hazelwood cautions against confusing low measurable intellect with stupidity. Disorganized offenders are capable of high animal cunning.

"My favorite example of this is a serial rapist I interviewed in a midwestern prison," he says. "I remember he was chained wrist to waist, and waist to ankle, and was considered one of the most dangerous inmates in the prison.

"He had attacked and beaten the deputy warden, and then sent him a letter saying that next time he hoped the official would put up a better fight.

"He was powerfully built, in his early thirties, about five-nine and two hundred forty pounds, all muscle. He had a full-scale IQ of seventy-nine, and spoke mostly in monosyllables."

The inmate's evident lack of intellect, says Hazelwood, masked a far more important asset—street smarts.

"He'd raped a series of women in Florida, and then fled to his hometown in the upper Midwest when he learned there was a warrant out for his arrest."

Searching for shelter, the rapist hit upon a foolproof way of hiding out. "He told me that he checked into a residential drug rehab program," Roy recalls. "Total confidentiality. No one would acknowledge he was there. Although he had never used drugs, he'd been around people who did, and was able to fake all the symptoms.

"Now remember, this guy has an IQ of seventy-nine. After several weeks in the drug program, he wanted a woman. He told his roommate he wanted one. The roommate says, 'Oh, no. You can't even get out of the building until you've been here six months.'

"'Bullshit,' the guy says."

As he later recounted the story to Roy, he faked a stomach pain and was sent with an escort to the city hospital for diagnostic work. Once there, the first thing he needed to do was get rid of the escort.

"Well, let's see," he said, "I gotta go to the seventeenth floor for X rays. Then I gotta go to the third floor for blood tests. Up to the sixth floor for urinalysis and—"

The escort interrupted: "I'll wait for you in the lobby," he said.

At this point in his narrative, the rapist stopped and asked Hazelwood where he would search for a rape victim in a hospital.

"The gynecology department?" Roy ventured.

"Nah. They're all pregnant in there, or have a disease. What you want to do is head for the women's rest room."

The rapist stood outside the rest room until a woman walked in alone, and then he followed behind her. After scratching "Out of Order" on a paper towel, which he affixed to the facility door, he returned inside and sexually assaulted the victim.

As he did so, a second female, ignoring the "Out of Order" sign, walked into the rest room, discovered the rape in progress, and ran out screaming, "There's a man assaulting a woman in the rest room!"

A crowd quickly gathered at the doorway. Meantime, as the rapist retold the story, he grabbed his victim by her hair and shoved her along in front of him, out the rest room door.

"And let me tell you something, bitch!" he screamed at her, "if I ever catch you screwing around on me again, I'm not only going to kill him, I'm going to kill you, too!"

His stunned audience "parted like the Red Sea," according to Hazelwood, and he escaped the rest room, the hospital, and the United States for Canada.

Typically, the disorganized offender commits his crime with any weapon available at the point of encounter with his victim. He will also leave her at the murder site, making little or no effort to conceal the body. He'll probably leave the weapon there, too.

Such an offender initially is apt to commit his crimes within walking distance of where he lives or works. However, if he is not caught and is mentally competent and capable of learning, he may soon stop taking such risks and evolve, over time, into an organized offender.

In a representative case Hazelwood consulted on in 1997, a young female was raped and murdered at home. The offender, who was personally acquainted with his victim, had kicked her and struck her with his fists before beating her to death with a steel rod he'd picked up inside her house. He left her body where he killed her and returned to his residence, which was less than a thousand yards away.

Roy immediately categorized the criminal as disorganized because he knew his victim, chose a weapon of opportunity, made no effort to conceal what he had done, and lived a short distance away from the murder scene.

The organized offender, by contrast, is a planner. He brings his own weapons or restraints, hunts away from where he lives or works, normally has no traceable association with his victim, and takes steps to conceal the body, as well as to remove evidence. He'll take care not to leave fingerprints, body fluids such as blood or semen, or spent cartridges and shells.

He is usually older, as well as more mature, than the disorganized offender. He prefers to commit his crime in seclusion, and often transports his victim to a second location for disposal. He is not necessarily concerned if she ultimately is discovered, because the publicity surrounding her death and its impact on the community can be highly exciting to him.

A case Roy worked on as a consultant in 1997 featured an organized offender. In the crime, a masked and gloved intruder, armed with a 9mm handgun, entered a retail business at closing time, taking six employees hostage. He had them bind one another, and then shot all six, killing three of them. After robbing the establishment, he collected the spent shells and departed.

This was an experienced, mature, and highly organized offender. He planned his crime, brought what he needed with him, concealed his identity, chose an advantageous moment (closing time) to strike, eliminated half the possible witnesses against him (the others were left for dead, his single oversight), and removed potential physical evidence (the shells) before leaving.

He still has not been caught, or even as yet identified.

Hazelwood also has characterized the organized offender as "a thinking criminal," and the disorganized offender as "not a thinking criminal."

Thinking criminals tend to be extroverted and articulate, use (but do not abuse) alcohol and drugs, and are highly narcissistic. They often take great care with their physical health and appearance, and can pass anything but a mirror.

Exceptions exist.

Ted Kaczynski, the Unabomber, obviously was highly organized, a thinking criminal. A Ph.D. mathematician, Kaczynski fabricated and exploded sixteen intricately built bombs over eighteen years, killing three people and injuring twenty-eight more. Yet he also was socially isolated, a hairy, ill-kempt hermit with few apparent social skills, who lived in a rustic shed in rural Montana.

Psychiatrists later diagnosed him as a paranoid schizophrenic.

Still another exception to the general rule is the disorganized offender who creates havoc, but in the midst of it also drops a clear hint of who he is and where he's been.

In one gory case that Roy worked, an offender had carefully extracted five green peas from his victim's eviscerated stomach and lined them up precisely on a plate.

Hazelwood surmised that the killer had once been institutionalized, and later was proved correct in his conjecture.

"How'd you get that idea?" a skeptical Dr. Dietz asked him.

Hazelwood explained to his friend the psychiatrist that in an institution where a person is totally controlled, a need for order in one's life develops. A patient, for example, might neatly line up books on a window ledge, even though his mind is chaotic.

The same patient, having just chaotically slaughtered a victim, might express that same craving for orderliness in the way this offender did, by arranging the green peas just so.

Organized offenders tend to remain organized over time, although again there are exceptions, such as Ted Bundy.

Bundy abducted and killed as many as a dozen girls and young women before the police discerned a pattern to their disappearances, or any of their remains—much less a crime scene—were discovered.

He murdered perhaps fifteen more victims before he was first arrested, by accident, and was charged with a kidnapping, not homicide. Even then there were no known witnesses to any of his abduction-murders, nor any fingerprints or other physical evidence that conclusively tied Ted to any of his twenty-seven or more sexual homicides.

Then Bundy began to unravel. On Super Bowl Sunday, 1978, in a bloody and wholly uncharacteristic spasm of spontaneous violence, he clubbed to death two sleeping coeds, and left two others for dead, in the upstairs bedrooms of the Chi Omega sorority house on the campus of Florida State University in Tallahassee. In his even wilder ultimate assault—for which he was caught, convicted, and executed—on February 9, 1978, Ted snatched Kimberly Diane Leach from her junior high school campus in broad daylight. He slit the twelve-year-old Florida schoolgirl's throat and deposited her partially clad body under an abandoned hog shed some miles away. Bundy was captured drunk, driving a stolen car, less than a week later.

Ted's final crime was hardly organized—at least not in the way his early kills were—but it wasn't entirely disorganized, either. It was "mixed," a third classification first proposed at BSU by John Douglas, Bob Ressler, and other agents who saw that not every crime fits exactly on one side or the other of Roy's original divide.

In fact, the Odom-Lawson case represented one important class of mixed offender cases, crimes in which two perpetrators of contrasting criminal type are involved.

The fact that Odom's and Lawson's victim was taken to a secluded spot argues for an organized offender. So would the serological evidence of semen found in her vagina; disorganized offenders are less likely to commit penile rape.

Yet the frenzied, postmortem mutilation and apparent indifference to how and when the body was discovered gave the crime a disorganized cast as well.

Multiple factors can be at play to create a mixed crime scene.

Sometimes what the investigator finds is behavioral evidence of a youthful disorganized offender in transition toward becoming organized. Sometimes, as with Odom and Lawson, mixed evidence actually points to two or more offenders.

The offender may also be mixed in that while he exhibits a disorganized criminal's typically short emotional fuse, he is also organized to the extent that he can assess his situation and adjust his behavior to avoid taking undue risks. Serial killer Jack Harrison Trawick typified this type of mixed offender.

The disorganized, organized, and mixed categories apply across the range of deviant criminality, including rape. However, Hazelwood's second major contribution to the classification of aberrant criminals was to divide rapists themselves into six groups. He adapted the system from a typology first suggested by clinical psychologist Nicholas Groth, author of *Men Who Rape: The Psychology of the Offender.*

Nick Groth was among the first researchers to observe that the underlying motivations for rape are principally power and anger, sometimes in combination. There are very few rapists for whom the primary motive is sexual.

The first of Hazelwood's offender types is the "power reassurance rapist," who is the most common example of a ritualistic, stranger-to-stranger rapist.

Familiar to newspaper readers as "the Gentleman Rapist" or "the Friendly Rapist" or any similar name that suggests what Hazelwood calls this type's "pseudo-unselfish" behavior, the power reassurance rapist is trying to do just that: reassure himself of his masculinity (which he deeply doubts) by exercising physical control over women.

The fantasy which fuels his behavior is of a willing, even eager, victim, the sort of sexual encounter he feels totally incapable of consummating in his day-to-day world. With a victim, however, he may play the part of ardent lover, fondling and complimenting her on her appearance, frequently inquiring solicitously if he's pleasing her.

The power reassurance rapist often produces a weapon, or claims to be carrying one. However, his fantasy is to express power through sex, not physical injury. He is the rapist least likely to apply more force than absolutely necessary to compel his victim's compliance.

His hallmarks are victims selected from within his own age range, whom he forces to remove their own clothing as a way of feeding his fantasy that they are his willing partners.

This offender generally spends an extended period of time with the victim, especially if he encounters a particularly passive female upon whom he can act out all of his sexual fantasies.

Afterward—and consistent with "pseudo-unselfish" behavior—he may apologize and even ask her forgiveness.

An example of the power reassurance rapist from Roy's casebook, one that he uses in his lectures, was an offender in Tennessee. After selecting a victim who lived alone, the rapist broke into her house through a bathroom window, pointed a knife at her, and said, "Do what I say and I won't hurt you."

The woman complied, as she later explained to Roy.

He kissed and fondled her, and within five minutes had committed a vaginal rape. Then he remained in bed with her for another forty-five minutes, head propped on an arm, speaking about himself.

The rapist explained that he was a college graduate and had been married until the day he caught his wife cheating with another man. Since then, he'd become a serial rapist, he said.

"That's the reason I'm committing these crimes," he told her, as if his unhappy personal history somehow explained, or mitigated, the degradation and trauma he was causing her.

As the conversation continued, his victim said she was engaged to be married.

He told her that he had parked his car six blocks away and left the keys in it. He said he hoped the vehicle wouldn't be stolen. He said he had a drunk friend who'd come with him, but that he wouldn't allow the fellow inside because he was drunk and he could not be responsible for his behavior. He advised her to repair the broken latch on her bathroom window.

After he finally left and she was calling the police, the victim discovered that four hundred dollars in cash had been stolen from her purse. Next morning, she opened her mailbox to find an envelope containing the money and a printed note from the rapist, executed in crayon in block letters.

In it, he first advised her again to fix the bathroom window lock.

He then wrote that he was "terribly sorry" his inebriated friend had sneaked into the house and stolen the cash, "and that he assures me that is all he took." He felt very fortunate to report his car had not been stolen, and wished her and her fiancé the best of luck.

Stealing four hundred dollars from a rape victim just to return the money in order to convince her you're really a good person illustrates the sort of complex and convoluted reasoning of which the power reassurance rapist is capable.

An offender in Hazelwood's next category, the "power assertive rapist," would find such a gambit wimpish, incomprehensible. Less common than the power reassurance rapist, and more violent, the power assertive offender, as Roy explains, "assaults to assert his masculinity, about which he has no doubts.

The key to understanding him is his macho self-perception. The most important thing in the world for him is for others to see him as a man's man."

This offender, who like the power reassurance rapist generally selects victims of roughly his own age, attacks in no particular pattern and at any convenient time and place. Unlike the power reassurance rapist, he will rip his victim's clothes from her body himself, and attack her repeatedly with no concern for her suffering.

Typically, he uses a moderate level of force whether or not his victim resists him. Experts in domestic violence have told Hazelwood that the power assertive rapist is most similar to the offender profile for date and spousal rapists.

One power assertive rapist whom Roy interviewed described to Hazelwood the time he came upon a female motorist stranded in her disabled car. She had her child with her, and was fearful. However, he was a well-dressed and well-spoken white male, and she soon relaxed a bit, grateful someone had stopped to offer his assistance.

He raised the hood and looked at the engine with an air of authority.

"You need a mechanic," he informed her, and offered the woman a ride to the closest garage. Because of his politeness and appearance, she risked accepting his offer.

They drove on, exchanging small talk as they went until she noticed he'd passed two exits without stopping. When she asked where he was going, the man produced a gun and told her to shut up. She screamed, and he struck her hard on the head with the gun. She momentarily lost consciousness.

When she regained her senses, her clothes had been ripped away, and he was raping her. She pleaded for him not to hurt her. At that he swore at her, struck her once more, and again told her to shut up.

Over the next two hours, he raped her three more times, and forced her to fellate him twice.

When he was finished, he threw her out of the car, nude.

"Show your ass and you may get some help," he said, and then drove away, leaving her nude by the roadside with her youngster.

Type number three, the "anger retaliatory rapist," ratchets up the violence even higher. He is angry at women for real or imagined wrongs, and lashes out against them, episodically. Typically, his assault is sparked by something involving a woman.

"But the problem is, that episode could be anything from a woman being elected to Congress to a female police officer issuing him a ticket to a fight with his wife," says Hazelwood.

This rapist uses excessive force; his victims often require hospitalization. He usually spends a very short time with them, often experiences sexual dysfunction (because of his extreme hostility), and is highly impulsive.

A classic example of the anger retaliatory rapist is the short and muscular rest room rapist mentioned earlier. A typical sexual assault he described to Hazelwood occurred in a supermarket parking lot at midafternoon. Seeing a woman loading groceries in her car, he walked up to her, pushed the cart out of the way, pummeled her, threw her in the backseat of her car and raped her, then got up and walked away.

The most dangerous of all to his victims is the "anger excitation rapist," the sexual sadist who is sexually stimulated by his victim's suffering.

None of these rare and enormously destructive offenders has left a fuller record of himself than Mike DeBardeleben, the so-called "Mall Passer" counterfeiter and subject of my book, *Lethal Shadow*. The Secret Service brought the case to Roy's attention after DeBardeleben was captured in 1983.

He left behind sheaves of handwritten notes, underlined passages in text, drawings, and tape recordings in which he created a detailed record of his desires and deeds.

"This is a tape, regarding my goals," DeBardeleben begins on one undated tape recording.

"Number one on my list of goals is to establish a new identity, complete with background, school records, employment records, driver's license, Social Security card, passport, checking accounts, savings accounts. Rent an apartment. Buy a car. Have a job—or a job front. All under a new identity. This new identity would not be able to be traced to me under *any* circumstances. It may have to be set up in a different location, a different city.

"Second on my list of goals is to buy a house; preferably, buy some land and build my own house according to my own *custom* specifications and needs. Number one would be a garage, one- or two-car garage, to completely enclose a car with no windows so that no one could tell if a car was there or not there. Also a basement area—or *work* area—which is hidden and unable to be detected by ordinary means.

"Naturally, of course, I would need as a requirement secret hidden compartments built into the house for stash areas, for various things . . . along with the secret work area for a press and darkroom facilities, a *fun* area—secret *fun* area—which would include a *cage* so that I could have an SMB [DeBardeleben's code for *sadomasochistic bitch*] locked *up!*

"Also of *prime* importance—top priority—would be an *incinerator* capable of incinerating at extremely high temperature—*total* incineration. This could be connected as the lower part of the fireplace in the living room above."

He also recorded torture sessions with his fourth wife, Caryn.*

"What are you going to do to me?!" the terrified woman is heard to say in a small voice on the tape.

"Huh?" DeBardeleben grunts.

"No!" Caryn screams. "What are you going to do to me?! Please! Please tell me! Please tell me! What are you doing?! *Tell me!*"

"C'mon," he drawls lazily.

"Oh, please don't do it again!'"

"You gonna be a crybaby? Huh?'

Caryn whimpers. "No, I won't."

"All right."

A pause.

"Please!" she screams again. "Untie my hands! Please, Mike! Don't fuck me in the ass! I wouldn't do something like that to you! *Don't fuck me in the ass!*"

The tape, a half hour long and edited in places, quite clearly depicts Mike DeBardeleben torturing and sodomizing Caryn. He forces her to beg for pain and humiliation, and giggles as she does so.

"Please let me die," Caryn pleads. "Let me die. Let me die. Let me die."

"Calm down. You gonna calm down?" her husband asks.

"Why can't I die? Why can't I die?" Caryn continues in a high-pitched singsong. "Why can't I die? Why can't I die? Why can't I die?"

"My mother died," DeBardeleben interjects.

"I wish I were her!" Caryn sobs. "I wish I were her and not me! I wish I were her, oh God! I want to die! Why don't you do it?"

DeBardeleben hated women and used sex to punish them.

He also exactly captured what could be called the sexual sadist's creed in written notes discovered by the Secret Service, and later published in court documents.

"Sadism," DeBardeleben wrote:

> The wish to inflict pain on others is not the essence of sadism. The central impulse to have complete mastery over another person, to make him/her a helpless object of our will, to become the absolute ruler over her, to become her god, to do with her as one pleases, to humiliate her, to enslave her are means to this end.

And the most radical aim is to make her suffer. Since there is no greater power over another person than that of inflicting pain on her. To force her to undergo suffering without her being able to defend herself. The pleasure in the complete domination of another person is the very essence of the sadistic drive.

"Investigators," explains Hazelwood, "find no other sexual crime as well planned and methodically executed as that committed by the anger excitation rapist. Every detail is carefully thought out and rehearsed, either literally or in the offender's fantasies. Weapons and instruments, transportation, travel routes, recording devices, bindings—virtually every phase has been pre-planned, with one notable exception.

"A sexual sadist will practice his brutality on his wife or girlfriend, but most of his victims are strangers. While they meet certain criteria established by the rapist to fulfill his desires and fantasies, they generally will not be associated with him in any way known to others. This is also part of his plan. He wants no ties that will connect him to the victim."

Of all Hazelwood's categories, the only type who may assault primarily out of sexual desire is the so-called opportunistic rapist, who usually commits his offense in the course of committing some other crime altogether, such as robbery or kidnapping. As his designation implies, he sees an opportunity and impulsively seizes it.

He generally uses minimal force and spends just a short time with the victim. It is common for the opportunistic rapist to bind his victim before leaving.

He often is drunk or high on drugs when he rapes.

About the last category, gang rape, Hazelwood has the least to say. "It is pathological group behavior in which the victim is almost always seriously injured," he says. "These rapists play to one another. There are multiple offenders, obviously. But there is always a leader, and always a reluctant participant, who often makes himself known to the victim. This is the offender whom law enforcement should focus on and attempt to profile."

EIGHT

"I'd Like to Pray
About This"

Following his AFIP fellowship, Roy returned once again to Fort Gordon, Georgia, to serve as a U.S. Army Criminal Investigation Division (CID) instructor. In a short time, he was placed in charge of all new agents training for the CID.

He had so far enjoyed his army career and had done well. However, Roy also knew the next step in his career path likely would be a desk job at the Pentagon, a prospect about which he was only mildly enthusiastic, even though it also meant another promotion, to lieutenant colonel.

He was ten years away from retirement, and had no expectations of staying in the army beyond that time. That meant at age forty-two he'd have to start looking around for a second career. "What am I going to do, sell real estate?" he asked himself. "Do prison work? Become a special investigator for a sheriff's department?"

Roy had reached another of those periodic junctures in his life when all he knew for certain was what he disdained. It was time once more for chance to intervene.

It finally did one day in 1970, when he drove a friend to an interview appointment at the FBI office in downtown Augusta, Georgia. Dressed in his uniform, Roy was seated in the lobby, waiting for his fellow officer to finish, when he was approached by an FBI agent.

"While your friend's in there, would you like to look at an application?"

"No, I'm happy," Roy said, gesturing at his uniform. "Career army."

"Well, just take an application," said the agent.

Hazelwood did, and went home and filled out the form "on a lark," he says. "I just wanted to see if the Bureau would accept me."

To his delighted surprise, the FBI did. An agent contacted Roy, advising him to resign his commission so he could depart immediately when the imminent appointment letter signed by J. Edgar Hoover arrived.

Major Hazelwood was too cautious for that.

"Wait a minute," he told the agent. "I have a wife and three kids. When I get that appointment letter, then I'll make a decision."

The appointment letter didn't come; although Roy was his recruiter's top choice, the Bureau was not hiring agents at the time.

In early 1971, he was selected to attend the FBI's National Academy program, a three-month course for veteran law enforcement officers from around the United States. Of the fifty members in each class, only two were military officers. It was a singular honor for Roy to be chosen.

Since an FBI interview was part of the preregistration process, Roy soon found himself back at the Bureau's Augusta office. He remembers how the special agent in charge (SAC) noticed on his documents that Hazelwood had been selected both to the National Academy and, pending appointment, for FBI agent training.

"Which would you prefer?" the SAC asked.

"FBI," Roy answered.

"Well, then, let's hold up this National Academy application," said the SAC.

The very next day, Roy received a special delivery letter of appointment to the FBI, signed by Hoover, informing Hazelwood he was scheduled to begin training November 29, 1971, nine months away. "That was their first opening," he says. "And I accepted it."

Roy remained an army major until Friday, November 26. Then he left Georgia for Washington, D.C., looking forward to what he believed would be sixteen weeks of top-level training in the world's preeminent law enforcement agency.

Hazelwood knew there would be some personal adjustments to make. For one thing, he was barely able to maintain the FBI's minimum weight, and for the next four months he made sure he was carrying a couple boxes of .38 ammunition whenever he was weighed.

The more serious potential difficulties were his age and experience. Not only would he be older than all but one of the twenty-five agents in his class; Roy also brought to his new work an impressive record of prior achievement.

He was a former military officer with extensive training and command experience. Plus Roy was a decorated Vietnam veteran, holder of the Bronze Star
and the army's Meritorious Service Medal, plus an Air Medal with three oak-
leaf clusters, awarded him for all the dangerous helicopter sorties he'd flown at
An Khe. He'd also been decorated by the Vietnamese government.

But if he thought starting over as a mere recruit was going to be a challenge,
by far the greater surprise was the indifferent quality of the classroom training
he received.

"I'd just come from what I considered the finest training for investigators
available anywhere in the world, U.S. Army CID," he says.

"At the FBI I can remember my counselor, Cliff Browning, asking me,
'Well, Major, what do you think of our training?'

"I said, 'Cliff, this is the worst I've ever received.'"

Hazelwood's disappointment did not extend to firearm training or to physical training in defensive tactics, which he thought were very good, or to the
hard work he was put through learning constitutional law.

But classroom instruction—conducted in Washington, D.C.'s old post office building—was for the most part an unending bore. "We learned everything by rote, and were tested by rote, too," he remembers. "They had very
few permanent faculty members, so we'd get supervisors pulled in from headquarters to teach this subject or that."

Roy finished his last class at 6:00 P.M. on a spring Friday in 1972. An hour
later, he was issued his credentials, a leather satchel, a pair of handcuffs, and a
.38 with a four-inch barrel, plus ammunition. He already knew his first assignment, the Bureau office in Norfolk, Virginia, where he was expected the following Monday morning.

There was no graduation exercise, nor was any diploma awarded.

"They just said, 'Good luck, gentlemen,' and that was it," he recalls. "You
walked out the classroom door, got in the car, and headed for your assignment."

Norfolk, a relatively small Bureau office that worked a large number of routine assignments inside the several nearby U.S. Navy installations, was not Roy's
first choice. He had hoped instead for a big-city assignment with more compelling challenges, such as terrorism and kidnapping and bank robbery cases.

But it was precisely because of his extensive army background that the FBI
first sent him to Norfolk. The Bureau figured that a man with Roy's military experience was a natural for working crimes on a military reservation.

While in time he would work bank robberies and kidnappings at Norfolk,
it was his very first assignment that nearly tore it for the newly minted agent.

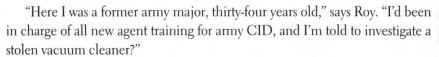

"Here I was a former army major, thirty-four years old," says Roy. "I'd been in charge of all new agent training for army CID, and I'm told to investigate a stolen vacuum cleaner?"

The appliance had vanished five years before from the community assistance equipment shed at the Norfolk Naval Station.

"Young navy couples were allowed to sign out equipment like chairs and couches and lamps," he explains. "Someone didn't bring this vacuum back."

"The people in the office weren't very concerned, so the matter just lapsed. Finally, during an inspection someone asked, 'Where's the vacuum cleaner?' And someone answered, 'We don't know. It must be stolen.' So they called the FBI. It was stolen government property on a government reservation and, technically, we had to investigate the case."

Hazelwood turned the matter into a personal challenge; he was determined to solve the so-far unsolvable mystery, and worked on it whenever time allowed.

He discovered that when the people who'd checked out the vacuum were transferred from Norfolk to a new base, they simply gave away the machine, piece by piece.

"So I tracked down everyone who'd ever come in contact with that vacuum cleaner," he says. "I got the nozzle from here, and the canister from there. It scared the hell out of some people when I knocked on their door. 'I'm with the FBI. Do you have a piece of this vacuum cleaner?'

"I spent a year at Norfolk, and in the last month before I left I walked into my supervisor's office, put the complete vacuum cleaner on his desk, and advised him what he could do with it."

Roy also coped in good spirits with the FBI's punctilious codes of behavior, a lingering legacy of the recently deceased J. Edgar Hoover. Instead of bucking the rules, Hazelwood bent them.

"People have asked me how I possibly could have worked in that environment," he says. "Well, I really enjoyed it. You just had to know how to beat the system."

Some rules, such as the requirement that all agents wear hats, could be safely ignored.

Others, equally silly if you took them seriously, had to be finessed.

Agents were forbidden to be at their desks for any reason for more than twenty minutes each day. They were supposed to be out in the field, working cases. Yet the paperwork somehow still had to be completed.

"Suddenly it dawned on me that libraries have air-conditioned reading rooms. So I drove to the local library with my paperwork and went inside and asked the librarian, 'Excuse me, can you tell me where your reading room is?'

"She said, 'You're with the FBI, aren't you? You must be new.'

"I said, 'Yes.'

"And she said, 'Well, it's back there where you'll find all the other agents.'"

In spite of—or perhaps because of—the strictly regulated work environment, camaraderie was strong.

Most agents dealt with the rule against commercial radios in Bureau cars by installing their own, and then removing them whenever inspections were held. When one Norfolk office agent neglected to do so in time, and was caught, he was suspended without pay for fifteen days, punishment also known in federal law enforcement parlance as being "put on the beach."

Without much need for discussion, fellow agents made up the offending employee's salary from their own pockets, while he volunteered to work without pay for the suspension period.

Says Hazelwood: "Everybody, including the Bureau, was happy."

The dos and don'ts of working cases were equally detailed, and sometimes distracting. Yet Roy discovered the artful agent had plenty of opportunity to innovate.

In one case, Roy and his partner were alerted that a pimp wanted for violation of the 1910 Mann Act—transporting women across state lines for "immoral purposes"—had been traced to an address in Norfolk. When the agents arrived at the modest residence in one of Norfolk's rougher neighborhoods, the only person at home was the fugitive's mother.

Although she grudgingly allowed the agents inside, this mother was having no truck with federal officers in search of her son.

Glancing around her living room as he listened to her speak, Roy noted a Bible open on a table, and a view of the Last Supper on the wall. On a table, he saw the weekly bulletin from a Southern Baptist church. He immediately knew how to handle the situation.

"Do you know what I'd like to do?" he asked. "I'd like to pray about this, and I'd like you to join me. Maybe it will help you to decide whether you should cooperate with us."

The woman agreed, as Roy expected she would, and they both knelt by the coffee table to pray.

"My partner," Hazelwood recalls, "looked at me as if I was nuts."

After an intense silence, the woman opened her eyes and gave Hazelwood a level look.

81

"You're right," she said. "I'll call my son and tell him to turn himself in to the FBI in New York."

"Uh," Roy replied, "we can handle that down here."

No sense in New York getting credit for the collar.

"Well, he's coming down tomorrow, but that's Saturday," she said.

"That's all right, ma'am. We work all the time."

At nine o'clock the next morning, Roy was waiting in the FBI's Norfolk office.

"And that guy pulled up with two of his girls," says Hazelwood. "He walked into the office and said, 'My mother told me I *had* to surrender.'

"And he did."

Roy left Norfolk in the spring of 1973 for assignment in Binghamton, New York, a medium-size community in the south central portion of the state, just north of the Pennsylvania border.

The Bureau had begun taking notice of Binghamton and the surrounding area in November of 1957, after a state police raid on a house near the village of Apalachin, just west of Binghamton, netted sixty-five Mafia thugs at a meeting there, including godfather Vito Genovese.

From 1973 to the middle of 1976, Hazelwood would work little else but OC—organized crime—in Binghamton, including extortion cases, gambling, and labor racketeering.

His partner was agent Bob Ross, also a veteran of Vietnam, where Ross had been an artillery captain.

Their adventures together included innumerable stakeouts. Sometimes Hazelwood and Ross posed as joggers, taking mental notes as they casually trotted around a suspect's house. Other times they'd pick a vantage point and sit together in an unmarked Bureau car, posing as lovers.

"Roy always wore the wig," says Ross.

One evening they followed a suspect into an Italian restaurant. Trying to be inconspicuous, the agents nursed cups of coffee at a table as their target sat down to a meal.

He was not fooled.

"You guys following me?" the suspect asked.

Ross and Hazelwood said yes, in fact, they were.

"Well, I'm going to stay here and eat," he told them. "If you guys want to get something, go ahead, instead of just sitting there with coffee."

Hazelwood asked what was good.

The suspect recommended spaghetti with olive oil and garlic — *ajo e ojo* — which he himself was enjoying that night.

Roy ordered the pasta, liked it, and has been ordering it ever since.

Much of the OC in Binghamton necessarily entailed the use of listening devices, called Title 3 cases after the federal statute that legalized the use of bugs. During the three years Hazelwood spent in Binghamton, he had a Title 3 listening device in place more than half the time.

In one case, Roy and an agent from the Utica office were assigned predawn street surveillance to cover an FBI black bag team installing a court-authorized bug in a suspect's carpet shop. As the two agents sat quietly in their car, watching the streets and maintaining discreet radio contact with the team inside, a man walking his Doberman pinscher came onto the scene.

"It was about four-thirty A.M., and the sun was going to come up in about forty-five minutes," Hazelwood recalls. "Instead of walking on with his dog, this guy decided to walk back and forth, back and forth, in front of the carpet store."

As time grew tighter and the first faint blue light of day streaked the eastern horizon, worried agents inside the carpet store began pleading with Hazelwood and his partner to *do* something about the man and his dog.

Finally, the Utica agent directed Roy to drive up alongside the man.

As they pulled even with him, Roy's partner rolled down his window.

"Hey, mister," he called.

"Yeah?" answered the Doberman's owner.

"Want a blow job?"

Man and dog vanished at once.

Another investigative target was a Mafia-owned travel agency, which arranged complimentary trips to Las Vegas for high rollers. In the event these players ran up bills they couldn't settle on the spot, the tour office became a strong-arm collection agency. That was illegal.

This particular set of gangsters operated above a bar in Binghamton. One night, a Bureau team installed a bug inside their office. Across a parking lot from the bar stood a paint store, where Roy and his fellow agents set up a second-floor listening post and photo surveillance operation.

"We photographed everyone who came and went," says Hazelwood. "We identified them, and then matched them up to their voices."

One day the conversation inside the travel agency turned to the FBI surveillance.

"We saw their boss point toward us and say, 'I think those are feebies.'

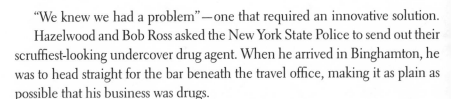

"We knew we had a problem"—one that required an innovative solution. Hazelwood and Bob Ross asked the New York State Police to send out their scruffiest-looking undercover drug agent. When he arrived in Binghamton, he was to head straight for the bar beneath the travel office, making it as plain as possible that his business was drugs.

"Then," Hazelwood explains, "we asked them to have a marked car full of troopers pull up in front of the bar. We wanted them to go in and arrest the drug agent. And we asked that on their way out they wave up at us."

The plan worked to perfection. The state police dispatched a longhaired undercover operative to Binghamton. Upstairs over the paint store, the federal agents made a busy show for the gangsters' benefit, snapping picture after picture of the narc as he entered the bar.

The state troopers arrived in a flourish about twenty-five minutes later. "They played it just right," Hazelwood recalls. "They checked out his license plate and then went into the bar. He put up some resistance. They used physical force to drag him out, cuff him, and throw him into the back of their car.

"Then they waved up at us, and we waved back and came downstairs and got into another car."

According to what the FBI picked up on the bug, Roy's ruse was a success. Because of it, they were able to leave the listening device in place for another six weeks. The photo surveillance team took up a new vantage point and continued spying on the unsuspecting thugs.

Hazelwood enjoyed his time in Binghamton, where outfoxing professional criminals seemed an agreeable way to earn his living. There was a component of gamesmanship that appealed to him, a contest of wits as well as will. "I loved working those guys," he says. "It was a challenge. I had a lot of respect for them, and they had a lot of respect for us."

Then fortune again intervened.

Roy was a capable street agent. "He was good at it," says Bob Ross. "Some guys aren't comfortable hitting the bricks, developing informants, running surveillance. Roy wasn't one of those."

But Hazelwood was ambitious for advancement.

In early 1976, he learned about MAP, the new Management Aptitude Program starting up at the FBI Academy at Quantico. Hoping to identify agents with executive acumen, the Bureau each month brought six of them back to Quantico, where they competed among themselves in the solution of management problems. The best and the brightest students could expect promotions.

"It basically was game playing," Roy explains. "In-basket problems. Employee problems. Industry used it. When I found out about it I said, 'Yes! I want to do that.'"

Hazelwood aced the competition, and was rewarded with an invitation to become a MAP administrator.

He enjoyed the assignment, and also discovered how much he enjoyed living in the wooded hills of eastern Virginia. When, after eighteen months at MAP, the Bureau seemed ready to relocate him again, Roy went shopping for another gig at the Academy, anything to avert another transfer. All that was available was the sex crimes instructor's slot at the BSU.

"I put in for it," says Hazelwood, "although I really had no particular interest other than I didn't want to leave Quantico."

Since joining the FBI, Roy had put aside his old fascination for extreme and unusual criminal behavior. While at MAP, he'd paid almost no attention to the Behavioral Science Unit, located in the subbasement of the Academy library, not far away.

"There was nothing special about the unit then," Roy recalls. "They taught classes like everyone else. I really had no particular interest in them."

Nor did he have an inkling of what he was getting into after his arrival at the BSU, January 1, 1978.

He discovered space was at a premium throughout the subterranean office warren. But at least most of the other agents' brick-walled cells were connected with one another by a hallway.

The esteem in which sex crime instructors were held at the BSU was forcefully brought home to Hazelwood when he came at last to his appointed workspace, a converted mop closet in the dreariest, darkest corner of the underground complex.

On his otherwise empty desk, Hazelwood's predecessor had left a box full of pornographic magazines, together with some nude glossies. Inside the box, as well, he found a collection of sex toys, bottles of oil, and assorted materials of indeterminate use.

For teaching materials, Roy discovered a robed statuette. If you pressed its head, its penis jutted out. There was low-grade fraternity humor everywhere.

Alarmed, Roy looked around the room to find a pair of women's black lace panties and a brassiere nailed to the wall behind his desk chair.

Affixed to the adjoining wall was a whip. A sign beneath it read: "Without Pain There Is No Pleasure."

NINE ✗

A Porno Show
for Cops

Prior to Roy's advent at the BSU, the FBI's approach to sexual crimes closely paralleled that of law enforcement in general: that is, the less attention paid to the subject, the better.

Part of the reason was turf. Unless a sexual crime occurs on a government reservation or in conjunction with a federal offense such as kidnapping, the FBI has no authority to investigate it.

"The Bureau always has been focused on its own jurisdictions," says Roger Depue, Hazelwood's former chief at the BSU. "Whatever you do, if it doesn't have any immediate relevance to an FBI investigative jurisdiction, it is going to be an uphill battle getting their attention."

The FBI paid practically no attention to sexual criminals until the late 1950s, when Walter McLaughlin, an agent in the Philadelphia office, began on his own to offer classes on the subject.

McLaughlin had a strong interest in criminal sexual deviance, and labored long to legitimize its study. But since he never published, McLaughlin endures as an influence today mostly in the recollection of his former Bureau colleagues and students. Even they do not fully agree on the nature and significance of his achievements.

"He was an immense influence on my life," says R. H. Morneau, Jr., a former agent and sexual crime instructor, now retired.

"He was an actor in the classroom," remembers Russ Vorpagel, another retired agent who worked for a time at the BSU. "He'd jump and down and giggle and laugh and scratch himself and we'd all think, Oh, boy. This guy is weird."

McLaughlin, diminutive and highly energized—"He was built like a little tank," recalls Frank Sass—did bring seriousness as well as showmanship to his presentations.

Working from both the scant textbook information then available on sexual crimes and his own investigative experience, McLaughlin devised what probably was the world's first sexual-crime classification system for law enforcement.

In it, he divided offenses into types—voyeurism, exhibitionism, rape, etc.— and then wrote a multipage discussion of each crime category, including a number of case histories for each sort of behavior. He even offered general advice on how best to handle victims.

The system ultimately was adopted as instructional material by agent instructors, a small victory. "He had a terrible time trying to sell the FBI administration on the need for police training in the field of sexual deviancy," says Frank Sass.

The Bureau instead steered an uneven course, alternating its approach to sexual-crime instruction between prudery and prurience.

Ken Lanning, a BSU agent who is an authority on the sexual victimization of children, recalls his own confusion and dismay at the FBI's state of knowledge in the early 1970s.

"I remember an in-service [class] at Quantico," he says, "when we were told we actually were going to be shown some real pornography. In order to see it, however, we had to leave the classroom and go to another room, where it was displayed for us on a table. We had to put our hands behind our backs and walk around the table, just sort of looking at it. That was a bizarre experience."

In the same period, Lanning began teaching the subject at field schools. He remembers being taken aside by his predecessor in the job.

"'Ken,' he told me, 'you're about to embark on probably the greatest topic the Bureau can teach. You can't go wrong. It'll be great. Let me just give you three bits of advice.

"'One, lots of dirty jokes. You have to have a dirty joke to go with every sexual perversion that you talk about.

"'Two, get lots of pornography. Dirty pictures. Magazines. Movies. Pass 'em out. The cops love 'em.

"'And three, never allow any women in the class.'"

Lanning asked why.

"Because if you have women," the other agent answered, "you can't do the first two things."

When John Douglas first arrived at the BSU in 1977, the situation had hardly improved. Douglas remembers an incident in a class taught by one of Roy's predecessors, an instructor infamous for his indifference to fact.

"This guy shows a slide and tells the class that it is one of the few instances of a female African American autoerotic fatality," he recalls.

"Well, after the instructor goes through the whole nine yards, describing the case, a hand goes up in the classroom. It was the investigator who'd actually worked the case.

"He says, 'Well, you got half the story right. She *is* a woman. But she's not black.'

"'What do you mean, she's not black? She has black features, black hair.'

"'No,' the cop says, 'she's in an advanced stage of decomposition. She's white and she's decomposing there.'

"Now that was embarrassing."

When Hazelwood arrived in 1978, he knew at a glance to drop the term "sex" from the course title. The class was renamed "Interpersonal Violence."

He cleaned up the classroom, as well. Instead of pornography and dirty jokes, he taught the nuts and bolts of sexual crime investigation, fundamentals such as interview techniques and the collection and preservation of evidence.

Later, Hazelwood and Ken Lanning would coauthor "The Maligned Investigator of Criminal Sexuality," a wide-ranging survey of law enforcement agencies' attitudes toward sexual crimes. Although the piece was respectfully worded, the agents took police organizations to task for their tendency to trivialize sexual crimes, sometimes stigmatizing sexual-crime investigators as "wienie waggers," sometimes compounding the victims' trauma by lack of empathy, sometimes forgetting how emotionally devastating these crimes can be.

They argued in the article that sexual-crimes investigators should be chosen from volunteers, not assigned to the work as punishment or discipline, as commonly has been the case. They also advised screening out those officers who are drawn to sexual crimes for the wrong reasons.

"Some investigators," Hazelwood and Lanning wrote, "are voyeuristic. . . . They get a vicarious thrill out of interviewing victims or viewing the pornography often associated with sexual crimes. They may demand sexual acts from prostitutes, ask a rape victim to describe her assault an unreasonable number of times, or make copies of seized materials for their private use."

The agents were equally adamant on the issue of confidentiality. "The investigator is absolutely dependent upon the victim for information pertaining to the crime and the criminal; he must not betray the victim's trust."

The BSU's "porno show for cops," as Roger Depue remembers it, soon became a legitimate and respected course at Quantico. From a ten-hour, non-credit elective class for National Academy students when Roy took over, by 1979 Interpersonal Violence had been expanded to a thirty-hour course for which the University of Virginia awarded two credits. The following year, the class was upgraded again to forty-four hours and three credits.

Hazelwood also sought out Howard Teten, the original guru of criminal personality profiling at Quantico, to learn the craft.

Teten, a veteran of the San Leandro, California, Police Department evidence unit, had joined the FBI in 1962. Later, Teten taught applied criminology to Bureau recruits in the Training Division's old post office building facility, where Roy had taken his classroom instruction.

When the Bureau opened its new Academy at Quantico in 1972, Teten came south to teach applied criminology in the newly established Behavioral Science Unit. Unlike the rote drudgery Roy had slogged through just the year before, the Academy offered new agents dramatically upgraded classroom instruction. Not only were the Quantico facilities the best in the world, but the quality of instruction improved dramatically, too. Teaching slots no longer went to the first available agent, but to the best-qualified agent.

The BSU's first chief was Agent Jack Kirsch, a former reporter for the *Erie* (Pennsylvania) *Dispatch Herald* who'd joined the FBI in 1950.

Kirsch candidly recalls that despite his determination to impart useful, practical information at the BSU, the new unit was not an immediate success with the police enrollees.

"A lot of our students were not outwardly hostile, but they weren't the most receptive group," he says.

Roger Depue, who arrived as a BSU faculty member in 1974, also encountered considerable skepticism among the students.

"The level of instruction was pretty basic, a lot of theory and war stories," says Depue. "Plus there was a natural animosity. Law enforcement officers back in those days did not trust the behavioral sciences.

"I remember they'd sit in the back of the room, arms folded, chair leaning against the wall with a 'What the hell is this guy gonna tell me?' expression. Often, their comments would begin with 'Bullshit.'"

One exception to the BSU's generally cool reception by its police-officer pupils was the Criminology Section, originally led by Howard Teten and agent Patrick J. Mullany, a former Christian Brother.

Teten was both a veteran investigator and an eager student of the detective's craft. He, as much as anyone, bent the BSU twig away from formal instruction toward profiling and active case consultation.

He sought out Dr. James Brussel, who'd helped capture George Metesky, New York City's so-called Mad Bomber of the 1940s and 1950s, and spent hours with the psychiatrist, reviewing cases and sharing lore. Teten also consulted Sir Arthur Conan Doyle's oeuvre, in search of whatever helpful insights the great Sherlock Holmes might offer.

Teten and Pat Mullany, who held an undergraduate degree in psychology, conducted informal case colloquiums at Quantico, meeting after class with students who brought with them strange unsolved cases in the hopes that either the FBI instructors, or perhaps their fellow students, might see something familiar or suggest an investigative strategy.

The consultations were strictly unofficial, and advisedly so. Although J. Edgar Hoover was gone, his shadow remained. The Bureau that Hoover built still operated by the book.

In the course of these discussions, Howard Teten added to his considerable fund of information and theory an enormous amount of new empirical evidence, a mass of specialized knowledge he graciously shared with Hazelwood.

As Roy delved more deeply into this strange new world of aberrant crime, the more intensely interested he became.

"Even though I hadn't given Harvey Glatman or what I'd learned at the AFIP any serious thought for years, I remember how quickly I felt at home at the BSU," says Hazelwood. "The old fascinations were still there."

TEN ✗

Atlanta

The BSU remained a little-known arm of the FBI until 1980, when Roy was invited by the Atlanta Police Department to consult in that city's infamous Child Murders investigation, one of the most massive, controversial, and socially divisive serial murder cases in the history of the American South.

The case began on July 28, 1979, along a scruffy section of Niskey Lake Road in southeast Atlanta, when a woman went out searching for redeemable soda cans and bottles discovered fourteen-year-old Edward "Teddy" Smith's leg poking out from a roadside tangle of vines.

Shortly thereafter, another African American youth, thirteen-year-old Alfred Evans, was discovered dead about fifty feet away.

Smith, who had been shot with a .22, and Evans, who most likely was strangled, were old schoolmates, although they no longer lived near one another. Atlanta homicide detective Mickey Lloyd, now a major in the department, found witnesses who put the teens together at a party several nights before their murders. But that was the end of the connections and useful leads. In time, the two unsolved cases moved to the back burner.

On November 8, a thirty-nine-year-old man in search of someplace to relieve himself entered an abandoned Atlanta elementary school and discovered stuffed into a hole in the building's concrete floor the decomposed body of another black child, eight-year-old Yusef Bell, who'd vanished on his way to the grocery store seventeen days earlier.

Bell's manner of death also appeared to have been strangulation. However, there was no immediate reason to link his death to those of Alfred Evans and Teddy Smith four months earlier.

The fourth victim, Milton Harvey, fourteen, was discovered dead a week later. Harvey had been missing since early September.

By the following spring, Atlanta's black community, and the police, noticed the pattern. Although poor children who live in big-city neighborhoods always suffer a higher incidence of violent deaths than their wealthier suburban counterparts, too many of Atlanta's youngsters were vanishing, only to be found dead, usually strangled, several days later.

A list of dead and missing children was begun. By June of 1980, there were ten names on it, eight boys and two girls.

Strange rumors circulated.

According to one, the local U.S. Centers for Disease Control was behind the killings. Scientists there supposedly needed the penises of recently deceased young blacks to obtain a chemical necessary for making the virus- and cancer-fighting protein interferon.

Much wider credibility was accorded rumors that the Klan or some other white supremacist group was behind the deaths.

By then, a parents' Committee to Stop Children's Murders had been formed. Lee Brown, the Atlanta public safety commissioner, announced a Missing and Murdered Task Force.

Although not yet a national story, the Atlanta Child Murders were generating fear and anger and dangerous stresses.

It was also in June of 1980 that Morris Redding, then deputy chief of the Atlanta Police Department and head of APD's Criminal Investigation Division, had an inspiration. Redding was generally acquainted with the BSU and the broad concepts behind criminal personality profiling. He also had heard much about Roy Hazelwood from officers who'd taken Roy's BSU class in Interpersonal Violence.

"So I said, 'Let's see if we can get Hazelwood down here,'" Redding recollects.

Roy arrived from Quantico a few days later.

The important assignment began inauspiciously when his wallet was stolen at Atlanta's Hartsfield Airport. Hazelwood had to borrow two hundred dollars from John Glover, special agent in charge of the FBI's Atlanta office.

Once he'd reviewed the cases, Roy had little trouble recognizing what Atlanta faced. "I was absolutely convinced a serial killer was at work," he says. A couple of the murders clearly looked like copycat killings to him. Others looked like a family member, or acquaintance, was the most likely killer. Roy deeply doubted that the serial killer had murdered either of the two young girls on the list.

But in the midst of the confusion and fear, the Child Killer certainly was out there, murdering for the sheer thrill of it, growing more confident and more skilled with each homicide. He was a classic lone wolf, and he wasn't going to be easily stopped.

Roy also was certain from the start that the killer was black.

"I drove with three black Atlanta police detectives to the neighborhoods where the victims lived, as well as where they disappeared and where their bodies were found," he explains.

"We were in an unmarked car, but I remember turning down one street and seeing everything just stop. People walking on the sidewalk stopped. People mowing their lawns stopped. People stopped talking to each other and stared at us. It was like one of those old E. F. Hutton ads on television.

"I asked, 'What the hell's going on?'

"These detectives said that it was me, that everyone wondered about the white guy in the car. I knew then that there was no way a white serial killer could have moved through those neighborhoods without being noticed. I knew the guy had to be black."

As the body count rose—two more young black males were added to the list in July—Roy felt both the pressure to make a positive contribution to the investigation, and the urgency of catching the Atlanta Child Killer before the city's strained social fabric began to tear.

"I called the BSU and I said, 'This thing's going to blow, and I'm going to need some help.'"

There didn't seem to be much interest at the other end of the line.

"So I called back about a week later and said, 'I'm telling you, this thing is going to blow.' That's when they sent down John Douglas."

Months had passed since Roy's first review of the case, and six more potential victims of the Child Killer had been identified. There was no consensus among the various law enforcement agencies involved as to just what sort of person, or persons, might be committing the killings.

Hazelwood and Douglas, in consultation with their colleagues back at Quantico, went to work on a profile.

Douglas immediately agreed with Hazelwood that the killer was an African American male, and that he probably was not responsible for all the deaths on the list—which would eventually reach thirty—especially not those of the two girls. While it is wise never to say never when it comes to aberrant offenders, Hazelwood and Douglas quickly isolated and analyzed enough behavioral evidence to have a firm sense of the offenses the Atlanta Child Killer would, and would not, commit.

His victims, many of them poor and streetwise, were disappearing routinely, yet there were no reliable reports that any of them had been forcibly abducted, or snatched in the night from their family's houses, except for one of the girls, LaTonya Wilson, who was taken from her bed.

The Child Killer was too cool for that. Hazelwood and Douglas knew he was using some variation on the con approach, an indication of intelligence.

They believed him to be in his mid- to late twenties.

"This type of offender has to relate to children," Hazelwood explains. "He can't be so old that he frightens them, or so young that they don't believe what he says. Whatever his lure, we said it had to be credible."

The agents' experience, and BSU research, led them next to conclude the killer probably was from a middle-class or higher background. These were not a poor man's crimes.

Self-evidently, his hobbies and pastimes would be attractive to children.

He also was single, and probably was sexually inadequate. The first conclusion flowed from his demonstrated sexual preference for boys. The second was an inference. Autopsies indicated minimal sexual contact between the Child Killer and his victims. In fact, the murders, at least the earliest ones, may have been caused by frustration and anger precipitated by his sexual dysfunction.

Finally, Hazelwood and Douglas knew that serial killers often are police buffs, and guessed that the Child Killer probably was one, too. He might even drive an old police car, or a vehicle that resembled one, and he likely had insinuated himself into the investigation.

He enjoyed the national attention, too, and would inject himself into the investigation to enhance that experience.

"We said that he not only was gratified in the commission of his crimes," Roy recalls, "but also in the authorities' inability to solve them."

In the midst of fitting these pieces together, Hazelwood and Douglas also had occasion to knock down the claims of at least one white Georgian who wished to take credit for killing so many black children.

The impostor placed a call to the police in Conyers, Georgia, not far from Atlanta, claiming to be the murderer. An unmistakably unreconstructed redneck, the caller mentioned the name of the most recent known victim, and said he'd left another body at a specific spot on Sigmon Road in Rockdale County, southeast of Atlanta.

After listening to an audiotape of the call with Dr. Dietz and recognizing it for a crude ruse, Hazelwood and Douglas devised a plan for flushing out the self-proclaimed serial killer. It seemed certain that the caller would monitor the Conyers police response to his information. Therefore, the agents suggested that police officers deliberately search the wrong side of Sigmon Road. The hope was that he'd surface to correct their mistake, either at the search scene or in another taunting—and traceable—telephone call.

The ploy worked.

Full of derision at the police's stupidity, the impostor ill-advisedly telephoned from his home to mock the Conyers Police Department, and stayed on the line long enough to permit a trace. He was arrested later in the day.

Hazelwood and Douglas delivered their joint profile of the Atlanta Child Killer in person to Morris Redding, Atlanta Police Department chief George Napper, Lee Brown, and a local psychiatrist who had been advising the task force investigation.

"There was a sigh of relief when we said we thought it was a black guy," Roy recalls. "One of them said, 'Thank God. We thought it was going to be a white guy. The last thing we needed was for these to be racial killings.'"

The profile proved accurate. Wayne Williams, who was arrested in June of 1981, was a single black musician and freelance photographer who lived at home with his parents, both schoolteachers. Hazelwood and Douglas seemed to get everything right but Williams's age. He was twenty-three at the time of his arrest.

Wayne Williams has never admitted to the Atlanta Child Killings, and those who have questioned his guilt point out that Williams never, in fact, was charged with killing a child. The deaths for which he ultimately was convicted were those of twenty-one-year-old Jimmy Ray Payne and Nathaniel Cater, twenty-seven, both clearly older than Williams's victims of preference, teen-aged boys (his youngest suspected victim was nine).

It is unclear why Payne and Cater were killed, but it is not uncommon for a serial murderer to occasionally select seemingly anomalous victims. John Wayne Gacy's oldest victim, for example, also was twenty-seven.

The local authorities closed twenty-three of the cases upon Williams's conviction, and left the remaining seven open, officially unsolved.

At the same time they presented their profile in 1980, Hazelwood and

Douglas also explained why they suspected one of the slain girls, Angel Lenair, had not been murdered by their UNSUB.

Lenair was found in early March 1980, next to a log near a stream with her hands tied behind her, not far from where she lived. An electrical cord was pulled tight around her neck. She'd been gagged with a pair of women's panties, not hers. The ME said the black child had died of ligature strangulation.

Sexual assault appeared unlikely. The only physical evidence of sexual contact was a very small scratch, as if made by a fingernail, detected on her vaginal labia.

"She was not beaten or otherwise abused," Hazelwood recalls. "I believe the autopsy showed she'd been fed potato chips and food of that nature during the days she was missing.

"We believed she had been abducted and kept in the same neighborhood. It didn't make sense to us that you would abduct someone, take them away, and then bring them back to dispose of the body.

"We thought that she'd been taken by someone with access to a nearby place where he could keep her.

"The panties found in her mouth might have come from his panty collection, we said. And it was our opinion he had little or no contact with women. The fact that he'd taken a little girl also led us to believe he was socially inept, with no confidence in his ability to capture an adult woman.

"We didn't think he was very intelligent, based on the way in which she apparently had been kept and fed junk food. We thought he would have spent time in a mental institution. The use of an electrical cord to strangle her was another clue. It was a weapon of opportunity.

"We suggested that the police canvass her neighborhood, asking kids if they knew anyone who acted strange, and hung around with kids a lot."

Such an individual in fact did live near Angel Lenair, in a derelict structure. As Hazelwood and Douglas had predicted, he also had been confined to a mental institution—a VA hospital.

Investigators discovered him hiding beneath his kitchen sink. He was clad in VA pajamas. In lieu of a belt, he was wearing around his waist a length of electrical cord identical to the ligature around Angel Lenair's neck. (There was, however, no conclusive evidence that connected this man to the killing, and the Lenair case remains officially open.)

"Do you know you have just described a paranoid schizophrenic?" the task force psychiatrist said after Hazelwood and Douglas were finished.

"That's absolutely correct," Roy answered.

"How do you know that?" the doctor asked skeptically.

"From the way he committed his crime," Roy said. "We try to think the way he thinks."

"And how do you do *that?*" the psychiatrist pressed.

"A lot of experience."

Then came the challenge.

"If I were to give you a series of tests, do you think you could test out with a particular mental disorder?" he asked.

Hazelwood and Douglas said yes, they thought they could.

"So we went to his office at night," Roy recalls. "He took John into one room and me to another. And he said, 'Okay, I want you to test out as paranoid schizophrenics.'

"And both of us did. He just thought that was amazing. He couldn't believe it."

ELEVEN

The Mindzappers

For a time early in the 1980s almost all the profiling responsibility in the BSU fell to either Hazelwood or John Douglas or the two of them together.

"We worked closely on so many cases," Hazelwood says. "I remember one year I did sixty profiles and he did eighty. And we traveled together on several homicides."

A Canadian double-murder case from the mid-1960s that Hazelwood and Douglas profiled together, two decades later, also was one of the oldest ever brought to their attention.

The Royal Canadian Mounted Police, who requested the BSU's assistance, reported that the victims were teenage sweethearts, Maurice* and Chloe,* who lived in a small town in eastern Canada. After failing to solve their double murder using traditional investigative methods, the Mounties hoped a fresh, behavioral approach to the twenty-year-old crime might yield results. Upon hearing of the new profiling service at Quantico, they decided to give it a try.

As RCMP agents recounted the story to Hazelwood and Douglas, one snowy Saturday night, Maurice and Chloe went bowling together with friends. Afterward, they climbed into Maurice's car and headed for his house. Chloe was to sleep over with Maurice's family and then drive to church with them the next morning.

They never made it home.

Maurice's car was found with its lights on along a little-used access road leading up a hill to his family's house. The wheels were pulled sharply to the right. Skid marks in the snow indicated the vehicle had stopped suddenly. The driver's door was open, as was the left rear door.

Two sets of footprints led from the car doors to the rear of the sedan. From there, the footprints and a trail of blood led to a ditch about fifteen feet away, where Maurice lay dead. He had been shot once in the back, and again in one ear at extremely close range, with a 30.06 rifle.

Chloe's footprints led from the car's closed front passenger door up the hill toward Maurice's house. The killer's prints led in the same direction from where he'd shot Maurice in the ditch, and intercepted Chloe's trail about 150 feet from the car.

There investigators found the girl, also murdered, curled in the fetal position. Chloe was surrounded by a series of wildly distorted snow angels, artifacts of her desperate fight with the killer, who had savagely clubbed her to death. He had not sexually assaulted her.

The keys to the car were in her right front pocket. The bolt from his 30.06 lay beneath her.

The killer's footprints then led away from the murder scene, back to the car, past the ditch, and past the dead Maurice and on toward the highway below, where his trail was lost.

Approximately thirty-six hours after the killings, the rifle was found, wrapped in an oilcloth. The killer had carefully placed the murder weapon in a garbage can within a block of Chloe's residence. The rifle's stock was split and broken. He had attempted to tape it back together.

Since the motive for the murders clearly was neither theft nor rape, Hazelwood and Douglas inferred that a deep personal rage lay behind the crimes. Although Maurice might have been the killer's primary target, the impersonal way he was dispatched suggested Maurice's death was incidental to his primary objective, killing Chloe.

Nor were these spontaneous murders. Chloe's killer did not hitchhike through the snow that night with his 30.06, hoping the two would pick him up. Nor was he waiting on the hillside in ambush: All footprints led away from the car.

The likeliest scenario was that the killer was hidden in the back of the vehicle when Maurice and Chloe emerged together from the bowling alley that night.

It was the agents' opinion that he waited until they turned up the hill, and then sat up and announced his presence. The reason Hazelwood and Douglas believed he waited until that moment was the sharp angle at which the car's wheels were turned.

"If I am holding a gun on Maurice the entire ride, and say, 'Now pull over,' he'd pull over," Hazelwood explains. "But if I rise up and say suddenly, 'Stop the car!' it will startle him, which explains the wheels being jerked."

The physical evidence told Hazelwood and Douglas that Maurice was marched to the rear of the car, where the assailant shot him in the back.

Hazelwood and Douglas surmised that as Maurice was killed Chloe grabbed the car keys and jumped out of her side, slamming her door behind her as the teen scrambled up the hill toward Maurice's distant house.

The mortally wounded Maurice, meantime, staggered a few feet to the ditch, trailing blood as he went. The killer followed him, and discharged a second round into the teen's ear. This murder was unemotional, detached.

Chloe's was not. It was clear from his tracks and the second crime scene that he ran after the girl and attacked her furiously. The later discovery of the rifle bolt under her body also suggested the power of his frenzy.

The weapon was extremely important to him, Hazelwood and Douglas believed. Although he'd smashed the stock in his assault on Chloe, he obviously carried the damaged weapon all the way back into town, and there discovered that he'd left the bolt behind.

"My bolt! Where's my bolt?!" the profilers imagined him wondering in distress, knowing he'd never find it in the snow.

The importance of the weapon to him was demonstrated by the fact that although he knew he had to get rid of it, he still carefully wrapped it in oilcloth.

He had been patient enough to hide himself in the back of Maurice's car and to bring his own weapon, but the crime scene was on balance disorganized. There was no attempt to hide or disguise what he had done—Maurice and Chloe would be found very soon—and he plainly was out of control when he killed the girl. Moreover, he had neglected to provide for his own escape, or even to improvise one. He simply walked away.

The combination of a disorganized scene and the victims' ages argued for a relatively young killer, nineteen to twenty-one years of age, the agents agreed. He didn't own his own car, or have access to one, or else he would have used a vehicle that night.

But he had developed a giant personal anger against Chloe. Combining all these factors, Hazelwood and Douglas concluded that he lived quite near her, probably with his parents.

What had generated such enormous hatred?

The only person Chloe had ever dated was Maurice. Both agents felt the killer was a socially inadequate loner who had created in his imagination a fantasy relationship with Chloe. She was his dream lover. Hazelwood and Douglas felt that over a period of time the fantasy grew increasingly important to him even as it became ever more untenable. He began to feel betrayed.

"She was his girlfriend," explains Hazelwood. "She didn't know that. But *he* knew it."

The agents told the Canadian investigators that the killer would have been very agitated in the days following the double murder. He'd be obsessed by the press coverage. He quite likely attended Chloe's funeral.

Six months after crafting this re-creation of the crime and portrait of the killer, Hazelwood and Douglas were contacted once again by the Mounties, who had exceptional news to share.

In a development unconnected with the BSU's consultation on the case, a woman had walked into an RCMP substation halfway across Canada from where Maurice and Chloe had been killed twenty years before, and asked if the murders ever had been solved.

A records check indicated it had not.

"Thank you," she said, and turned to leave.

"Oh, ah, wait a minute," the Mountie on duty asked. "Why do you want to know?"

She decided to be frank.

"Because my brother may have done it."

The woman explained how her family had lived near Chloe's house in Eastern Canada. Her brother, Antoine,* had startled her after the murder, she said, by confiding that Chloe was his girlfriend, when she knew that to be untrue. After the murder, he had begun constantly bathing and washing himself. She had been further troubled by Antoine's obsessive interest in the crime's aftermath. He carried around a photo of Chloe in a notebook he filled with newspaper clippings about the case.

All of this had come back to her twenty years later, she went on, because Antoine, who still lived with her, seemed to be repeating the same behavior. He was fixated on a restaurant waitress, although he hardly knew her.

Once the broad outlines of her story checked out, and the Hazelwood-Douglas profile was consulted, the Mounties reexamined their physical evidence. Looking closely at the wrapped rifle stock, preserved in an evidence locker for two decades, they discovered a human hair—Chloe's—wedged in its splinters.

Then the Canadian authorities looked at the photos they'd taken of Chloe's funeral. Sure enough, Antoine appeared in one picture, leaning against a telephone pole across the street, looking on intently.

The Mounties subsequently informed Roy that Antoine was tried and convicted for the double murders.

At about the same time they were working the Canadian double homicide, Hazelwood and Douglas also were assigned a serial prostitute murder case with its own unique twist: For a while, it appeared that the two profilers inadvertently had shared their special expertise with the killer himself.

The bodies of five prostitutes—all strangled to death with ligatures—had been discovered, one by one, dumped in remote spots progressively closer to a military base in a large western state. In each murder, a souvenir was taken, a watch or a piece of jewelry.

There had been no witnesses and no useful physical evidence left behind. The victims apparently had not struggled. This killer was careful and patient—organized.

The homicide detective in charge of the investigation—who in twenty years had never failed to solve a killing—was sent to Quantico to work directly with Hazelwood and Douglas on the case.

His identity and certain facts of the investigation must be kept a secret. The investigator has never been told that for a while his own department suspected he was the killer they were looking for.

"We spent three days with him," says Roy, "and we went over the cases in great detail. I remember it was our belief the killer was someone at the military installation. Because the bodies were found out in the wilderness, we assumed he was familiar with the terrain and comfortable in it.

"We surmised that he was an outdoorsman, and we believed he was a noncommissioned officer. It seemed to us that an enlisted man probably would have been too young to commit such mature murders.

"Beside the profile, we told the detective what the UNSUB's postoffense behavior likely would be. We also offered some proactive techniques, investigative suggestions, and interview suggestions should they develop a suspect."

During the intense three days in Virginia, word came back to the investigation that two more bodies had been found. "He was just devastated," Hazelwood recollects.

"Then the guy went home and the murders stopped. He called us for more ideas. We told him that maybe the killer had left town, and suggested he check transfers from the base."

From hot rods to the military police—Roy as a Texas teenager (above), a second lieutenant at Ft. Rucker in Alabama (below), and in Vietnam (right).
Roy Hazelwood

Harvey Glatman, the Lonely Hearts Killer—A prototypical modern
sexual criminal, Glatman in the 1960s was a dark mystery to Roy and
everyone else in law enforcement. UPI/Corbis-Bettmann

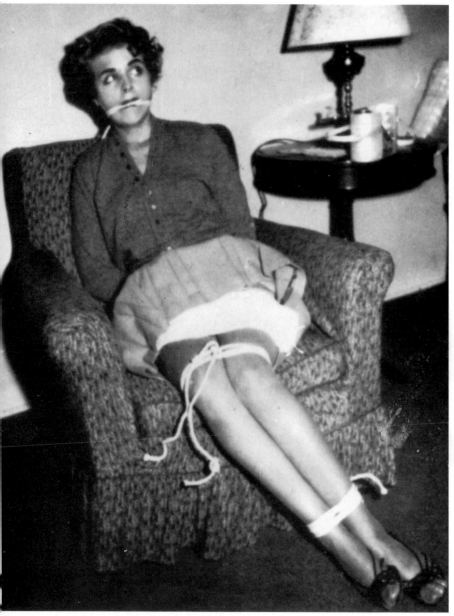

Fear—Glatman's victims believed he was photographing
them for detective magazine covers. Pierce Brooks

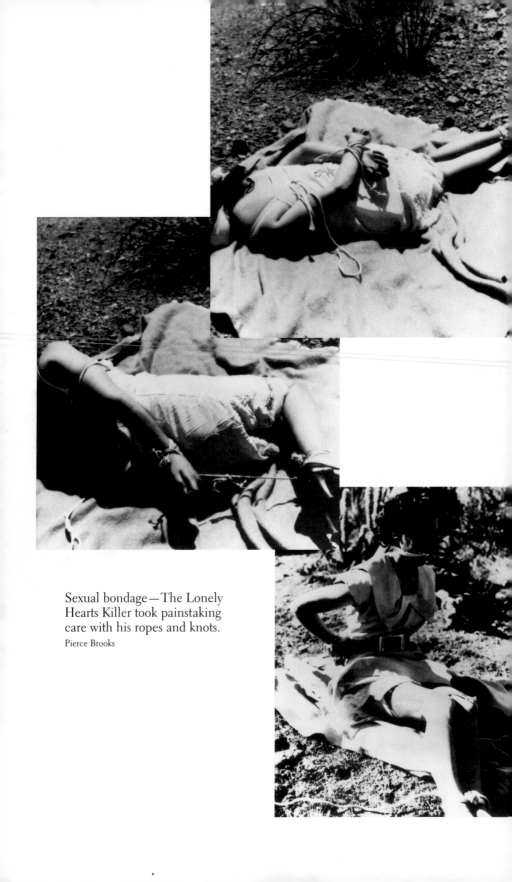

Sexual bondage — The Lonely
Hearts Killer took painstaking
care with his ropes and knots.
Pierce Brooks

Death in the desert—After securing the women, Glatman strangled them.
Later he led investigators to their bodies. Pierce Brooks

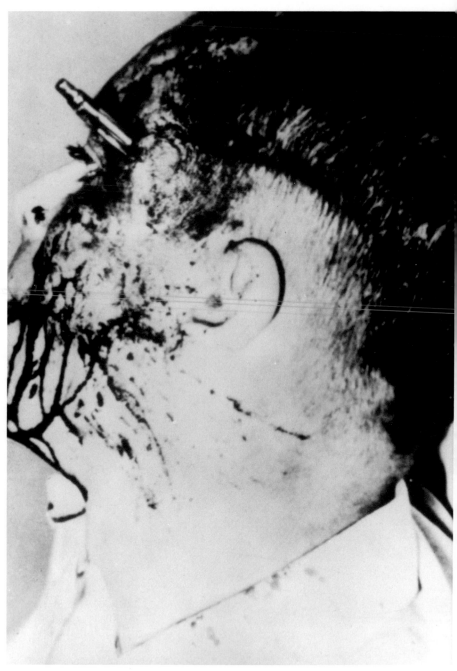

Macabre victims—Roy's study of aberrant behavior began with a fellowship to the Armed Forces Institute of Pathology. The cutting and stabbing syllabus he wrote there included this bizarre suicide by ballpoint pen. Roy Hazelwood

Dangerous solo sex—Roy's
first project at the FBI's
Behavioral Science Unit was
his unique, comprehensive
study of autoerotic fatalities.
Roy Hazelwood

The BSU in 1978—Front row: Roy is at far left, John Douglas at far right. Second row, far left, is Roger Depue. Next to him is Dick Ault. Third from left (partially hidden) is Bob Ressler.

FBI photo

About six months later, an emergency call came down to the BSU from FBI headquarters in Washington, D.C. Director William Webster had been contacted directly by the detective's superior with deeply disturbing news.

The investigator's girlfriend had turned him in as a suspect in the killings. The woman related how she'd seen a box of women's watches and jewelry among his possessions. On nights that the victims had disappeared, she said, he'd been hyper, couldn't sleep, demanded sex. She recalled driving out into the woods with him, where he'd point out sinkholes, and remark how ideal they were for secreting bodies.

There were some other oddities as well. Hazelwood and Douglas had told the detective that his killer probably hung out in bars near his victim disposal sites. But they hadn't predicted how strange his behavior became.

"One day," says Hazelwood, "he recovers the body of a teenage girl whose parents lived on the base. He puts her body in the trunk of his car, and drives to this bar. He forces everybody inside to come out and look at the body in his trunk. Then he drives to her parents' house, brings them out to his trunk, and asks them if that is their daughter."

Director Webster ordered that Hazelwood and Douglas fly at once to consult with the suspect officer's superiors.

"Oh my God, we've given the store away," Hazelwood said to Douglas on the plane. "He knows *everything* we think!"

The profiling partners then pondered the situation for a moment. "Of course, this is going to be *extremely* interesting," Douglas then added hopefully.

"Yeah!" Hazelwood agreed, also looking for some positive spin on a grim dilemma. "And from a teaching standpoint, the story is great. We're always talking about how killers inject themselves in the investigation. Well, here's an example!"

The jollity ceased when Hazelwood and Douglas reached the local FBI office.

"The only two people there who knew why we'd come were the SAC and the assistant SAC," says Hazelwood. "Everybody else in the office was hinky. They thought one of them might be in trouble, and here were two mindzappers from Quantico coming in to tell management how to screw with the guy's mind."

Working in secrecy, Hazelwood and Douglas reviewed every shred of available evidence. "We spent days going over his personnel file and everything else known about the man," says Hazelwood. "There was nothing that remotely suggested a propensity toward violence, temper, authoritativeness, or abuse of his position. We even interviewed his ex-wife. 'He is not a violent person,' she told us."

The fact that the detective's girlfriend had no concrete evidence to offer against the accused also had important weight in their deliberations.

"We thought he'd shared the facts of the case with her, but that she hadn't actually seen anything," says Hazelwood. "We felt she was repeating what he had described. And we also guessed she was angry at him because he'd broken up with her and she was trying to get even. That turned out to be the case."

And the macabre scene with the dead girl in his trunk? "We believed he was exhibiting signs of stress. We thought he was close to a nervous breakdown, caused by his inability to solve this string of killings."

At Hazelwood's and Douglas's suggestion, the detective's girlfriend was approached in a low-key, nonthreatening manner.

"We suggested they bring up that there was nothing to corroborate her story, but not to make her suspect that they didn't believe her over their fellow officer.

"We felt they should say something like, 'We certainly appreciate your bringing this to our attention. We have put a lot of man-hours into this case. So far, we've simply found *nothing*. Can you give us *anything* to corroborate what you say?'

"The rest of the advice was to tell her how the thing was escalating, that there was going to be a major political impact. We felt she needed to see how the case was going well beyond her specific problem with him."

The detective's girlfriend at last conceded she'd fabricated the story, putting the investigation back where it started.

Soon thereafter, however, *another* woman came forward to report *her* suspicions of *her* boyfriend. This time the doubt and worries proved well founded.

As the profile had predicted, the suspect was an NCO and avid outdoorsman. According to his companion, before his recent transfer to another post, he used to take her on frequent camping trips. While they were out alone together in the woods, she said, he'd disappear for hours. On these occasions, she sometimes would catch him hiding off in the distance, pointing his crossbow at her.

She also enjoyed sunbathing in the nude, the woman continued, but she did not enjoy it when he sneaked around with his camera, clicking pictures of her.

When authorities checked to see when her friend had been transferred, they discovered the date coincided with the last known prostitute murder in the series.

Again, Hazelwood and Douglas offered interview tips to the investigators. One of the most important suggestions, the profilers stressed, was to confront the suspect when he was out of uniform.

This type of offender, Hazelwood and Douglas said, closely identified himself with the military. In uniform, he'd be self-assured. In mufti, he'd be far more vulnerable.

So the investigators in fact did wait for a Sunday, when they found their suspect in his civvies. Under questioning, in his walking shorts, he confessed to the killings.

TWELVE

"My Intentions Were
to Inflict Fear"

Intimate as a profiler becomes with an offender in the process of studying his crimes, the relationship between BSU agent and UNSUB usually is remote and short-lived.

Hazelwood was the first profiler to routinely bridge that distance by conducting a series of research projects on violent sexual criminals.

The first of these encounters was with Jon Barry Simonis, the Ski Mask Rapist, who would prove as challenging, and enlightening, as any offender Roy has ever interviewed.*

Hazelwood entered the case in 1980, when he received a request for assistance from the police in Baton Rouge, Louisiana.

For the past year, Baton Rouge and jurisdictions in many other states had shared a common problem, a particularly vicious traveling sexual criminal and thief known as the Ski Mask Rapist.

A white male, about six feet two inches tall, with a slender frame and dark hair, the Ski Mask Rapist targeted residences exclusively. He habitually entered a house between dusk and 1:00 A.M., gaining access through open or unlocked doors and windows.

He usually was armed with a gun or a knife. In his later attacks, he occasionally carried both. He sometimes struck when victims already were home. Other times he waited in their darkened houses for them to return.

*Simonis granted the author permission to use his name.

After gaining their attention with his weapon, he would reassure his victims that no one would get hurt. Once they were bound, however, he sexually assaulted the women. He commonly committed these attacks in full view of their husbands, fathers, brothers, or boyfriends, a key behavioral clue in Roy's subsequent profile.

Afterward, he usually robbed the household, and he frequently fled in the victim's car, which he ditched many blocks away.

Roy agreed to prepare a profile, and asked the police for official reports and victim statements from five of the Ski Mask Rapist's earliest known cases, plus five cases from the middle of his criminal career, as well as five of his latest offenses.

In this way, Hazelwood hoped both to produce a behavioral portrait of the UNSUB and possibly to predict his future patterns.

Roy noted among the early assaults that the rapist used a screwdriver or some similar tool to enter his victim's residence. He'd capture her, bind her with her own articles of clothing, and sexually assault her. But he did not subject his early victims to any added, gratuitous, physical assault. He stole mostly home appliances: stereos, microwaves, and televisions—all easy items to pawn.

In the middle group of crimes, the Ski Mask Rapist began bringing his own handcuffs with him (a sign to Hazelwood that this criminal was capable of learning and improving his MO) and began to physically assault his victims. He demanded anal sex and forced women to fellate him. He punched the women, often in their breasts.

The level of violence applied by a sex offender is part of his ritual, not his MO.

"How much physical force a rapist uses against his victim is a matter of satisfying himself, not simply to overcome her resistance," Hazelwood explains.

The Ski Mask Rapist therefore seemed to Roy to be evolving from a power assertive rapist, who applies moderate force or coercion, toward sexual sadism. His psychosexual needs were changing. A whole new criminal character was emerging.

In one case, he forced a woman to fellate her date, and then to fellate him, while her date watched.

In another, he surprised a thirteen-year-old baby-sitter, whom he forced to perform oral sex.

Afterward, when she warned him that he better run because he was in a police officer's home, the Ski Mask Rapist seemed delighted. "No shit?" he said, "What time does he get home? I'll wait for him."

When the officer and his wife did return, the intruder forced them to hand-cuff one another. Then he vaginally raped the woman.

"Are you all right?" her husband asked her at one point.

"Yes, he's being a gentleman," his wife replied.

At that, the Ski Mask Rapist grew enraged and began brutally pummeling the woman's breasts. So serious were her injuries that a double mastectomy later was necessary.

Roy recognized that the UNSUB was highly macho. Hazelwood based this conclusion on the offender's deliberate habit of committing his sexual assaults in front of his victims' male companions.

"That told me he was extremely confident," Roy says. "He was not at all threatened by the male's presence. In fact, he wanted to humiliate him. That is an unambiguous expression of macho. He thinks of himself as macho, and he projects a macho image."

Roy enumerated several corollaries to that core judgment.

The Ski Mask Rapist probably consumed alcohol and/or used marijuana, Hazelwood said, because in the rapist's perception that is what real men did. Likewise, he would be athletic, a sports participant as well as a spectator, who took care of his body, worked out, and exercised a good deal. Appearance meant a lot to him. He liked to show off his muscles.

Roy speculated that the rapist had served in the military and had chosen the ground forces—the army or marines—because to him those were the most manly services to join. His car would be a reflection of that macho image, too: a fast, flashy vehicle. The Ski Mask Rapist would not drive a sensible four-door sedan.

Roy profiled the UNSUB in his late twenties or early thirties, roughly the same age range as his victims. "Based on my research, I know that rape is basically a young man's crime," says Hazelwood. "He would assault females who were about his own age. Also, macho offenders do not rape preteens or old people."

The Ski Mask Rapist was single and never married, Roy believed, for the same reasons. Loving and being true to one woman did not suit his self-image. Marriage was for suckers.

His demonstrated ability to learn indicated he was of at least average intelligence. Based on the BSU's familiarity with other offenders who fit this profile, Hazelwood further believed the rapist's education or training extended beyond high school, possibly including college. He either was currently employed in a job requiring some sort of special skill, Roy thought, or once had worked in such a position.

Although never married, the Ski Mask Rapist had ongoing consenting relationships with various women, again a conclusion based on BSU research, but he would never be faithful to any of them.

Roy's final conclusion was in fact an admonition. The Ski Mask Rapist was growing ever more violent. Hazelwood predicted that unless he was caught, he seemed likely someday to cross the threshold and become the Ski Mask Killer.

On the night of October 29, 1981—approximately one year after Roy submitted his UNSUB profile—a policeman in Gonzales, southeast of Baton Rouge, noticed a bright red Pontiac Trans Am parked alone in a city lot. The vehicle struck the cop as suspicious, out of place in the neighborhood.

That same night, a ski-masked gunman surprised three women, recently returned from shopping together, in a Gonzales residence. He bound all three, plus one woman's husband, with ligatures he'd brought with him. Then he robbed the females of their jewelry, raped all three of them, and departed in one of the victims' cars.

The Gonzales police officer learned of the assaults over his car radio. On a hunch, he returned to where he'd seen the red Pontiac. It was gone. But parked near where the Trans Am had been was the rape victim's missing car. On the ground nearby, police also found a pair of men's gloves similar in description to those worn by the rapist that night.

Members of the multijurisdictional Ski Mask Rapist Task Force, only recently formed, immediately were told of the incident in Gonzales. Several reported back that a distinctive red Trans Am also had been seen in their communities prior to assaults believed committed by the Ski Mask Rapist.

A regional BOLO (be on the lookout) bulletin was issued for the car.

Weeks passed. Then on the Monday before Thanksgiving, off-duty Louisiana state trooper Herman Rogers saw a bright red Trans Am in Lake Charles, near the Texas border, and jotted down its license number.

The owner turned out to be thirty-one-year-old Barry Simonis, a former all-state high school quarterback, army veteran, and onetime hospital cardiovascular technician.

Hazelwood's profile had been dead on.

After identifying Simonis, the police surveilled him for nearly a week, keeping the suspected Ski Mask Rapist in their sights while investigators all over the

Southeast and Southwest worked to see if they could connect him with their known cases.

"He loved to drive," state police lieutenant Butch Milan told a reporter. "He would drive right by us and never look at us. He just wandered aimlessly."

As Simonis enjoyed Thanksgiving dinner at his mother's house, the investigators made do on 7-Eleven fare.

When they finally had their affidavits and arrest warrants in order, they tailed him to a Lake Charles convenience store and grabbed him as he walked out.

Simonis was barefoot as he stepped from the store, carrying a loaf of bread and two packs of cigarettes.

"State police," Butch Milan said as he approached the suspect. "You're under arrest. Are you armed?"

Simonis was not.

The capture received wide press attention—Barry Simonis confessed to rapes and burglaries from coast to coast. Roy learned of it back at Quantico, and was gratified to see that his profile had been so accurate. Hazelwood decided he wanted to talk to Jon Barry Simonis should the opportunity arise.

It did, almost three years later.

On a fetid summer day in 1984, Simonis welcomed Hazelwood and Ken Lanning to his permanent address, the Louisiana State Prison at Angola. The penitentiary is set down in remote and forbidding backwaters along the Mississippi River, where the lower portion of the state of Mississippi juts westward into Louisiana like Homer Simpson's upper lip. Angola itself is too small to warrant its own dot on most atlases.

Swamps surround the facility, where consensus wisdom has it that if would-be escapees from the prison are not shot, the snakes or the alligators will get them.

At the time of Roy's visit to Angola with Lanning, there were only two air-conditioned areas within the prison. The warden's office was one. The wood-paneled conference room where Simonis met with the agents was the other.

Hazelwood and Lanning wore suits and ties, and sat opposite one another. The mustachioed Simonis in his white prison-issue T-shirt sat between the two agents. Coffee cups and ashtrays were scattered around. At Roy's nod, a video camera started recording, and the conversation began.

"What are you incarcerated for?" Roy asked.

"A series of armed robberies and rapes," Simonis answered evenly.

"What's the total number of those, combined?"

"I think we have a figure of one hundred forty robberies and rapes and robberies and rapes combined."

Simonis was unprepossessing, serious and alert and responsive, but with almost no edge to his voice, or much light in his eyes. That was intentional. The Ski Mask Rapist had learned the value of not being noticed.

He explained to Hazelwood that when he first arrived at Angola in 1982 the older cons advised him to deliberately score low on the standard IQ form so that prison authorities wouldn't expect too much of him, or watch him too closely. Simonis had scored a 108. When Roy had him retested by a psychologist, he scored a 128.

"And how many were rapes, specifically?" Hazelwood asked.

"Between forty-five and fifty rapes. Actual sexual assaults probably would get a little higher, anywhere between sixty and seventy-five."

"And what would you include in sexual assaults?"

"Uh, somebody who would perform oral sex, masturbation, any kind of a sexual act other than intercourse."

The discussion had the air of an employment interview, a tone that Hazelwood set deliberately. If they had any response besides clinical interest in what Simonis was saying, neither Hazelwood nor Lanning would betray it.

"And in what states did these take place, and what period of time are we talking about?" Roy continued.

"My first assault took place in November of 1978," Simonis answered, "and it ended in November of 1981. It went from Florida to Georgia, North Carolina, Ohio, Michigan, Wisconsin, Mississippi, Louisiana, Texas, Oklahoma, and California."

"Would you say there was a progression, or an escalation of aggression or violence associated with your attacks?"

"Oh, yes," Simonis answered. "It started out very mild and progressed quite heavily."

This part of Simonis's behavior already was evident from the case reports. The question that remained for Roy was how commonly did rapists' violence escalate? Was Simonis a rarity? The evidence from police agencies on this point was anecdotal and unscientific, a collection of memories and impressions, as is true for much investigative lore.

Hazelwood asked Simonis to describe his first assault. The Ski Mask Rapist didn't hesitate.

"The first one started out to be a burglary," he said. "I entered a house and

111

was confronted by the lady who lived there—who I'd followed from a shopping center earlier that day.

"After confronting the woman I kinda let her know that I was in control. After I got the money from her and I kind of bound her hands, I took her into a bedroom and had her perform masturbation on me. I was unable to do vaginal intercourse because I was unable to get an erection at the time. I was very nervous."

"You did not physically assault her?"

"No sir."

"How," Roy asked, "would that assault have occurred two to three years later?"

"Near the end of my criminal activities it got to be a much more violent thing, a form of degradation toward the women, making them feel completely dominated. My intentions were to inflict fear into them, to force them to do things they wouldn't ordinarily do."

Ken Lanning asked if Simonis's preparations for his crimes evolved as well.

"I progressed into a more disguised way," Simonis explained. "My face was covered. I wore gloves. I also wore baggy clothes, like coveralls, to kind of conceal my build. I also took into the place a pistol and precut lengths of rope to bind the victims with, or handcuffs. Duct tape to blind them, maybe tape their mouths. A pocketknife in case I needed to cut anything."

"What precautions did you take when you left?" Roy asked.

"I'd usually cut the phone and make sure they were tied securely where they couldn't get loose anytime soon. Sometimes I'd slash their tires to prevent them from traveling."

In this exchange, Simonis had provided Roy with his first glimpse of one of the serial rapist's central distinguishing characteristics. He is typically an intelligent offender, who reflects not only on the sexual assault itself, but also on all the details of his pre- and postoffense behavior in order to perfect his crime, heighten the psychosexual experience, and minimize the possibility of capture. Simonis was a perfect example of the highly organized offender, a thinking criminal.

Hazelwood asked how much money, in all, Simonis made from his thefts.

"After fencing the stuff, about a quarter million dollars," he guessed. "Retail it probably was worth three to four million."

"Was it necessary for you to work, as well?"

"Not at all. When I worked in the hospital as a cardiovascular specialist I was maybe making somewhere from fourteen thousand to eighteen thousand a year. I'd sometimes make that much in a month from thefts."

"Barry," Lanning said, "how did you identify your victims?"

"There were different ways. They usually were wealthy. As I drove through an area I'd pick out a house that looked to belong to a financially secure couple. Sometimes I'd pick somebody driving around in an expensive car. Or I might see somebody inside a store who might be wearing a gold watch or a large diamond. I'd wait outside in my car and then follow them to where they lived.

"If I didn't hit them directly, I'd probably hit somebody else in the neighborhood where they lived."

"What about a woman attracted you?"

"Attractive ones had an appealing effect on me. It wasn't always the motive for following them, but it was a major one. I figured that if a woman was attractive and her husband was well off, he'd do things to keep her happy. Buy her expensive jewelry and other nice things.

"This was the initial reason for a lot of the attacks. I'd rob and take what I could. The assaults and rapes usually took place afterward."

"Tell us your understanding of why you did these things," Lanning asked.

"It's pretty complex. I think there was a multitude of things involved. Money was a motive. Sex was a factor. Urges just came on to me to the point that I was uncontrollable near the end. The effects on me when I saw women had more of a hold on me than I had on them."

"Did the robberies and burglaries, entering homes, satisfy some of your urges?"

Here, Simonis confirmed what many experts on criminal behavior have observed. Offenders get a psychic jolt from danger. They don't just rob for the money, or assault out of anger or a need for power. There's an adrenaline rush that lifts the experience to a higher plane for them.

"It got me high just going into a place that belonged to somebody else," Simonis explained. "Any kind of illegal activity, knowing there was a risk of being caught, created stimulation. It was a turn-on, so to speak. But it was a different high than the sexual aspect. They kind of coincided with one another."

Prior to his arrest as the Ski Mask Rapist, Simonis's rap sheet included a 1978 arrest near Lake Charles for making indecent telephone calls. In a statement he gave police, he admitted window-peeping as early as 1975. Later, as a soldier in Europe, he said, he repeatedly exposed himself to women.

The obscene telephone calls, Simonis said, had begun in late 1977, when he was working at Lake Charles Memorial Hospital, operating a heart-stress machine. He denied ever having committed a rape to that point.

Roy probed Simonis's paraphilias, or perversions, as they were once known, realizing they likely were manifested much earlier than his arrest record showed.

"You began deviant sexual behavior at fifteen? Is that right? With window-peeping?" he asked.

"Yes."

"How long did you continue to window-peep?"

"Oh, off and on until the times I was actually going into the houses."

"You stopped at that time?"

"Well, I classify window-peeping as just looking, and not doing anything else. There were lots of times I'd peek in a window and see women who might be undressed but it was more to get an idea who was home, and where they were at. It wasn't just looking and leaving."

What about the exhibitionism?

Simonis said it started when he was in Europe in the army at age twenty-four.

"How long did that go on?"

"Off and on for about three years."

"The purpose was to get a response from the women?"

"Exactly. A lot of times I got a stimulating feeling just on the reaction of people. A lot of times it was to induce fear, or surprise, and see how they responded to it. I would feed off this fear. It was like a source of fuel for me."

Lanning asked about the telephone scatology.

"Ah, yes. That was around '77 or '78, around in there."

Neither Hazelwood nor Lanning at first fully comprehended the importance of what Simonis had revealed about paraphilias: that they do not appear in isolation from one another. This important disclosure would later be borne out in research conducted by Dr. Gene Abel, an Atlanta mental health expert who specializes in the study and treatment of child molesters. Roy would be among the first investigators to make practical use of it.

"You also said you masturbated a considerable number of times," Lanning said to Simonis. "What kind of fantasies did you have during masturbation?"

"It was a multitude of things. It might consist of bondage or the fantasy of a rape, or maybe multiple males and multiple females."

"And how long did you masturbate?"

"Sometimes four or five times a day. But there were times when it was as much as ten or twelve times."

"During the time you were committing your rapes," Roy asked, "were you also having consenting sexual relations?"

"Yes. Quite a bit."

"Did you ever live with a woman?"

"Several of them, yes."

This, Hazelwood would learn, was not atypical for rapists. Of the forty-one in his survey, only one was not in a consenting sexual relationship at the time he was also raping.

"Why do you think you were so successful for such a long period of time?" Lanning asked.

"I think it was just a natural instinct I developed, and relied on heavily. It always paid off for me.

"It got to be a cat and mouse game with the police. I knew they were after me by 1980. From there on I figured that if I kept on going I just could not create a definite pattern. I had to stagger my attacks and my robberies in different states. Always change my clothing, have new stuff after every job. Throw the old stuff away. Never kept any evidence.

"I tried to think like the cops would think. For instance, after I left one job I figured they'd probably block the interstates. So I used the back roads. It was a kind of guessing game with them."

Both Hazelwood and Lanning locked on to what Simonis was explaining. Both agents knew that criminals refine their MO over time, but Simonis was saying that an important part of the process was the guessing game he played with the police.

Clearly, just as the seasoned bank robber or jewel thief might alter his MO in order to avoid capture, so, too, did the more intelligent deviant offenders.

The message for police was not to become too predictable. If the investigators followed repeat patterns, the smart criminal would pick up on that and use it to his advantage, as Simonis did.

"Was traveling in a lot of jurisdictions part of those efforts?" asked Lanning.

"Oh, yes. Spreading them out. There was less chance of people associating those crimes with me."

"Did you ever use your occupation to select victims?"

Here, Simonis had chilling news.

"Oh, yes. When I worked in a hospital I had access to all the medical records. I knew where the patients lived; what their husbands did; whether he worked in or out of town; who was home during the day, and who wasn't.

"Also, if they were having surgery, I'd have access to their keys, which they usually left in their nightstands by their beds. I'd go down and have a copy made and return the original and copy down their address and later on use that to get in their house."

"Did you ever take advantage of patients under sedation?"

"Oh, sometimes. I had neurology patients we had to sometimes sedate. So there were times for that, yeah."

Halfway through the daylong interview three lunches arrived from the prison kitchen. Word was around Angola that the two suits talking to Simonis were federal agents, meaning that a surprise very likely was hidden somewhere in their meals, probably bodily excretions contributed by one or more inmates in the Angola kitchen.

Simonis advised Hazelwood and Lanning of that possibility, and was thanked for his consideration.

Lunch was returned to the kitchen untouched.

"What was the youngest victim you sexually assaulted?" Lanning resumed the questioning.

"Agewise I really don't know," Simonis answered a little warily. "About thirteen or fourteen."

Consistent with his hypermasculine point of view, Simonis was careful that the agents didn't think him a baby raper—the lowest form of life in the prison class system—or that he preyed on the elderly, also the sort of crime that is beneath the virile self-image of the macho offender.

"And the oldest victim?"

"There was one in Houston who was fifty," he answered, then added, "but she was really well preserved. She looked more like thirty-eight or forty."

"You mentioned that you would take things that were easily transportable, easily concealed," said Hazelwood. "Why?"

"Well, in the beginning I took a lot of things like televisions and video recorders, but I was exposing myself to the chance of being caught. Later on, I started taking just jewelry. Easy to conceal and lightweight. It didn't bog me down in case I had to move or run or get away quickly."

"What type of vehicle did you drive?"

"I started off driving a '78 Buick Regal. It was gray and I had it painted black. I also had a '79 Kawasaki motorcycle that I'd use especially out in the country, where I could conceal it quite well.

"Later on, I sold the Buick and the bike and bought an '81 red Trans Am."

"Did you like to drive?"

"Oh, yes. I put about eighty thousand miles on it in ten months."

"Why did you like to drive so much?"

"I just liked to travel. It gave me a sense of freedom. I didn't have to worry about what I did. I didn't have to worry about answering to people."

Ken Lanning leaned forward, fingers clasped together.

"Barry, you indicated earlier that you had these tremendous urges that kind of drove you. Yet in some cases you'd rob and burglarize and not sexually assault. What are some of the factors that determined whether or not you sexually assaulted a victim?"

"The victims herself plays a part in that," he answered. "If they'd show fear or apprehension, sometimes I'd feed off that. That might cause me to make a sexual attack. Some I had no sexual contact with at all. I don't know why."

"Were there ever practical reasons why you wouldn't sexually assault?"

"Well, sometimes if the assault jeopardized getting away with the robbery, I wouldn't."

"Did you ever take anything that wasn't valuable?" Hazelwood wondered. He knew that many sexual offenders take away souvenirs of their crimes.

"Just some articles of clothing, and maybe a driver's license on a few occasions. They were just temporary things to hang on to."

"And what did they represent to you?"

"Like a trophy. Kind of a reminder. It helped me visualize in my mind the scene when I reenacted the fantasy in my mind."

"You said you'd dress in a particular way for your assaults. What would you do with that material later?"

"Oh, I'd always discard it. Put it in Dumpsters. Rip it up and throw it out the window along the interstate. Usually, this was a long distance away. I'd never dump it right there in the community where I committed the crime."

"What would be your first response when a woman resisted you?" Roy asked, lighting his second or third Lucky Strike of the afternoon.

"In the early stages, if they would have put up a scream it probably would dissuade me from sticking around."

"What would happen later on?"

"It would have been a point of agitation to me and I would probably have retaliated by taking a physical action against them."

"Such as?"

"Beating them. Or kicking them. Or burning them. Any way to inflict pain to get them to be quiet."

Lanning asked Simonis to describes the assaults.

"Well, their hands were tied, and usually their feet were, too, but not always. Uh, I'd slam my fist to their breasts or into their stomach. Sometimes I hit them across the face. There were times I'd light a cigarette and touch it to their breasts."

Roy reminded Simonis of the police officer's wife.

"She said you were being a gentleman, and then you assaulted her."

"Correct. I struck her across the mouth a couple times."

"What was the reason for that?"

"I felt she was trying to patronize me. Like she was talking down to me. Treating me like a child. It irritated and agitated me. I decided to let her know I was in control and she would not dictate to me what was going on."

Simonis's sharp loathing for women was evident. What he said reminded Roy of Mike DeBardeleben's extended reflections on the same subject, handwritten and tape-recorded material he just recently had analyzed for the Secret Service. DeBardeleben and Simonis had much in common.

"You mentioned compulsive urges just a moment ago," said Lanning. "Yet you were able to control the urge so as not to bring harm to yourself. If you had an urge to assault but you knew the area to be dangerous, what would you do?"

"My safety came first. If I thought I could pull it off, I would pull it off. If not, I'd go somewhere else, or try from a different angle."

"So you did not have an irresistible impulse?"

"No. Not total domination. Later on it did get to where it controlled me a lot more than I wanted it to. But I wasn't at its mercy completely."

"I'd like to talk a little bit about pornography," said Lanning. "Did you ever view or collect it?"

"Yes. I had a small note binder full of different pictures I'd get from *Playboy* magazine and other skin books."

"How did you use these pictures?" Lanning asked.

"I'd look at them for masturbation."

"Did you ever view pornography when you were younger?"

"Yes, I did. But not to get off on it. I was about six or seven, I think, the first time I actually came in contact with any kind of pornography. It was something like *Stag*."

Simonis explained that from his very earliest memory, sex was connected to violence and pain in his imagination.

"It had an artist's conception of a woman, completely nude, with her hands tied together and bound above her head, tied to a rope that went up to the ceiling, and there was a man standing there with a smile on his face, holding a large knife. It looked like he was getting ready to inflict bodily harm, a form of mutilation, almost.

"It wasn't so much the nude woman that excited me. It was the overall picture."

"Do you think the picture had an impact on you?"

"I think it did. It's stayed in my subconscious all these years. I'm not saying it was a contributing factor to me doing the things that I did. I have to take full blame for that. But I think it does contribute in some way."

"A while back we were talking about sexual bondage," Roy said, "and you mentioned tying your victims in a variety of positions. Where did you get the idea for that?"

"From magazines."

"Was it your goal to inflict pain on your victims?"

"Yes, that was the most stimulating part, I guess. To inflict pain and terror to a woman. The attacker kind of feeds off it. It's kind of like adding fuel to the body. The more you see it the more it stimulates you, the more it gets a person going."

"Is the pain itself the goal? Or is it the victim's response?"

"I think it's the initial response that they give off, that's produced by their pain. That is what the sadistic person's actually looking for. It's not that he doesn't enjoy inflicting the pain, but the final product is the reaction you get from it. If you inflicted pain and they showed no response whatsoever, it would be like making sex to a dead person. You'd get no thrill out of it."

"What was the turn-on?" Roy asked. "Was it sexual intercourse or control?"

"It was a multitude of things. The rapes were a sexual thing a lot of the time, but it was also mainly the idea of being dominant, having complete control, having the woman at your disposal and mercy to do what you wanted to do."

The interview continued for another seven and a half hours.

"Barry, will you tell us what your sentence is?" Roy asked in closing.

"I'm not sure I remember them all. I have about twenty-one life sentences, plus an additional 2,386½ years to go."

"Any possibility of parole?"

"Zero possibility."

Off camera, Simonis made several further disclosures to Hazelwood. He said that although he had no chance of ever legally walking free of Angola, he was glad in a way to have been stopped when he was. Rape, said Simonis, was beginning to bore him. About the time Lieutenant Milan arrested him outside the Lake Charles convenience store, his fantasies increasingly were of murder.

THIRTEEN

"I'm Going to Have
Sex with You"

A worry preoccupied Hazelwood as he came away from his meeting with Barry Simonis. He could not erase thoughts of the terrible pain the police detective's wife had endured for simply saying that Simonis was a gentleman. The incident alerted Roy to a potential problem he hadn't fully considered before.

All over the United States, he knew, women receive advice on how to react when confronted by a rapist. Allegedly authoritative voices on television and radio and in newspapers and magazines counsel all sorts of responses, from the use of weapons to pleading pregnancy to claiming you are infected with a sexually transmitted disease.

Thinking about the detective's wife, Hazelwood realized that hundreds, if not thousands, of women around the country might say exactly the same thing in the same situation, because they had been told that was the best strategy to pursue with a sex offender.

Roy's rapist typology, however, indicates there should be no blanket strategy for rape victims. Avoiding, or minimizing, harm depends on several variables.

In the subsequent paper he published with fellow BSU agent Joseph A. Harpold, Hazelwood identified three "critical variables" that he believes women should be trained to assess before deciding what their most reasonable course of action is.

First of the critical variables is location. A woman confronted at midafternoon in a grocery store parking lot obviously has different options than she would at 4:00 A.M. along a deserted roadway.

Hazelwood points out that screams or noisemakers—whistles and the like—might help the former victim, but be useless to the latter.

The wisdom of carrying a weapon or a disabling chemical such as Mace also varies according to the situation. A cocked gun stuck in his ear would easily dissuade many would-be rapists. However, the armed woman might place too much faith in her weapon and forget her native caution. She might neglect to lock a door, or forget to peer into the backseat of her vehicle before getting into it, thus raising her risk of a potentially deadly confrontation.

A false sense of security might lead her unthinkingly into places that common sense tells her to avoid.

The second variable is the victim's personality.

Anyone advocating vigorous verbal or physical resistance to the threat of rape, for example, should recognize that not every victim can be combative on cue. It may not be in someone's nature to behave that way. Conversely, Hazelwood says, "an independent and assertive individual will be hard-pressed to submit to a violation of her body without a struggle, even if she has been advised that passivity is her best course."

The third and most important variable is the offender himself.

Knowing how best to respond entails understanding the type of rapist confronting you.

Acquiescence might only encourage a power reassurance rapist by feeding his fantasy of consenting sex. In a similar vein, pleading for mercy from an offender such as Barry Simonis might be, as Simonis told Hazelwood, "the most stimulating part" of the assault.

In a case from his serial rapist survey that Hazelwood sometimes uses in his lectures, a power reassurance rapist approaches a teenage girl in a parking lot.

"Do you want a ride?" he asks.

"No."

She walks on.

The stranger drives up again, this time blocking her way with his car. He pulls a gun from his T-shirt.

"I think you better get in the car," he says.

This particular girl has attended rape classes where she has been taught not to let a would-be attacker depersonalize her. She has learned not to antagonize him, but to encourage him to see her as a real person, to talk to him.

As Roy explains, "Now, you have a rapist whose fantasy is a consenting sexual relationship, and you have a victim who's been told to try to get the offender to relate to her as a human being, rather than as an object. She begins telling him about her family, and how she skipped school that day. And she asks him what he's going to do.

"'Well, I'm going to have sex with you,' he says.

"'When you're finished, will you take me back home?' she asks.

This technique, designed to help her survive a rape, actually feeds her rapist's fantasy.

In the end, Roy and his coauthor called for multidisciplinary programs to train women to quickly and competently assess their peril and then to finesse or overcome it.

"We know of no such comprehensive training program," they wrote, "but we know that one is possible."

The more encompassing consequence of his encounter with Simonis was Roy's decision to undertake his serial rapist survey. It was a natural next research step for the BSU after John Douglas's and Bob Ressler's serial killer survey and Roy's book on autoerotic fatalities. Serial rapists are a clear and serious problem for law enforcement. Until Hazelwood's prison study, they also were largely a mystery.

"There'd been hundreds of rape studies done," says Hazelwood, "but no one had ever looked at serial rapists."

He had three major research objectives that grew out of the Simonis interview.

"One, I wanted to find out what made serial rapists so successful," he explains. "What traits did they have in common? Two, I wanted to see if they varied their MO or rituals over time. Three, I wanted to test whether rapists escalate the violence of their crimes. Simonis did. But I wasn't sure about other serial rapists."

In order to gain valid trend information and to ensure there were no fluke inclusions in his study, Hazelwood set the bar high.

Generally, a rapist is considered a serial offender if he commits three or more sexual assaults. To qualify for inclusion in Hazelwood's study, the offenders must have committed at least ten documented sexual assaults.

"You can't look at just three or four rapes and gauge why someone was so successful, or if they changed over time or if they escalated their violence," says Hazelwood. "I set the figure arbitrarily at ten in order to capture this behavior."

To recruit his subjects, he combed the records from prisons in twelve states, and found forty-three men who met his criteria. All were guaranteed confidentiality. All were also advised not to mention any past crimes for which they had not been charged, or of which the police were unaware.

It was Roy's version of don't ask, don't tell.

Out of that group, only two men declined to participate. Both explained to Hazelwood they had nothing against him or his research, but they did bear grudges against the authorities in general, and that included FBI agents.

The forty-one rapists who sat down for the open-ended interviews, which lasted between four and a half and twelve and a half hours, were a predictably strange, and highly various, group. In all, they had committed 837 known rapes, plus an additional 400 attempted rapes.

One of Roy's biggest surprises in a survey that would be full of unanticipated results was that only one of the offenders said that he himself had been sexually abused as a child.

Yet by their responses to his next question—"With whom and at what age did you have your first sexual experience?"—it was evident that thirty-one of the men, 76 percent of the sample, were in fact sexually victimized as youngsters.

One rapist said that his first sexual contact occurred at age fifteen with his girlfriend's mother, who began a yearlong affair with him. Although she was a willing bed partner, she forced him to withdraw from her before he spent himself. She then would masturbate the boy to ejaculation.

Later, when he started raping, he also would have his victims masturbate him—in handcuffs.

"I was seven years of age when my mother hired a knockout baby-sitter, who was twenty-one," said another. "She taught me how to go down on her."

A third inmate said that his initiation to sex came at age nine with a child molester. Each week at the movies, he told Roy, he had allowed the older man to fondle him in return for a ticket, refreshments, and two dollars.

Overall, sexual abuse committed against these men by family members was fairly evenly divided between male and female relatives. Sexual abuse by outsiders, however, almost invariably was committed by males.

One offender, Tim,* described how he had been repeatedly raped by his father until Tim was eleven. That's when Dad, a serial rapist, found other uses for his boy.

He took his son with him into bars (shades of M.P. Reddick) where Tim drank Cokes and watched as his father chose his prey for the night. At closing time, Dad would suggest to a woman that she join him and his son for breakfast. Tim's presence usually put the intended victim at ease, and she'd agree.

But instead of heading for an IHOP, his father would drive to a graveyard, where he raped and tortured the woman in the backseat as Tim looked on in front. Once finished, Dad would direct Tim to carry out an assault of his own.

At first, the boy was frightened.

"I was terrified," he said. "But I remember one woman telling me to do what my father said, 'or he's going to hurt me worse.'"

"Was there any significance to the choice of graveyards?" Roy asked.

"Police don't usually patrol them," he answered.

By about age thirteen, Tim said, he had changed. He started looking forward to the attacks, hoping his father would finish quickly, "so I could have her."

It wasn't until he was fourteen and began to discuss sex with his peers in school that Tim learned sexual intercourse ever occurred with warmth and affection between willing partners. This was a profound revelation for him.

Two years later, his father raped Tim's girlfriend, and the young man finally broke away from home. But his pattern had been set. Tim was by now a habitual rapist himself, different from his father only in that he always stopped short of physically brutalizing his victims.

To him, that was an important distinction, he told Roy.

He continued to rape even after enlisting in the army and becoming a military policeman in Korea. After returning to the United States, Tim joined a major East Coast police force. While a cadet officer in the training academy, he committed so many sexual assaults that a special task force of his fellow officers was created in the unsuccessful hope of hunting down the phantom UNSUB.

They never did.

Tim finally quit the police department, he told Hazelwood, because of the huge physical cost of working during the day and raping at night. "I was so exhausted, I couldn't stay awake," he said.

Finally he was captured, convicted, and sentenced to prison, where he served seven years. Upon his release, Tim found a job managing a bowling alley, and married.

All apparently went smoothly for him for two years and Tim began to believe he had conquered his deviant urges. Then one night, he called his wife to say he was picking up a couple steaks and a bottle of wine. She was to "get ready," he said.

As he was driving home, Tim stopped at a light where he happened to glance at a woman in another car. Suddenly, the old violence was reawakened in him and Tim chose not to resist it.

Instead of continuing on home to his waiting spouse, Tim followed the woman, stopped her, and raped her.

"My boyfriend's going to kill you for this," she said after he finished.

Again, the old behavior boiled up. Tim mercilessly beat the victim with his fists, and raped her again, this time anally.

However, even as he was committing the assault, Tim was hit with a horrifying realization.

"My God, this is exactly what my father did," he thought. "I'm turning into my father!"

With that he stopped, walked to his car, and drove away, allowing the victim ample opportunity to write down his license number, which she did. He subsequently was caught, convicted, and sentenced to life in prison.

"Why did you allow yourself to get caught?" Roy wanted to know.

"I didn't care anymore," Tim answered.

Another serial rapist taught Roy that even deviants can have a code of conduct.

This inmate recalled the night his mother had bailed him out of jail. She later helped him celebrate his release with some marijuana and a bottle of Jim Beam.

Mother was dressed only in her bra and panties.

In time, she passed out, or at least she seemed to. Her son thought to exploit the situation, and began to undo her bra.

She stirred at his touch.

"What are you doing?" she asked him.

"I'm gonna fuck you," he answered.

She slapped him hard several times. "No son of mine is going to do that!" she shouted.

"So I stabbed her three times and killed her," he told Roy.

Hazelwood nodded, then asked, "Well, did you rape her?"

The inmate stared at Hazelwood, a confused, hostile look in his eye.

"Did you hear what I said?" the rapist finally said.

"You said you stabbed her three times, but did you then rape her the way you originally intended?"

"Jesus no!" the prisoner finally snapped, shocked that this FBI agent would think him capable of both incest and necrophilia.

"I didn't rape her! I just killed my own mother!"

There were thirty-five white males, five African Americans, and a single Hispanic in Roy's sample. They had committed between ten and seventy-eight sexual assaults each, and ranged in age at the time of their interviews from twenty-three to fifty-five years.

The youngest victim was five years of age; the oldest was sixty-five.

The first apparent clue to their success was intellect. Of the thirty-three for whom intelligence testing was available, all but four scored average or better. Nine were "bright normal" and eight more were "superior or very superior."

Part of that intelligence was expressed in their eagerness to learn.

"Some of them told me that they went to rape prevention seminars to find out what women were being told," says Hazelwood. "They wanted to figure out ways of circumventing what experts were suggesting to women."

The rapists' second important shared characteristic was patience. They were, for the most part, organized offenders like Barry Simonis. Fewer than one in four described his assaults as impulsive or opportunistic.

But there was also an important subgroup that Hazelwood identified, a handful of impulsive rapists with low IQs who nevertheless had been quite successful in avoiding arrest.

Their key to success was more difficult to quantify. Roy calls it street smarts, the kind of animal cunning displayed by the anger retaliatory rapist who recounted to Roy the violent rape he committed in the hospital women's room.

Most of the forty-one told Hazelwood they adjusted their MOs over time. Across their early, middle, and late-stage assaults, the rapists learned that one of the best places to assault a woman is in her home. They gradually reduced the number of riskier attacks they committed on the street or in alleyways.

"Many of the rapists told me, 'The woman feels safest in her home, but when I get her in that bedroom, there's four walls and me, and that's all there is.'"

The serial rapists also consistently assaulted strangers, rather than acquaintances or neighbors who might be able to identify them.

Roy asked the rapists about their initial contact with victims, a critical component of their MOs.

He differentiates an offender's approach into three general types: "the con," "the blitz," and "the surprise."

The con, just as the name implies, is the friendly, at-ease advance, something as simple as asking a woman for directions, or if she'd like to dance. Any pretense will do. Impersonating a police officer is a very common con approach.

"Prior to his arrival in Florida, Bundy used the con approach," Roy explains, "as part of his ritual to select 'worthy' victims. Actually, it was practically a necessity for him to convince them to go willingly with him."

The second type Roy calls the blitz, although the term has nothing to do with suddenness. The blitz assault is brutal, whether short-lived or long. It might be as instantaneous as a stunning blow to the victim's head, or as protracted as strangulation to unconsciousness, then choking and then application to the victim's mouth of a fatal dose of anesthetic, such as chloroform.

The blitz approach is frequently seen among anger retaliatory rapists.

The third method is the surprise approach, in which the offender selects his victim and then lies in wait for her—in her car, in her residence, in her backyard garden, anywhere he can get her alone for a moment.

Typically, he will come upon the victim from behind, produce a knife, and promise her she will not be hurt if she does as he says. The surprise approach is most often used by the power reassurance rapist. He relies on the threat of harm, not pain or injury, to secure his victim's cooperation.

For the forty-one serial rapists in his study, the incidence of blitz attacks dropped from 23 percent in the early offenses to 17 percent among the last rapes. Surprise approaches fell from 54 percent to 44 percent, while the most sophisticated approach, the con, rose from 24 percent to 41 percent.

Those who used minimal physical force and relied instead on the threat of violence to control their victims did so consistently across all three phases.

Yet the survey showed that a minority of offenders, like Barry Simonis, do escalate their violence. Ten of the forty-one rapists increased their violence over time.

Roy zeroed in on these ten, hoping to find root causes for their escalation. He was surprised to find none. There were no significant differences in these rapists' personal histories that were predictive of escalation. Whether or not a parent was physically abusive, for example, would not necessarily determine if their son would be violent, too.

However, those who did escalate their violence also committed the most rapes; increasers averaged forty victims, while nonincreasers averaged twenty-two.

They also assaulted more frequently, every nineteen days as opposed to every fifty-five days.

"It's obvious," says Hazelwood, "that a police jurisdiction should give priority to UNSUBs who are increasing the level of violence each time. They'll assault twice as many victims as a nonincreaser in about one-third the time."

None of the forty-one decreased their violence over time.

The most common nonsexual offense on the serial rapists' rap sheets was breaking and entering or attempted burglary. Reason: "If law enforcement can't prove attempted rape," Roy explains, "they'll charge him with something they can prove."

About three-fourths of the rapists reported multiple paraphilias, as Simonis had. Twenty-one of the men were compulsive masturbators. Twenty-six said they collected detective magazines and violent pornography.

The responses suggested these rapists commit their crimes largely indiscriminately. Of the forty-one rapists, 15 percent said the victim's attire was a reason for the assault; 39 percent cited race; 95 percent cited gender; and all but one rapist said that victim availability was the reason she was assaulted. A quarter of the survey sample said they had no specific criteria at all for choosing victims.

The best-educated of the group was a black professional, who stands out as one of Hazelwood's more intriguing interviews, too.

"When I walked in the door," Roy recalls of this visit, "I said, 'My name is Hazelwood.'

"He said, 'I know who you are. You're Roy Hazelwood.'"

Roy asked why he knew his name.

"When I was raping I did a literature search on you," the inmate answered. "I've read everything you've written."

Martin Mason* was one of only five serial rapists who would not allow his interview to be audiotaped.

As a youth, he had been something of a black Horatio Alger hero, extremely bright and highly motivated. His father was imprisoned when Mason was young. His mother, a professional woman, made tremendous personal sacrifices to make sure her son made it through graduate school and into his highly paid profession.

The first of Mason's paraphilias to surface was voyeurism.

He told Roy he used to window-peep his mother when she played bridge with her friends. He also peeped on his favorite male schoolteacher as he ate dinner or watched television with his family.

Mason said his fantasy was to walk up to this teacher's door with a .38 and shoot him. When he told his mother about the fantasy, she said, "Well, you'll grow out of it."

Mason was full of self-loathing and anger.

"What I could discern from that interview was that he believed he was eventually going to screw up *because* he was black," Hazelwood remembers. "And he felt there was nothing he could do about it."

Mason told Roy he tried in various unsuccessful ways to cope with his deviant impulses. When he raped for the first time, he rationalized that if he acted out every one of his fantasies—which included torture and simulated murder (Mason was a sexual sadist)—then perhaps he'd be sated and could stop.

When that didn't work, he tried audiotaping an assault.

"Then anytime I wanted to rape I reasoned I could play it back and masturbate to it," he said to Hazelwood.

However, what he heard was so horrendous he could not bear to listen. So he erased the tape.

"Did you destroy it, too?" Roy asked.

"No, I just erased it," Mason answered.

"Why?"

"Because I'm obsessive-compulsive. I'd never destroy it."

The far deeper question was why Mason committed his crimes in the first place.

"If I knew why some people act out and others don't, I'd retire today," says Hazelwood, who nevertheless believes the answer has to do with self-perception.

"One of the reasons that we all don't act out is that we have inhibitors, or brakes, to control desires," he says. "They can be social status, religion, personal values, or fear of jail.

"Those who do act out are losers. They are convinced they are losers, so they don't see how they have anything more to lose by yielding to their desires.

"Basically, that is what Mason was saying to me. 'I know I'm going to screw up. Regardless of how successful I may appear to be, I know I'm going to screw up. So why not go ahead and do it and enjoy it? I'm going to give in to it.'

"I frequently run into this theme with offenders. Sexual sadists. Serial rapists. It is a common theme."

FOURTEEN

Who Hanged Andrew McIntyre?

The case was peculiar from the outset.

Gloria Bruno of Hilo, Hawaii, was senile, according to her doctor's diagnosis, and required care and supervision. Yet the eighty-four-year-old grandmother insisted upon living alone, even rejecting her son and daughter-in-law's repeated offers to move in with her and see to her needs.

Then Gloria Bruno vanished on an October afternoon in 1981.

She was seen several times that day, wandering around the neighborhood in an apparent mental fog. Local business owners reported Bruno walked into their stores throwing leaves about, saying they would keep Satan away. One young man told police of encountering her along a rural roadway. He recalled that the octogenarian had been shielding herself from the intense Hawaiian sun with a newspaper.

Five days later, Mrs. Bruno was found dead in the woods not far from her home. She was discovered in the thick underbrush, supine and partially undressed. Her blouse had been removed. Her camisole was wrapped around her neck. The waistlines of her pants and underpants were even with her pubic arch. Beneath her heels, officers found indentations in the soil.

She had not been sexually assaulted, nor had her two rings been stolen. At autopsy, Hilo medical examiner Dr. Alvin Majoska found a band of purplish discoloration on Bruno's throat.

Scrapes were evident on her feet, arms and thighs. She was bruised above her left ear and right eye.

Twenty-five feet away from the body, searchers found her sweater and blouse, neatly folded. A nearby depression in the earth suggested she had rested there. The police later recovered Bruno's new shoes along a gravel road approximately a half mile from where her body was found.

Dr. Majoska believed the disoriented victim had kicked off her shoes and wandered alone into the woods, where she became lost. The pathologist was unable to pinpoint just when she died, but he attributed her death to "asphyxiation following ligature strangulation" in what Majoska ruled was "a probable homicide."

But by whom, and for what motive?

Gloria Bruno was well known in Hilo. Her sudden death thoroughly appalled the city, and confounded police investigators. There was nothing remotely similar to the case in anyone's memory. Nor was there a viable suspect anywhere in town, on the island, in the state of Hawaii, or anywhere else.

The community struggled with its puzzle for fifteen months, and might had done so indefinitely if not for a serendipitous visit to Hilo by Roy Hazelwood, who came to town to conduct an FBI field school. In the course of his lectures, Roy was approached by Sergeant Roy Luis of the Hilo police, who asked if Hazelwood would review the case and profile the offender.

Back in the BSU bunker, Roy began with Dr. Majoska's autopsy, and considered the fact that Bruno had not been sexually attacked or mutilated. Nor had she been severely battered or stabbed. Nothing was stolen.

Since there is no such thing as a wholly motiveless crime, Hazelwood concluded that Bruno probably had not been murdered. Somehow, she'd killed herself. And since suicide seemed unlikely, the only possible answer was that she'd died in some sort of personal mishap.

Yet how?

As Hazelwood saw it, the keys to reconstructing Gloria Bruno's death were the sun and her dementia. He agreed with the medical examiner that she probably removed her uncomfortable new shoes along the gravel roadway and then wandered on, randomly, into the roadside brush, probably in search of shade from the intense Hawaiian sun. She would have discarded, or mislaid, her newspaper sunshade near where she first entered the brush.

Hazelwood pictured her lost and dazed by the noonday heat, possibly dehydrated, and increasingly disoriented. He suggested in his report that she might have groped along a barbed-wire fence that ran parallel to the road, hoping to find her way out of the rough terrain. Later investigation disclosed that bits of her hair and clothing were caught on the fence.

Roy believed that, unable to regain the roadway, and desperate for relief from the sun, Bruno then lurched deeper into the fields, where she finally found a clearing under a large tree. She shed her blouse and sweater there, folding them to serve as a pillow as she rested—hence the indentation—before moving on.

She didn't get far.

In the nearby copse where her body eventually was found, Bruno apparently continued to disrobe. Hazelwood believed that as she pulled the camisole over her head, it became entangled in the branches around her head. Bruno must have panicked and struggled, which would explain the scratches and bruises on her extremities and head.

The camisole also would have constricted her throat where, as those who practice autoerotic sex know, even slight pressure on the jugular vein or carotid artery can induce instant unconsciousness. Possibly, the exhausted woman simply collapsed from her exertions.

Hazelwood surmised that as Bruno slumped to the ground, her camisole caught fast on the surrounding branches, pulling it tighter around her neck, asphyxiating the frail grandmother, and creating what later appeared to be a purple ligature bruise.

As she struggled to loosen the garment, her heels would have dug into the earth. Her subsequent exertions would have caused her pants and underpants to slide down her waist and hips, later creating the impression they had been pulled. The lightweight camisole might then have slipped free of the bushes, but remained closely wrapped around her neck as she collapsed to the ground and died.

Roy's conclusion confirmed a rule of criminal investigation first promulgated in Arthur Conan Doyle's Sherlock Holmes stories, and made part of the BSU canon by Howard Teten: Once all other possibilities are eliminated, whatever is left, however improbable, is what happened.

And if Gloria Bruno's demise was bizarre, Hazelwood's explanation of it was appreciably less sinister than what the citizens and police of Hilo had feared.

In their subsequent review, the local authorities found nothing to contradict Roy's assessment, and much circumstantial evidence to support it. As a result, both the Hilo police and Dr. Majoska concurred in Hazelwood's conclusions, and the Bruno case was closed, reclassified as an innocent, if horrifying, accidental death.

Roy employed what he calls "equivocal death analysis" to explain Gloria

Bruno's mystifying demise. Built on deductive principles he first worked out while parsing autoerotic fatalities, equivocal death analyses differ in the main from criminal personality profiles in that the analyst must solve multiple variables, and must have a broad range of knowledge and experience to competently attempt one.

"They are more complex," he says, "because you have more than just the question of who did the crime. You have to determine if a murder occurred at all.

"Secondly, there is more risk involved. If a profile is wrong, no one gets hurt. But with equivocal deaths you face the same set of potential problems you do with autoerotic fatalities: insurance questions, religious questions, and a lot of emotions. You have to pay very close attention to what you are doing. You've got to capture every detail."

Never in Roy's career was that maxim more plainly true than in another equivocal death investigation—probably the strangest case he's ever encountered.

At about 4 A.M. on July 6, 1985, June Smith,* twenty-four, and the mother of two young boys, was found dead, lying face up next to a parked car in her neighbor's driveway, about sixty feet from her front door. Smith was shoeless, dressed only in a pair of slacks and a blouse, which was saturated with blood. Her left arm, the source of the blood, had been nearly severed at the shoulder, and rested beneath her.

Her scalp was shaven from her forehead to the midline of her skull.

A trail of blood led circuitously back from where she lay to her neighbor's porch and then to Smith's front door, tracing what appeared to be June Smith's last few faltering steps before she collapsed and died in the night from loss of blood.

Inside the Smith house, police found six plastic bags arranged together in the living room. In the center of each was a plate of uneaten food and a glass of milk.

Smith's older son, aged four, lay asleep on the couch. He was unharmed, although a substance that appeared to be blood was discovered on the shoulder of his pajamas.

The kitchen was littered with food, milk containers, more plastic bags, dirty plates, and clothing. Two newly baked cakes, both untouched, rested incongruously on the top of the stove.

Investigators found Smith's younger child, her one-year-old baby boy, safe and asleep in his bed.

Next came the bathroom.

A pile of June Smith's hair lay at the threshold. The walls were spattered with blood. The floor was slick with it, as were the sink and the shelves on both sides of it. Three more plates, each accompanied by a pair of forks, were arranged on either side of the sink. Behind the water faucets was a Bible, opened to the Book of Psalms, chapters 22 to 26. A cross attached to a chain was affixed to the wall to the right of the bathroom mirror.

Opposite the sink, the bathtub was partially filled with clean water.

The forensic pathologist who autopsied Smith concluded from the pattern of her wounds that they were self-inflicted. And from his own attempts to duplicate the near-total amputation using the same knife Mrs. Smith had used, he estimated she had spent two hours hacking at her left shoulder in the bathroom.

He also noted in his report that she had several superficial bruises of recent origin on her right arm.

The victim's family could not conceive of such a horrible rite of self-destruction. They pressed for a fuller explanation from the local police, who called on Hazelwood and Park Dietz to consult in the case.

Roy concurred that amputation is a highly unusual form of killing somebody, or oneself; and that it is especially so for a woman, and particularly in the deliberate way Smith seemed to have gone about it. No one reported hearing a sound from the Smith residence at any time that night, meaning she would have endured epic pain without uttering any cry much above a whimper.

Yet Hazelwood was not primarily interested in the way that June Smith died but in whether she'd killed herself, or been killed. While conceding that pills or gas are a more common way for females to kill themselves, Roy cautioned that women do occasionally inflict horrible injury on themselves. He mentioned in his later report a case in which the victim hacked herself to death with a machete.

Roy emphasizes that the first rule of equivocal death investigations is to never let the severity of the trauma determine the manner of death (i.e., homicide, suicide, or accident).

"Studying the victim," he says, "is the most crucial factor in analyzing equivocal deaths."

June Smith's pertinent history began in her late teens, when she left her family and friends and a comfortable suburban life to marry a fisherman and live with him and his parents in a modest house in a small and isolated coastal village.

Her husband often was gone to sea for months at a time, leaving his wife to make do in an alien culture. June Smith complained in letters of her boredom and lack of privacy.

In 1980, her first son was born. The following year, Smith suffered a miscarriage, then became pregnant again, only to learn the fetus was afflicted with a gross brain abnormality for which death would be the certain consequence within days of its birth. She elected to abort.

Two years later, Smith gave birth to her second son, and immediately went into a severe postpartum depression, according to her in-laws.

Around Christmas, 1984, she began ignoring both her little boys and took up Bible study. Soon thereafter, Smith set several fires in the house, claiming she was combating an evil spirit. She also heard voices calling out to her in the dark, "I want you, I want you."

Mrs. Smith at last was sent to a mental institution, where doctors diagnosed her condition as schizophrenia. According to her chart, the staff frequently heard her chanting "I love Jesus" and proclaiming her sinfulness. She was discharged in late January 1985.

A gap in Smith's personal history extends from her release date until late in June 1985. All that Hazelwood could learn of her story over that period was that she quit taking a powerful antipsychotic drug prescribed for her in the hospital, and that her in-laws had taken care of the boys.

Ten days prior to her death, she moved into a duplex. There was no available explanation why. Then her husband set out for a three-month fishing trip, leaving the psychologically fragile June Smith alone, and solely responsible for her children.

On the afternoon of Friday, July 5, 1985, the day before her death, she and the boys paid a surprise visit to the home of a local pastor. All three were neatly dressed, although the pastor noted that Mrs. Smith and her boys were barefoot.

The clergyman later described her as highly distraught. He said she told him that she'd suffered from both AIDS and cancer, but had been cured. She also insisted that God had led her to him. She was going to die soon, she explained, and wanted to be baptized in some unspecified magical way that would ensure her passage to heaven.

He explained that baptism required approval by church authorities, and that he wouldn't be performing any that day. The minister also gave June Smith the Bible later found in her bathroom, and advised her he'd be in touch.

Dr. Dietz wrote in his report that "it is possible to conclude with a reasonable medical certainty that [Mrs. Smith] was psychotic hours before her death."

The forensic psychiatrist additionally observed that "the disarray of her home . . . and the ritualistic and bizarre elements in her head-shaving and arm-cutting are additional evidence that she was psychotic at the time she inflicted the lethal wounds upon herself."

Besides the victim profile he assembled, Hazelwood's analysis included the observation that Smith had suffered no apparent defensive wounds, and there was no physical evidence that she had been incapacitated by, for example, a blow to the head. He noted the bruises on her right arm doubtlessly were suffered as she stumbled out the door, her bloody left arm dangling at her side. She probably fell repeatedly before she collapsed and died from blood loss.

Furthermore, there was no physical evidence of a struggle in the bathroom, or of another person in the house, although June Smith's four-year-old may have witnessed some part of the night's horror. Months after his mother's death, he asked his grandmother if God owned a knife.

Roy also saw something else at the scene that to him suggested Mrs. Smith committed suicide, behavior that a less knowledgeable or experienced investigator would not have known how to interpret correctly.

It was the plates of food surrounded by garbage bags in the living room, and the two fresh cakes sitting on the stove.

In and of themselves, the two discoveries are of no investigative consequence. But taken together with the rest of the evidence, they pointed away from homicide and toward suicide.

Roy refers to such indirectly corroborative evidence as the "feminine touch."

He has seen several cases where women have cleaned house or washed and ironed the family's clothes before killing themselves. Such behavior usually is not associated with murder or accidental death. Roy also noted that in the case of the woman who hacked herself to death with a machete, the victim first cleaned her house, washed and ironed clothes, bought a new dress, and had her hair styled.

In June Smith's case, Hazelwood theorized that the garbage bags placed around the plates of food in the living room were a matter of maternal tidiness. Mrs. Smith had set them out in the middle of the night, he believed, so as to catch crumbs and other debris from messy eaters, her two little boys, whom she meant to consume the milk and food when they awoke.

The two recently baked and untouched cakes were his second example.

In Roy's opinion, Mrs. Smith may have been deeply disturbed, intent on taking her own life, but she was still a mom.

That left her grisly wounds, her shaved head, and the scene in the bathroom to interpret. Hazelwood believed explanations were to be found in the Bible.

June Smith clearly was preoccupied with religion, a well-documented obsession underscored by the cross and Bible she'd brought to the bathroom scene of her autoamputation.

From the bloodied facing pages of Psalms 22 to 26 propped in front of her that night, the psychotic Mrs. Smith might have symbolically reenacted verse 20 of Psalm 22: "Deliver my soul from the sword."

If suicide was her intent, then she was delivering her soul *via* the sword, her knife.

In the familiar Twenty-third Psalm, the phrase "He leads me beside still waters" was reflected in the partially drawn bathtub, where she might also have intended the baptism denied her by the neighborhood minister.

Later, "Thou preparest a table before me in the presence of my enemies" could have inspired her to arrange the plates and forks on either side of the bathroom sink. June Smith certainly perceived enemies in her disordered world, the unseen evil spirits that threatened her in her in-laws' house.

"Thou anointest my head" may have precipitated the decision to shave hers. Head shaving traditionally is associated with penitence.

Finally, June Smith could have read "and I shall dwell in the house of the Lord forever" to mean the promise of immortality for the amputation, in her tortured mind an ultimate act of expiation.

Her death officially was ruled a suicide.

Homicide or suicide also was the issue in another of Hazelwood's equivocal death inquiries where victimology once again proved a decisive factor in Roy's analysis.

In this case, Hazelwood questioned the official view that eighty-two-year-old Andrew McIntyre* took his own life. Roy and the victim's family believed a killer might be on the loose.

Andrew McIntyre lived alone in a small town for nineteen years, ever since his wife died of cancer.

He was deeply religious and very active in his church. McIntyre was also a model of probity and restraint, deliberate in everything he did, from dating grocery cans and boxes as he purchased them to making sure that his dog never left the house unleashed.

He was a kindly old man, according to his friends, family, neighbors, and acquaintances.

They described McIntyre to Hazelwood as "a very calm, loving, and gentle man," "very quiet, but friendly," "like family," "one of the most dependable men I've ever met," "considerate," and "a very godly man who lived what he believed."

McIntyre was security conscious, too. Five weeks before his death, he installed a motion detector on his front porch. A similar device already had been installed in his garage.

One Tuesday, June 4, 1995, his youngest daughter, Joyce,* drove her father to a doctor's appointment. McIntyre recently had been very ill, which kept him in bed and unable to eat for days. The old man was depressed by his lingering incapacity. "I just wish I could die, but I can't," he told Joyce.

Yet by June 4 McIntyre had regained his vigor and good humor. He asked his doctor if he might resume his daily one-mile constitutionals.

"Sure, just take it easy," said the physician.

Andrew McIntyre had no other medical problems that his doctor knew of.

On the morning of June 5, he spoke by telephone with his friend and neighbor, Mabel Lowe,* who fixed Andrew his late-afternoon supper most days. Lowe would remember McIntyre saying he felt stronger, better.

Later in the day, he went into town to buy a get-well card for his ailing pastor, and also mailed an RSVP for his granddaughter's wedding in three weeks. Also on his forward calendar was another granddaughter's dance recital on June 18, and the father-son dinner scheduled for the eighth at this church.

At about 5:30 that afternoon, McIntyre spoke by telephone with his daughter Carla,* who lived nearby with her husband. Dad seemed in good spirits to Carla.

His next reported contact was a brief conversation with Mabel Lowe. The two spoke for maybe half an hour in the alley between their houses. Andrew inquired about Mabel's eye, which had been bothering her. She assured him it was better.

About ninety minutes later, around 8:00, Lowe heard again from McIntyre, by telephone. Once again he asked about her eye, which seemed odd to Lowe, and he made no reply whatsoever when she explained again, that her eye was okay. In retrospect, Mabel Lowe believes Andrew McIntyre was trying to send her some sort of signal with the call.

Joyce McIntyre was scheduled to leave on a business trip the next morning. That evening she expected her father to call her as he always did just to say, "Have a good trip! I'll be praying for you."

When she did not hear from him, she called at approximately 8:15.

No answer.

Joyce then remembered that Wednesday night was prayer meeting night.

Well, he must have felt pretty good tonight, so he went to the prayer meeting, she thought to herself.

She kept calling at half-hour intervals. When her father still wasn't home by 10:00, Joyce guessed that a fellow parishioner had invited him out for a piece of pie, a not unlikely possibility.

However, when her father still did not answer at 11:00, Joyce began to worry. She called Carla at 11:15.

"Have you seen Dad, or talked to him?" she asked.

Carla, who'd been asleep, told Joyce of her 5:30 conversation with their father.

"Well, he's not answering the telephone," Joyce said.

"Do you want me to drive over and see how he is?" asked her sister. Carla had made similar checks in the past, each time discovering nothing was amiss with their father.

"I don't know," Joyce said. She considered calling the police, but decided against it.

If they go driving up there with their lights and sirens, it'll frighten him, she thought.

Joyce told Carla she didn't think the trip was necessary.

She continued trying to reach her father for another two hours as she packed for her trip. At one point, she called the local telephone company to ask if there was trouble on the line. Joyce was told that such checks no longer were done.

Finally, trying to put her mind at ease, she hit on a possible explanation.

The previous day, Andrew McIntyre had told his doctor in Joyce's presence that he was having trouble sleeping, and wondered if it was okay for him to take Tylenol PM. The physician had said yes.

Driving home, Joyce had asked her father how many Tylenol PMs he took. Two, he had answered.

"That's what he's done," she said to herself. "He's taken two Tylenol PMs and gone sound asleep."

The next morning at 7:30 Carla telephoned their father. Still no answer. Fifteen minutes later, she arrived at the old family house. The front door was closed but unlocked, which was completely out of character for Andrew McIntyre. His dog was loose in the house, and highly agitated.

Deeply concerned, Carla walked outside to the detached garage, also un-

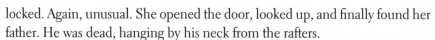

locked. Again, unusual. She opened the door, looked up, and finally found her father. He was dead, hanging by his neck from the rafters.

Andrew McIntyre, dressed in gray trousers, black belt, blue socks, an undershirt, and underwear, still wore his gold wedding ring.

A stepladder stood next to the body. The dead man's shoes rested alongside a box in the front of the garage. His glasses lay atop it.

His daughter was stunned speechless — "in a state of shock," she says. Carla was barely aware of telephoning Joyce, or of summoning the police at 7:55 that morning.

The single officer who responded to the call arrived six minutes later. There was no suicide note, and no signs of foul play or physical struggle in the house. After what Carla describes as a perfunctory look around the residence, the officer said, "Well, it's obvious what happened here," meaning suicide.

Not to Andrew McIntyre's family. He simply was not the sort of person to kill himself, they believed, and certainly not in the way the police thought McIntyre had killed himself. For one thing, his body was hanging in front of a windowed door, so that anyone passing by that morning could easily have seen him.

McIntyre was as private as he was proper. His family knew Dad never would allow himself to be discovered in that way. Moreover, he had been in an automobile accident not long before, and had suffered a shoulder injury which made it very difficult for him to raise one arm above his head. Joyce believed it was physically impossible for her father to have attached the ligature to the rafters unaided.

Yet who could have murdered him? McIntyre had no enemies. There was no evidence of a robbery. No one in the family stood to gain by his death.

Later that day, however, as his children and their families prepared to gather at his house, another possibility was raised. Carla's husband telephoned Joyce to remind his grieving sister-in-law of something she'd shared with the family many months before.

In late 1995, Joyce's then-husband, Mike Jones,* had threatened to kill her father, she claimed. George now reminded Joyce of the incident, and asked her to think about reporting it to the police.

Andrew McIntyre's death overwhelmed Joyce so completely that she hadn't thought of her ex-husband, or the threat, until the moment Carla's husband mentioned it.

Once reminded, however, she needed no time for reflection. "There's no thinking about it," she said over the telephone. "I'll call the police right now."

"You need to take my father's death very seriously," Joyce told the police, "because his life was threatened by my husband."

The story begins in a restaurant bar.

Joyce was visiting an out-of-town friend, and the two were enjoying a meal together when a strange man several years Joyce's junior "zoned in on me," as she puts it. "He wasn't bad-looking, although he had big ears."

Joyce was not interested in a relationship. She had married her first husband at age nineteen. Three years later, he died accidentally. A second marriage lasted sixteen years before she filed for divorce. Highly dubious of men under any circumstances, Joyce had vowed at the time she definitely was through with marriage.

But she hadn't reckoned with the likes of Mike Jones.

That evening, Jones told Joyce and her friend that he was a professional and produced a business card that said so.

The following night, he took both women out to dinner. Then the three of them took a day trip together.

Joyce had hoped Jones would focus his considerable energies on her friend. However, she was hardly home and back to work the next week when Mike started calling, frequently. Soon they were chatting together for three or four hours a night. He told her he'd graduated from a prestigious midwestern private college, and that he was a former soldier with top-security clearance. Mike had the papers and card that seemed to prove these claims, too.

Weekend visits soon began.

"I said I'd never get married again, but I guess he knew what I needed to hear," says Joyce. "He played me like a violin."

Joyce married Mike within months of their first meeting. In retrospect, she says she should have sensed something was a little wrong when none of his relatives or friends attended the wedding.

But Joyce was blinded.

"Mike was everything I ever thought I could ever want," she says. "But two days after we got married he started physically abusing me. I didn't tell anyone for quite some time because I was so ashamed."

In the eighteen months they were together, Joyce estimates that Mike physically abused her eight times or more. He never left marks, and never sexually assaulted her.

"He would terrorize me," she says. "Lock me in my room and not let me out. Pin me down. I remember one time he pinned me on the bed and held a pair of scissors over me like he was really going to stab me."

Once at a movie, "Somebody was killing somebody on the screen, and was putting his arm around the guy's neck. Mike looked at me and said, 'It only takes a second.' The way he said it just gave me the creeps."

Overdrafts on her personal checking account soon began to appear. Joyce attributed them to confusion at the bank. Several months later, however, the manager of the bank where she kept her corporate account informed Mrs. Jones that Mike had kited seven thousand dollars worth of checks on that account. Joyce paid the amount due, went home, and ordered her husband of six months out of the house.

Mike left, but was back shortly. "He played on my sympathy," says Joyce. And her fortune.

Like many people who routinely receive credit card solicitations through the mail, Joyce dumped the unwanted offers in the trash. Mike would retrieve the applications, fill them out, and have the new plastic mailed to a post office box he maintained. Then he'd max out each card before moving on to a new one.

About a year into their marriage, Joyce went searching in the basement for some old tax return documents. As she worked her way through the accumulated papers, she discovered that Mike had filed for unemployment benefits the month they were married, and also had filled out a bogus automobile accident report.

Now genuinely alarmed, she hired two private investigators to look into her husband's past. They found that Mike had not gone to college. The security clearance was a fake. He'd operated at various times under two or three Social Security numbers, and four different birthdays. Mike's mother later told Joyce that her son's military experience was confined to the National Guard.

The PIs also turned up Mike's rap sheet. It went back more than a decade, and included guilty pleas for forgery, receiving stolen property, theft of services, and theft by deception. Mike had done two years in prison.

Frightened and confused, Joyce tried not to betray what she'd learned as she considered what to do about it. However, Mike must have sensed something.

On a vacation cruise some weeks later, he got drunk and began slamming her against their cabin wall.

He told Joyce that with a phone call he could empty her house of its possessions that night. Then, coldly, he added: "I will destroy you, starting with your family. Nothing will happen to you because I want you to stand by and watch."

She was resolved to file for divorce the next morning, but delayed doing so in order to attend, with Jones, a religious pageant that her brother had organized.

Mike capitalized on the moment. "God spoke to me here like he never has before," Mike told Joyce. "I'm going to change."

He didn't.

Over the holidays he was arrested on a drunk driving charge. Back home, he assaulted Joyce, tearing her sweatshirt in the process. She filed a report with the police that night, and Jones was taken off to jail.

Joyce finally filed for divorce in the spring. She last saw her husband when he came by to pick up some tools. Her Dad died in early June.

McIntyre's family soon discerned that, despite assurances to the contrary, the authorities dismissed out of hand their murder theory of the case.

The first autopsy seemed to confirm the official point of view. The local medical examiner, a forensic pathologist, discovered minor abrasions on the backs of both Andrew McIntyre's hands, as well as small bruises on his right shoulder and upper right arm.

While the marks could have been defensive injuries, the ME found the weight of the forensic evidence—including ligature abrasions on the victim's neck—was consistent with suicide.

McIntyre's children paid for a second autopsy, also conducted by a forensic pathologist, who was less dismissive of their father's unexplained injuries.

"I fully agree with you," the doctor wrote Joyce, "that there are many troubling factors concerning your father's death which could lead an objective observer to question if he died as a result of suicide."

Neither autopsy addressed the victim's time of death. However, McIntyre's bedside medicine dispenser had a single tablet left in it, a pill he was to have taken at 9:00 P.M. Since he definitely was still alive at about 8:00 P.M. (when he made his strange telephone call to Mabel Lowe), whatever impulse or incident had led to his death apparently occurred between 8:00 and 9:00.

Two months after his death, one of his granddaughters hit on an idea. She lived in eastern Virginia with her husband, and was aware via the local media that Roy Hazelwood, late of the FBI, also resided in the area. In fact, her family and the Hazelwoods attended the same church.

One Sunday in August 1996, she approached Roy after services and explained the McIntyre family's dilemma.

Would he review her grandfather's death?

Roy said he would look into it.

A couple of weeks later, Carla came to Virginia and laid out for Roy everything the McIntyres knew. Unable to resist such a mystery, Hazelwood agreed to undertake an equivocal death analysis for the family, cost free.

After conducting his survey and reviewing all available investigative records—the local police gave Hazelwood a one-page single-spaced "Incident Data Sheet," but the medical examiner refused to share Andrew McIntyre's autopsy photos—Roy constructed two detailed lists, one of factors consistent with suicide, and another of factors consistent with homicide.

Those elements that supported a conclusion of suicide included first of all the manner of death. "Hanging," Roy wrote, "is a highly lethal and frequently observed means of suicide."

There was also no evidence of a struggle anywhere in the house or garage, nor were there any scratch marks on McIntyre's neck to indicate he had resisted the noose. Roy also agreed with the police that the tidiness with which his shoes (and glasses) had been placed by the box in the garage was consistent with suicide.

There was no evidence McIntyre had been bound, drugged, or incapacitated in any way, and there was no evidence of an associated crime, such as robbery or burglary.

McIntyre *had* said recently he wished he could die, although he apparently was only temporarily despondent over his sickness.

The strange call to Mabel Lowe at 8:00 P.M. could be interpreted not as a veiled plea for help, but as a farewell. Suicides often say good-bye in such ways.

Two days before his death, McIntyre also had written to a female member of his church, apologizing for something he'd said to her in a parking lot "some time ago." He informed the woman that he'd sought God's forgiveness for what he'd said.

The old gentleman was highly sensitive to other people's feelings. If he was contemplating suicide, Roy knew it would be in character for him to attempt some sort of closure over the perceived personal offense.

Finally, Andrew McIntyre cleaned his house and did his laundry the afternoon before his death. This again is behavior consistent with suicide. However, as Roy noted in his list, the victim also *normally* performed these chores, and had put them off for some time because of his illness.

On the other side of the question, homicide, Roy found much to consider.

To begin with, there were the unexplained scratches and bruises on McIntyre's hands and body. While not conclusive proof he had struggled with his killer, the marks were consistent with an attempt to defend himself. In a forty-five minute telephone conversation, the pathologist hired by McIntyre's family told Roy he could not rule out the possibility that the victim's injuries were defensive injuries.

There was no suicide note. Although such notes are not typical, or even common, Andrew McIntyre's children did not believe their father would take his leave in such a way without explanation.

He was experiencing no special stresses at the time of his death, save for what appeared to be a minor misstatement of some sort to the woman in the parking lot.

He had been ill, and despondent about it. But at the time of his death, he was physically improved and feeling better. His doctor reported McIntyre was suffering no other medical problems.

"People contemplating suicide typically do not make plans for the future," Roy noted. Then Hazelwood listed all the forward-looking actions Andrew McIntyre had taken, from accepting an invitation to his granddaughter's wedding to recently spading his garden, readying the earth for planting. He also had ordered prescription refills, and groceries in bulk amounts. Never one to waste or overspend, Andrew McIntyre had thirty boxes of breakfast cereal on hand at the time of his death.

"The preponderance of the behavioral evidence indicates that *if* Mr. McIntyre killed himself, it was a highly impulsive act," Roy wrote. "Mr. McIntyre was not reported to be an impulsive person."

What was more, the means of death—a ligature looped over three rafters and a stepladder—were inconsistent with impulsiveness. If Andrew McIntyre had decided suddenly to kill himself, his abundant supply of pills would have been a much more likely means.

Suicides typically telegraph their intent, either directly ("I ought to kill myself") or indirectly ("I can understand why someone would kill himself"). As far as was known, McIntyre made no such statements.

He was a religious man, who centered his life on his church and Bible. McIntyre's faith made suicide a sin.

The garage door could be locked from the inside, but wasn't. "Suicides typically take steps to preclude interruption," Hazelwood observed.

"Mr. McIntyre was very conscientious with his dog," Roy added. "It is probable that had he intended to take his life, he would have arranged for the animal to be taken care of, or ensured that it was restricted to a room with food and water."

Finally, there was no history of suicide in the McIntyre family, nor had he ever been treated or medicated for mental problems. Nor was the date of his death of any particular significance in his life.

On balance, Roy concluded in his analysis, which later was forwarded to the local police by the McIntyres, "the circumstances of Mr. Andrew McIntyre's death appear to be more consistent with a finding of homicide than suicide."

His daughter Joyce has one theory how such a murder could have occurred.

"My father would have let Mike in the house," she says. "All he would have to say is that he thought he'd left some tools in the garage. Once they were out there, I believe that all Mike had to say was that he'd hurt me or other members of the family if my father didn't do exactly as he told him."

In his report, Hazelwood politely suggested that "further investigation of Mr. McIntyre's death is justified to more definitely eliminate the possibility of homicide. This opinion is based upon Mr. Hazelwood's education, experience and consultation on similar cases."

No further investigation was conducted. Andrew McIntyre's official cause of death remains suicide.

In a postscript to her disastrous third marriage, Joyce McIntyre received a bill for approximately eight thousand dollars from the Internal Revenue Service, which claims Mike Jones filed no tax return the year they were married.

She's still arguing with the IRS over the back-tax assessment. If she loses, she reckons her ex-husband will have bilked her out of forty thousand dollars or more.

A month after receiving the IRS's unpleasant news, Joyce heard from the state police. A body had been found, the trooper told her. He said he had been contacted by a young flight attendant who had been dating her ex-husband, and who believed the dead man could be Mike Jones. Would the former Mrs. Jones care to talk to the woman?

No.

Then a second woman contacted Joyce. Identifying herself as an attorney in a western state, she said she'd met Mike the previous autumn.

"How much did he take you for?" Joyce asked.

"About fifteen thousand dollars," answered the lawyer.

Joyce then called the flight attendant, who lived in the same general area. She said she had known of Andrew McIntyre's death, that she met Mike Jones very soon thereafter, and that she quickly found him living with her.

"She said she felt he was hiding out, like he was hiding from some people," Joyce recalls.

In time, the lawyer also learned of Andrew McIntyre's death, and called Joyce once again.

"I feel you have to know this," she said. "Mike used to tell me that the easiest way to kill somebody was to wrap a wire around their neck and jerk their head back."

Mike Jones next surfaced in a large southwestern city, leasing an apartment from a couple he'd met. He didn't have the full rent immediately, he explained to them, because he was paid quarterly. They accepted Jones's word that he would catch up on the rent as soon as his check came through.

Meantime, the ever personable Jones attended a big Christmas party with his landlords, and met one of their friends at the affair, a flight attendant who'd flown in especially for the party.

As the couple later told the story to Joyce, her ex-husband went right to work.

"I'm thinking of driving to Mexico next week," he told the woman.

"If you do, stop by on your way," she said.

Here Joyce interrupted the report.

"Let me guess," she said. "He stopped by and never left?"

"That's right," came the reply.

Jones reportedly lived with this woman for about four months, long enough for his former landlords to start wondering about the back rent he owed them. They searched the apartment, discovered a name and telephone number for the lawyer, and through her found Joyce.

"They got scared after they heard about Dad and everything else Mike had done to me," Joyce recalls. "So the guy got on a plane and flew out to see the flight attendant. They were all good friends and he didn't want anything to happen to her.

"He said he told Mike, 'Pack your bag, you're coming with me. You owe us money.'"

About that time, the flight attendant received a call from a bank asking if she authorized a five hundred dollar charge against her card.

Joyce's most recent information, current as of late 1997, placed Jones with yet another female acquaintance he reportedly met in a bar there.

Apparently she loaned him fifteen hundred dollars, which he repaid with a bad check.

FIFTEEN

"We Changed
the Rules"

The USS *Iowa* was an awesomely potent weapon.
Launched August 27, 1942, at the Brooklyn Navy Yard, the huge
battleship with its crew of fifteen hundred was armed with the biggest, most
powerful guns of any U.S. warship ever: nine 120-ton leviathans, each sixty-
eight feet long, capable of lofting 2,700-pound explosive projectiles onto targets nearly twenty-three miles away.

The giant rifles with their sixteen-inch bores could be fired twice a minute
in a complex series of steps requiring a five-hundred page manual to describe.
They were safe, too. Through several wars and innumerable engagements
across decades of service, not a single sailor inside a sixteen-inch gun turret on
any U.S. naval craft had ever been killed due to a misfiring.

Not until April 19, 1989.

That morning the *Iowa* was conducting routine gunnery exercises in the
Caribbean, about three hundred miles north of Puerto Rico. Turret One fired
four times without incident. Then it was Turret Two's turn to fire.

Instead at 9:55 A.M., before it discharged a single round, Turret Two was
rocked by an enormous blast that annihilated all forty-seven sailors working inside.

The navy at once placed Rear Admiral Richard D. Milligan, a former battleship captain himself, in charge of investigating the unprecedented explosion.

At first, the official probe was entirely technical, focused on *how* the fatal
explosion might have occurred. But in early May, a letter from Ohio abruptly
redirected everyone's attention.

Kathlene Kubicina, introducing herself as the sister of twenty-four-year-old Gunner's Mate Clayton M. Hartwig, one of the forty-seven who'd perished, informed the navy that her dead brother had taken out a double-indemnity life insurance policy. The beneficiary, wrote Kubicina, was Kendall Truitt, another sailor aboard the *Iowa.* Kubicina was curious to know if Hartwig's family qualified for part of the $100,000 benefit, too.

Kathy Kubicina's letter came just as the navy's technical investigators were reporting that although they did not know what had caused the fatal detonation, the *how* apparently was no accident.

Confronted with the possibility that the navy now should be searching for a *who,* quite possibly Clay Hartwig—gun captain in Turret Two that day—Admiral Milligan called on the Naval Investigative Service for help, asking the NIS to probe Hartwig's past for any possible clues. NIS investigators crisscrossed the country in search of both physical evidence and anyone with a connection to Hartwig, from Kendall Truitt to the dead sailor's boyhood pals.

Meantime, agent Dick Ault at the BSU received a call from an old acquaintance, NIS commander Tom Mountz.

Ault, a former marine whose specialty at the BSU was spies and espionage cases, had met Mountz in the course of interviewing more than thirty traitors for a secret government research project. Now Mountz wanted to know if the BSU would do an equivocal death analysis on the *Iowa* explosion.

Ault, who had done several such analyses in partnership with Hazelwood, approached Roy to join him. In what would prove a fateful decision for both agents, Hazelwood agreed to team up.

Roy had already learned from the Tawana Brawley fiasco (see chapter 18) that the search for simple truths in a complex criminal investigation is easily subverted, and then overwhelmed, when other agendas intervene. In the *Iowa* case, Ault and Hazelwood would discover the price of promulgating an unpopular point of view, especially at their level in the federal food chain.

"I knew at the time what probably was going to happen," Roy recalls.

"Either we would make the navy unhappy, or the politicians and the media and Hartwig's family would attack us. We were going to get hammered one way or the other."

Hazelwood and Ault's assignment was essentially interpretive; they were to create for the navy what the late Dr. James Brussel called an "inferential mosaic" from evidence supplied to them by the NIS. Neither Hazelwood nor Ault took any part in the field investigation or witness interviews.

Nor did either agent ever consider the possibility that the explosion aboard the *Iowa* was an accident. The navy confidently informed them it was not. Their only concern was whether enough behavioral evidence was available for Hazelwood and Ault to decide if possible among three options: Had Petty Officer Hartwig committed a suicide, or a homicide, or a suicide/homicide? If so, for what reason?

As gun captain in Turret Two on April 19, Clay Hartwig was stationed near the gun breech, the perfect spot to do mischief. Later forensic investigation would show that Hartwig was bent at the waist, peering upward through the open breech, when 660 pounds of gunpowder packed in five silk bags exploded back down the barrel at him.

Accelerating to nearly twice the speed of sound at a temperature of three thousand degrees Fahrenheit, the blast reached Hartwig in about one-twelfth of a second. He was killed in an instant.

Clay Hartwig didn't feel a thing.

He was the third of three children in the family of Evelyn and Earl V. Hartwig, a navy veteran. Both of Clay's older siblings were girls.

One sister told the navy that her younger brother was considered a loner within the family, that Clay spent most of his boyhood by himself in his room. She described him as nonathletic, friendless, and estranged from his family, but not overtly hostile toward them, either. She could not recall a time where Clay ever had lost his temper.

This description of Clay Hartwig wouldn't vary in significant detail among the many people who spoke to the navy interviewers. They uniformly characterized Hartwig as aloof and immature—a disgruntled loner.

He collected combat-style knives and guns, and read *Soldier of Fortune* and similar men's magazines. Young Clay also purchased many books about World War II, with specific interest in warships.

In his junior year in high school, Clay befriended Brian Hoover, then a ninth grader. Hoover would tell the NIS of how the older boy described making pipe bombs and blowing up trees with them. Hoover said that he and Hartwig together built a makeshift Molotov cocktail from detergent and gasoline. They detonated the device in an open field.

The NIS investigators uncovered little to suggest that Hartwig ever was interested in girls. The one female friend from his youth they did find was four years his junior, a seventh grader he met about the same time he met Brian Hoover.

The violent subtext in Hartwig's personal history included a self-destructive streak. Hoover once walked into Hartwig's room to discover his friend intently stroking a sharp knife blade across his wrist.

Hoover told investigators that he took the knife away, and that Clay believed his friend's intervention saved his life. So grateful was Hartwig that he wrote out an informal will, leaving Brian Hoover everything he owned. NIS investigators later found the document tucked in one of several Bibles in Clay's old room at home.

According to those who knew him, self-dramatizing gestures of this sort were typical of Hartwig, who also was apt to bear bitter grudges against those he believed had wronged him.

When he joined the navy out of high school in 1983, Hartwig began sending Hoover two hundred dollars a month. He kept up the practice for eighteen months, until Brian disclosed to Clay that he'd had sex with a girl of their mutual acquaintance.

Hartwig immediately suspended the monthly stipend to Hoover.

The young sailor's sexual orientation became a public issue within weeks of his death when a television network reported he was homosexual. The questions had been raised before.

There were whispers on board the *Iowa* that Hartwig and Kendall Truitt, his life insurance beneficiary, were physically intimate, rumors that Truitt has repeatedly denied.

Hartwig's rumored homosexuality is not an idle question for the purposes of understanding what occurred in Turret Two, however. Statistics indicate homosexual males commit suicide at a substantially higher rate than do heterosexual males in the same age group.

In any event, Hartwig apparently had scant sexual experience with females. A woman in Norfolk, Virginia, the *Iowa's* home port, told the NIS that Hartwig impulsively proposed marriage to her on their second date. They'd gone to bed together, but he had kept his pants on and nothing happened between them.

Another of Hartwig's very few known female acquaintances said she had notified Clay by letter that she expected them to consummate their relationship on his next return from sea. Reticent as he was about the subject, her demand for sexual performance may have unnerved him.

It was not Clay Hartwig's habit to discuss intimate matters directly with anyone. Instead, he wrote letters and notes, hundreds of them, to both men and women he regarded as friends.

Hazelwood and Ault read a wide assortment of them.

"One thing about me is I show very little emotion," he wrote in an undated note to Truitt, ". . . and I never express my feelings out loud. But it's different when I write it down. It's much easier for me to do it that way."

When Clayton Hartwig did talk about himself, he was given to exaggerations and outright lies, confecting a fantasy life altogether different from the world Hartwig actually inhabited. He wore unauthorized insignia on his uniform, and showed off a navy SEAL membership for which he did not qualify. On and off the ship, Hartwig bragged about the hush-hush high-level assignment in London he'd been promised if he reenlisted.

No such special assignment existed. In fact, his performance reviews suggested he lacked the aggressiveness to be a good leader.

Hartwig persevered nearly to the end of his six-year enlistment in the navy, even though he appears not to have succeeded particularly well, or to have enjoyed navy life.

He was scorned and ridiculed by shipmates, according to Kendall Truitt. Another *Iowa* seaman recalled Clay calling the warship "a damn pig."

Nor did his fascination with violence subside. Hartwig owned two handguns. Found in his possessions after the explosion was a technical manual, *Improvised Munitions*. His sister Kathlene reported that in the summer of 1988 Clay came home on leave with what he described as explosive materials from the *Iowa*, substances used "to shoot the big guns," he said.

Reportedly, Hartwig also said when he was home that if an explosion occurred inside the *Iowa*'s gun turrets, there'd be no survivors.

After her brother's death, Kathlene found in Clay's typewriter a list of all the crewmen assigned to Turret Two. NIS investigators also discovered in his room an album devoted to newspaper accounts of ship disasters.

Death seemed to have been yet another preoccupation.

According to Truitt, when Clay discussed death it was in a context of extreme violence, including mutilation.

In December of 1988, ten months after Hartwig took out his double-indemnity life insurance policy naming Truitt as beneficiary, his younger friend married.

Aware that Hartwig disliked his fiancée, Kendall did not invite Clay to the wedding. Hartwig's response to what he must have considered a painful snub is unrecorded. However, just as he had suddenly shunned Brian Hoover, Hartwig ceased all communications with Truitt, although he did not drop or otherwise alter the insurance policy.

Two seamen reported to the NIS that Hartwig told them he wished to die in the line of duty.

Another shipmate who was working through some personal problems of his own said that he, too, had discussed death with Hartwig. The two sailors de-cided that he quickest way to go would be in an explosion.

"He just said he imagine[d] that he wouldn't feel a thing and he'd never know it," said the seaman. "He said he kinda knew what I was going through, because he had tried to commit suicide at one time. So we kept talking and talking and he confided in me that . . . he still thinks about it some-times."

Still another shipmate reported he'd seen an electronic detonation device in Hartwig's locker.

In all, the remarkably consistent behavioral evidence left little doubt that Clay Hartwig had the mind-set, the ability, and abundant motive for commit-ting suicide, as well as both the expertise and the opportunity to blow up Tur-ret Two.

There was no one else aboard the *Iowa* that day in which all these critical factors were so richly present. If the blast was deliberate, then Clayton M. Hartwig was the man who did it.

Hazelwood and Ault in their report to the NIS described Hartwig as "a trou-bled young man" with low self-esteem "who coveted the power and authority he felt he did not possess."

They opined that he'd been "emotionally devastated" by "real and per-ceived rejections of significant others" and was facing a "multitude of stres-sors"—from a young woman's sexual demands to his unavoidable exposure as a sham. That there was no special assignment waiting for him would be clear at the close of the *Iowa's* cruise.

Suicide, which appears not to have been far from his mind in any event, now might appear as an escape route, even a morbid form of affirmation, the kind of death he'd read about in *Glorious Way to Die: Kamikaze Mission of Battleship Yamato, April 1945*, a volume Hartwig had checked out of the li-brary two years before.

Even the month, April, seemed propitious for such a deed.

Hazelwood and Ault believed that the combination of stressors in Hartwig's life "virtually assured some type of reaction."

And they were unequivocal in what they believed it was.

"In this case," they concluded, "it was suicide."

The agents submitted their analysis on June 16, 1989.

On September 7 Admiral Milligan called a press conference to announce the navy's determination that "a wrongful intentional act" had caused the explosion in Turret Two. Milligan added that Clayton Hartwig "most probably" had committed the act.

"We have an FBI profile by FBI psychologists with the opinion he took his own life and hoped it would look like an accident," said the admiral.

The expected reaction was swift.

"I never believed it from the start," Hartwig's sister, Kathy Kubicina, told a reporter. Of Milligan's press conference, she added, "I didn't really hear anything I didn't hear before."

The Hartwig family lawyer called for a congressional investigation.

"I think the navy is at a loss," said Kendall Truitt. "They are looking for scapegoats."

The allegations touched a chord both in the press and on Capitol Hill, and in retrospect it is simple to see why. In the aftermath of Vietnam, Watergate, and the Reagan administration's secret sale of U.S. arms to Iran to finance the Nicaraguan contras, when significant numbers of people still doubted that Lee Harvey Oswald or James Earl Ray acted alone, it was not difficult to believe the U.S. Navy capable of conspiracy, too.

When hard scientific evidence of sabotage aboard the *Iowa* was not forthcoming, both the U.S. House and Senate announced their own investigation of the explosion, no doubt mirroring constituent sentiment.

Although there were dark variations on the theme, the thrust of the skepticism was that the technical experts couldn't figure out exactly what had happened, so instead of accepting that there might be something intrinsically amiss aboard the *Iowa*, the navy chose to place the onus on a dead man.

Clay Hartwig looked like a convenient patsy.

This idea surfaced everywhere in the press.

The New York Times unloaded several salvos, lambasting the navy's "unproven, probably unprovable charge that one dead crew member was the culprit."

Syndicated columnist Lars-Erik Nelson, a former colleague of mine at *Newsweek*, derided Hazelwood and Ault's analysis as "quack evidence."

The intelligent and thoughtful Lester Bernstein, a former editor for whom I worked at *Newsweek*, turned up during the *Iowa* debate as an angry voice in *Newsday*, accusing the navy of scapegoating Hartwig as a consequence of the service's "hidebound commitment to its four half-century-old battleships."

In still another fusillade from West Forty-second Street, the *Times* scolded the navy for its decision to "smear a crewman's memory on flimsy evidence" and for relying on a "libelous psychological profile of Mr. Hartwig."

Members of the House Investigations Subcommittee were hardly more polite. While the FBI was accustomed to taking its licks in the press, deserved or otherwise, Capitol Hill usually was friendly territory, particularly for the BSU.

It hadn't been too many years since Roy, John Douglas, Roger Depue, Ken Lanning, and others from Quantico had come before another House committee, testifying under the legislators' beneficent nods to the encouraging progress the BSU was making toward identification and apprehension of aberrant criminals.

The agents' presentations had been earnest and professional and highly persuasive. The Reagan White House and a Democratic Congress responded with a $4 million appropriation to fund VICAP, the BSU's computer-based Violent Criminal Apprehension Program.

But the beneficence soured to balefulness by December 1989, when Hazelwood and Ault sat down before the subcommittee, accompanied by assistant FBI director Anthony Daniels, then in charge at Quantico.

Roy read into the record a summary statement which laid out the eight main factors, plus buttressing evidence, that had led him and Ault to their conclusion.

1. "Hartwig was a loner" with only six known friends, the document explained. "Hartwig believed that four of the six individuals had rejected him, and the fifth was applying pressure on him for an intimate relationship that he was not capable of."

2. "Hartwig was dissatisfied with life." Here, Hazelwood and Ault reviewed the evidence, from Hartwig's subscription to *Soldier of Fortune* to the false intimations he made about his expected reassignment to naval security work in London to the amateur "war games" he and others played while stationed at Guantánamo Bay in Cuba. "He had a fantasy life that went far beyond the realities of his true life," the agents noted.

3. "In the writers' opinion, Hartwig believed that he had good reasons for not returning from the cruise." If he killed himself, he wouldn't have to face discovery of his lies, or the pending sexual demands. Finally, there'd be relief from the onboard ostracism, as well as the rejection he felt.

4. Clay Hartwig had a revenge motive. He disliked the ship and his shipmates. He had also been disciplined aboard the *Iowa*, taken before a so-called captain's mast and reduced one grade in rank.

5. "Hartwig had a history of immature reaction to change in his life and interpersonal problems. He was also known to carry a grudge against those who he believed wronged him."

6. "Hartwig was experiencing a number of stressors at the time of his death." Besides all his other unsolved problems, he was broke, his car needed repair, and his telephone had been turned off.

7. "It is the opinion of the writers that Hartwig had suicide ideation." He had talked of suicide, and seemed to be thinking seriously about it the day Brian Hoover discovered him in his room, playing with the knife.

In what proved to be his last letter to the woman in Norfolk, Hartwig closed with "Love always and forever, Clayton" instead of his usual "Clay," and added, "I'm sorry I didn't take you home to meet my mother!"

To another woman, who accused Hartwig of "hiding" aboard the *Iowa*, he wrote on April 9, 1989, "I don't think the 1200 men that went down on the USS *Arizona** were hiding, or the 37 sailors that were killed on the USS *Stark* in the Persian Gulf in 1986! I could become one of those little white headstones in Arlington National Cemetery any day!"

8. "Finally, Hartwig possessed the knowledge, ability and opportunity to ignite the powder in the same fashion that occurred on the USS *Iowa*."

Nothing contained in the agents' thirteen-page summary report or their testimony seemed to make much of an impression with the lawmakers.

After wondering aloud what made BSU agents any better at making psychological evaluations than, say, teachers or insurance agents, Indiana Democrat Frank McCloskey asked if it was unusual for someone working around explosives to believe he or she might die in an explosion.

"No sir," Hazelwood agreed. "But it is unusual for them to say 'I *want* to die

---

*Clay Hartwig's story is dotted with curious coincidences. He would have known that the battleship *Arizona* was sunk at Pearl Harbor on December 7, 1941. The surprise attack by the Japanese began at 7:55 A.M.

The coup de grace against the *Arizona* was a high-altitude bomb that crashed into the ship adjacent to Turret Two and exploded belowdecks, detonating the main battery magazines.

April 19 is a special date as well. Timothy McVeigh would choose April 19, 1995, to blow up the Murrah Federal Building in Oklahoma City, killing 168 people. McVeigh is widely believed to have selected April 19 because it was the second anniversary of the federal assault on the Branch Davidian compound at Mount Carmel, near Waco, Texas, in which David Koresh and eighty of his followers perished. It is also an important historical date on right-wing militia calendars, a fact that Hartwig might well have been aware of through *Soldier of Fortune* and his other reading. It is the anniversary of the 1775 Battle of Lexington and Concord, where colonial Minutemen—on whom many present-day militias profess to pattern themselves—first skirmished with the British redcoats, marking the start of the American Revolution.

in the line of duty,' not 'I may die,' not 'I'm in danger of dying,' but 'I want to die in the line of duty' to two different people. That is unusual, yes sir."

The final subcommittee report excoriated Hazelwood and Ault's analysis for "doubtful professionalism" and declared "the false air of certainty generated by the FBI analysis was probably the single major factor inducing the Navy to single out Clayton Hartwig as the likely guilty party."

Curiously, Roy remembers one hectoring questioner raised the reverse possibility, that Hazelwood and Ault had gone into the tank for the navy. At that Anthony Daniels rose to ask for a clarification. Was the congressman accusing the agents of lying? Daniels asked. No, came the quick reply.

As Roy told the committee, a BSU profile or analysis "can be used or discarded or discounted" by the requesting agency, in this case, the navy. That Petty Officer Clay Hartwig deliberately blew up Turret Two "is simply our opinion," he added.

The House committee also asked the American Psychological Association to form a committee to review the evidence as well as Hazelwood's and Ault's findings. Of the fourteen panel members, several were dubious of the FBI analysis, although only three asserted that Clay Hartwig was probably guiltless in the matter.

The other members were generally supportive. Dr. Roger L. Greene of the psychology department at Texas Tech University in Lubbock said he detected "a number of potential problems with the logical links between the evidence and the conclusions drawn in the FBI equivocal death analysis."

This was a not unreasonable *academic* criticism of purely practical exercise in speculation.

Dr. Elliott M. Silverstein, a forensic psychologist in Chapel Hill, North Carolina, wrote, "Presuming all the evidence is true, the psychological profile drafted by the FBI is very plausible."

Dr. Alan L. Berman of the Washington Psychological Center was less equivocal. "It is most reasonable," wrote Berman, "to conclude that Hartwig sacrificed his own life in a planned suicide–mass homicide to accomplish a variety of ends."

Hazelwood and Ault's next engagement was with the Senate Armed Services Committee, where the reception was only marginally more civil.

William Cohen, then a Republican senator from Maine and later to be Bill Clinton's secretary of defense, was patently skeptical of both agents.

"Let me ask you," said Cohen, "is it abnormal for members of the navy to have subscriptions to *Soldier of Fortune* magazine?"

"I recall very few of my fellow marines who subscribed to *Soldier of Fortune* magazine," Dick Ault replied.

"Very few of your fellow marines were driven to violence? Don't they teach you a lot of violence at marine boot camp?"

"They teach us to hate the enemy."

Cohen pressed on. "You indicated that [Hartwig] only had three close women friends . . ."

Ault completed the senator's sentence: ". . . with whom he never had any sexual contact, as far as anyone could tell. He proposed to one woman on their second date. She turned him down."

"Well," asked Cohen, "what's so unusual about that?"

"She was a dancer in a strip joint," interjected Hazelwood.

Cohen was undeterred.

"Another factor I think that you drew some significance from was that he said he could hide his hurt inside and never reveal it."

"That's what he said, yes sir," Roy answered.

"Is that unusual?"

"When you combine that with the fact that people never reported seeing him angry, never seeing him violent, that to us is a danger sign.

"We've seen it on too many occasions where they've just stored it up and then went out and murdered fourteen people at a college, or blew up a ship. . . . Yes, sir."

Cohen, like McCloskey, also fixed on Hartwig's expressed desire to die on duty.

"Is that unusual?" he asked.

"I was in the army for eleven years, and never once did I or any of my friends make the statement, 'I'd like to die in the line of duty.'" Hazelwood replied. "No sir. I didn't want to die in the line of duty."

The closest any of the questioners came to sympathy for the FBI men was John Warner, Republican of Virginia.

"Thank you, gentlemen," said Warner at the close of the session, and then he appended a small marvel of understatement: "Tough job that you've had to perform."

The FBI stood by its own.

After the hearings, Hazelwood and Ault both received personal telephone calls of support and congratulations for a good job well done from Director William Sessions and Associate Director John Otto.

Roy stands by the analysis.

"I'm as convinced today as I was then that we were correct," he says.

"As I told one of the senators, it would take new forensic evidence to convince me otherwise."

Several subsequent reanalyses of the technical data, plus a wide array of other experiments, were undertaken by both the navy's Naval Sea System Command (NAVSEA) and the Sandia National Laboratory in New Mexico.

None of the tests could scientifically establish whether the explosion in Turret Two was an act of suicide or an accident. However, there was unexplained foreign matter recovered from the gun's barrel. This material was consistent with a chemical detonator being used to ignite the powder. But it didn't prove it.

Despite the lack of hard new evidence, on October 18, 1991, Admiral Frank B. Kelso, chief of naval operations, announced at a Washington news conference that the navy had changed its mind.

After spending $25 million in an unsuccessful search for conclusive evidence, Kelso announced, "There is no certain answer to what caused the tragedy. Accordingly, the opinion that the explosion resulted from a wrongful intentional act is disapproved."

Asked about Admiral Milligan's previous announcements on several public occasions that the blast was deliberately set, Kelso explained, "I had a different set of evidence than he had, and we changed the rules."

The navy's final conclusion, said Kelso, would be "exact cause cannot be determined."

The admiral also issued an apology. "I extend my sincere regrets to the family of Hartwig," he said. "We're sorry Clayton Hartwig was accused of this."

Admiral Kelso's choice of October 1991 for reversing course would later strike both Hazelwood and Ault as ironically apt. Within days of Kelso's pronouncements, NAVSEA issued its own final report, reasserting that the navy had been right all along.

"The review of the original investigation," read the report's executive summary, "has not produced any information, data, or analysis that supports any material change to the conclusions of the original technical report."

The summary continued: "In the absence of a plausible accidental cause and having found material consistent with a chemical device, the NAVSEA team concludes that an intentional act must be considered as a cause of the incident."

A month earlier there had been what would prove to be another watershed event in Admiral Kelso's career.

September 1991 was the month of the infamous Tailhook convention in Las Vegas, where drunken navy fighter pilots allegedly groped, molested, harassed, and verbally abused scores of women.

Kelso had attended the convention.

According to a *Washington Post* article by reporter John Lancaster, in September of 1993, then navy secretary John H. Dalton reportedly tried to fire Kelso on the grounds that as senior officer at the convention, Kelso was responsible for the pilots' behavior.

Lancaster reported Dalton was overruled by Defense Secretary Les Aspin. In his former life as a Republican member of the House Investigations Subcommittee, Les Aspin had joined in the hostile grilling of both Hazelwood and Ault.

Aspin subsequently succumbed to a heart attack.

Admiral Kelso took an early retirement from the navy in February of 1994.

SIXTEEN ✳

The Fetishist

Nikia Gilbreath was by all accounts a contented country housewife, an attractive brown-eyed brunette who lived happily with her husband, Billy Joe, known as Joe, and their infant daughter, Amber, on a sixty-eight-acre farm in the mountains of extreme northwest Georgia, about an hour's drive south of Chattanooga, Tennessee.

Life in the mountains was measured and quiet. Neither Nikia nor Joe had any sense of foreboding or knew of any reason to worry that August 17, 1989, was going to be anything but another routine day in the young family's well-ordered existence.

The name James Ray Ward meant nothing to the Gilbreaths.

They arose early as usual that Thursday, careful not to awaken Amber. Nikia, who was five months pregnant with the Gilbreaths' second child, a boy, fixed her husband his lunch and then retired once again in her oversize T-shirt, panties, and maternity briefs.

She needed her rest even more than usual. That night, Nikia and her mother, Linda Tucker of Dalton, Georgia, were to drive to Florida for a short vacation with Amber. Nikia was trying to spend as much time as possible with Amber before the new baby's scheduled arrival in January. She particularly wanted her daughter to get her first sight of the ocean that August.

Joe Gilbreath was out the back door by 6:00 and behind the wheel of his pickup, headed north over country roads to his job as a welder at Salem Carpet Mills in Ringgold, twenty-five miles away.

Joe did not speak with Nikia by telephone that day, which was not out of the ordinary. Nor was Joe at first surprised when he returned home at about 4:45 to find the family Oldsmobile missing from the front driveway. He assumed Nikia had gone to the store.

When Gilbreath walked inside the open back door, the telephone was ringing. It was Nikia's younger brother, Jon Tucker, who said he had been trying to reach Nikia by telephone all afternoon, with no luck.

As they spoke, Joe saw Amber in the living room, still in her pajamas from the night before, clearly hungry, wearing a very wet diaper. Suddenly, a dark perplexity began to close in on Joe Gilbreath. He apprised his brother-in-law of his discovery, and rang off. Then Joe changed and fed his daughter, put her in her three-wheel stroller, and headed out for the roadway to search for Nikia, not really knowing what else to do.

Jon Tucker, meanwhile, called his mother, who was in Chattanooga, with the disturbing news.

"Good lord, Jon, get help," Linda Tucker told her son. "Something's wrong."

Nikia's mother jumped in her car and "flew" down the highway, as she recalls. "I could not for the life of me imagine what had happened," she says.

Fixed in Mrs. Tucker's mind was a single immutable fact: Under no circumstance would her daughter ever willingly leave Amber alone in the house, or anywhere else, for a moment.

Arriving at the farmhouse, Tucker saw a sheriff's deputy sitting outside in his car. His presence was reassuring. Walker County sheriff Al Mallard, a former FBI agent, was a Tucker family friend.

Mrs. Tucker remembers asking the deputy if he had any news of her missing daughter.

"Ma'am," he answered, "there'll be twenty-four hours before there's any search."

"We're not waiting twenty-four hours," Tucker corrected him.

"Now ma'am, don't get excited," advised the deputy.

"Honey," Tucker told him evenly, "you ain't seen me excited."

The Gilbreath house was filling with worried family and friends. One cousin reported he'd driven by at 7:30 that morning on his way to work and noticed that Joe and Nikia's gray '89 Cutlass wasn't parked in the driveway as usual.

Al Mallard then arrived, and went into earnest conversation with Joe Gilbreath. Joe's mother-in-law quickly surmised why. Linda Tucker knew that when a husband or wife vanishes and there is a suspicion of foul play, the first person police suspect almost always is the remaining spouse, and for good reason. Often, he or she is the guilty party.

"All eyes went to Joe," she says. "He really took a lot. I know a lot of people assumed he'd done it."

She searched for Nikia for as long as the light held, then drove the seventeen miles home to Dalton. Linda Tucker slept poorly for a few hours before arising to resume her search for Nikia.

She still did not know what to make of the situation. Nikia had no history of emotional instability. To the contrary, she was levelheaded and strongwilled. If someone had tried to abduct Nikia, Tucker knew her athletic daughter most definitely would fight, and fiercely, to protect herself and her family.

She had married Joe in early 1987, and bore Amber that same year. It was a wonderful time for the Tucker family until days after Christmas, 1987, when Gary Tucker, Linda's husband of twenty-five years, was killed in a hunting accident.

Within a year, Linda Tucker had become a mother-in-law, a grandmother, and a widow.

Gary Tucker, a construction contractor, had come up with the name Nikia for their firstborn child. Nikia, in turn, planned to name the boy she was carrying Garrett, in honor of her dead father.

It was midmorning on Friday, the eighteenth, as Linda Tucker again neared her daughter's house. A number of dirt lanes fed onto the main country road she was traveling. She paid no attention to them until she was within about a half mile of the farmhouse.

Then one particular dirt track caught Tucker's attention. There was nothing special to distinguish it from any of the other lanes, except that some invisible power Linda Tucker cannot explain forcefully drew her to it.

She backed up and turned down the track until she reached a large rock. From there, Mrs. Tucker continued on foot, still sensing she was being drawn along, when suddenly she saw the Gilbreath family Cutlass in front of her. The car was abandoned. One of its doors (she cannot remember which) was half open.

Tucker hurried away to report her discovery, and returned to the scene with Joe and the sheriff.

They saw that the driver's seat had been pushed back, doubtless in order to accommodate someone much larger than the five-foot five-inch Nikia. The keys were in the ignition, which was turned forward to the "Accessory" position. The Oldsmobile's battery was nearly dead. A second set of tire tracks led toward the main road through the weeds and grass past the abandoned car.

There was no sign of a struggle in the car or around it.

Everyone's attention then fell on the closed trunk. Mrs. Tucker, Joe, and the rest of family waited impatiently, fearfully, for the authorities to open it, praying that it would not disclose the dead Nikia.

It didn't, and everyone relaxed briefly. But the family's sense of foreboding was not dispelled. Nikia was still missing. She obviously had been brought by someone to this secluded place. How had this happened? And where had he taken her?

A check around the Gilbreath residence, which stood on a low hill about one hundred feet from the main roadway, revealed no signs of forced entry, no footprints in the dirt around the windows (even though it recently had rained), and no direct evidence of a struggle inside the house.

The back door was unlocked, as was customary; Joe had left it unlatched when he went to work. However, the front storm door, normally ajar because of the difficulty in closing it over a newly installed porch carpet, had been pulled shut. The screen door inside it, normally latched, was unlatched.

In the living room, the blue telephone cord had been ripped from its jack in the wall near the sofa, and was gone. Missing as well was a patterned nylon bedspread from the Gilbreaths' unmade bed.

The spread would be unmistakable to anyone who saw it, Joe and Linda told sheriff's investigators. Because the nylon bothered Joe's skin, his mother had hand-stitched a white sheet to the underside of it, creating a distinctive and unique article of bedding.

Two days ensued with no further developments in the case. Then on Sunday, as Joe and his mother-in-law were searching through the Gilbreaths' bedroom, looking for anything that might assist the investigators, they jointly discovered that the dresser drawer where Nikia stored her underwear was completely empty. Whoever had abducted Mrs. Gilbreath had taken every last pair of her panties as well.

No one could make any sense of the unnerving discovery, except Linda Tucker. It didn't tell her who had taken her daughter, but now she knew who was not responsible—Joe. Whatever her son-in-law might be capable of, it didn't include stealing his own wife's underwear. That was a certainty.

"Until then I hadn't really thought about it," she remembers. "But if Joe had done it he would not have taken that underwear. Uh-uh. At that moment, I knew for sure that a stranger had taken Nikia."

Several hours later that Sunday, Nikia Gilbreath's body was discovered in a garbage dump, approximately eight miles north of the Gilbreath residence.

She was still dressed in her T-shirt, briefs, and panties, and was lying on her back. No care had been taken to conceal her body.

Her jewelry, a silver wedding ring and a gold heart-shaped pendant on a gold chain around her neck, was untouched.

There was no evidence of sexual assault. However, Mrs. Gilbreath's back was extensively bruised. Three of her ribs were broken as well. There were ligature marks on her wrists and ankles. Yet, she bore no defensive wounds or broken fingernails. There had been no fight for her life, or to protect her daughter.

She died, according to the medial examiner, of asphyxiation from three wads of paper toweling that had been shoved down her throat, obstructing the airway at Nikia's pharynx.

Besides Joe Gilbreath, about whom some investigators harbored misguided suspicions for months, there were no likely suspects in the homicide, and for several months the local authorities made no progress toward solving the case.

Then in December, a Walker County sheriff's detective named Keith Smith had a fortuitous encounter with agents of the Georgia Bureau of Investigation. Smith traveled to the GBI office in the little town of Calhoun, in neighboring Gordon County, to have a polygraph test conducted in an unrelated matter.

He struck up a conversation with the GBI agents, who told him of an unusual abduction-rape case they were working on, which involved a Gordon County suspect. The more he heard about the offense, the surer Smith became of a connection to the Gilbreath killing.

The victim was a thirty-two year old Laura Grant,* a divorcée who lived with her nine-year-old daughter in a trailer park a short distance south of Walker County in Rome, Georgia.

At approximately 5:30 A.M. on Friday, December 8, Grant and her daughter were asleep in their separate bedrooms when an intruder slipped through her trailer's unlocked back door. She awakened to the sight of his stocking-covered face and saw his knife.

He placed a hand over her mouth, and told Grant that her child would not be hurt if she did not make a sound. He handcuffed Grant and walked her out the front door to his truck, parked a block away. On the way out, he glanced at the modest tabletop tree she'd decorated for Christmas, and remarked that she deserved something a bit grander.

When Grant's daughter awoke at 6:30 that morning to discover her mother missing, the little girl called the police.

Meantime, the intruder drove her mother to an empty house, where he demanded she masturbate him, as well as fellate him. He in turn fondled Grant and performed cunnilingus on her. Then he raped her.

In between the assaults, he told Grant a preposterous lie, that he actually had been sent to kill her, but found her so likable and alluring that he'd protect her, and planned to argue before his unnamed coconspirators that her life be spared.

It was by now full light outside. The rapist put away the knife and took off his mask. Grant already knew he was big—six feet seven inches and 245 pounds. Now she could make out his features, including a beard, mustache, and bushy hair.

He drove Grant to a second unoccupied residence in Gordon County. There he handcuffed her to a chair, left for a short time, and returned carrying a number of women's teddies. He ordered her to model them for him.

She did as she was instructed.

The man watched as she posed for him in the lingerie, became highly aroused, and raped her several more times. Finally, he drove her back to Rome, leaving Grant near her trailer park about fourteen hours after first abducting her. On the way, he said he'd like to see her again, and asked his baffled victim if he might call her.

Two days later, he pulled into her driveway in his truck and placed a Christmas tree on her porch. Grant's father, who lived across the street, witnessed the unlikely scene and recorded the vehicle's license plate number. The police soon arrested its owner, a thirty-three-year-old well digger named James Ray Ward. Grant identified Ward in a lineup as her abductor.

Once Linda Tucker heard of Ward's arrest, she rushed to the Walker County sheriff's office with a photo Nikia had taken of Amber resting on the Gilbreath's missing nylon bedspread with its attached bedsheet. If the killer still had the spread, she told the officers, the photo would help them identify it when they searched Ward's house.

Al Mallard's men thanked Mrs. Tucker, but made it plain they had no expectation of recovering such a damning piece of evidence so many months later.

They were mistaken.

There were several searches of the unfinished structure that Ward, known as Ray, shared with his wife, Jamie, and their two children. The investigators found the telephone cord missing from the Gilbreath residence, plus the unusual bedspread (which Ward had tried unsuccessfully to burn), and one other surprise item, the bottom part of a two-piece Bill Blass swimming suit Linda Tucker had purchased for her daughter. As luck would have it, Tucker still had the top to the suit.

Roy in 1993—After sixteen years with the BSU, Hazelwood's casebook included more than 10,000 deviant assaults, murders, and other crimes.

Roy Hazelwood

Jon Barry Simonis in custody—Roy and fellow profiler Ken Lanning spent nine hours debriefing the Ski Mask Rapist inside Louisiana's Angola Prison.
UPI/Corbis-Bettmann

Nikia Galbreath—Her murder stumped investigators for nearly four months.

John C. Bass

A close-knit family—Nikia with her father and walking her daughter, Amber, with her mother, Linda Tucker. John C. Bass

The damning evidence—
Investigators discovered
approximately $3,000
worth of plastic-bagged
lingerie inside Ray Ward's
partially built house, as
well as part of Nikia's
swimming suit and the
Gilbreath's missing
comforter.
John C. Bass

Bob Rhoades as a sex slave—A class sexual sadist, Rhoades tried gradually to destroy Debra Davis.

Debra Davis

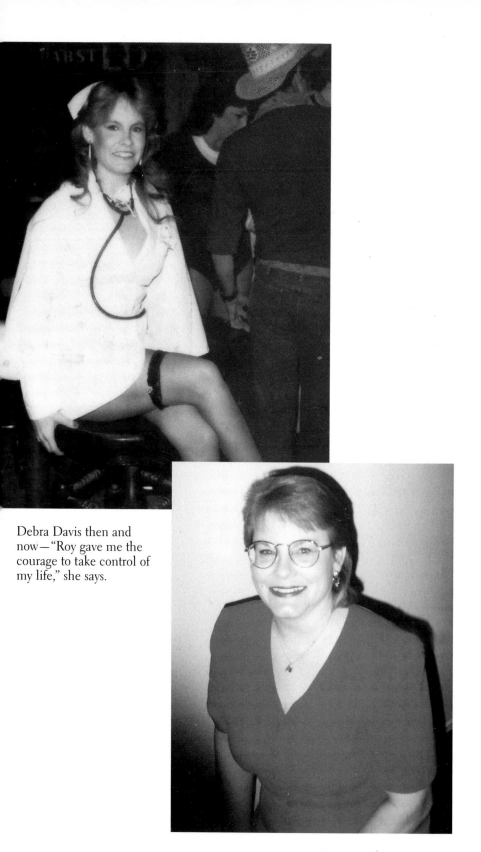

Debra Davis then and
now—"Roy gave me the
courage to take control of
my life," she says.

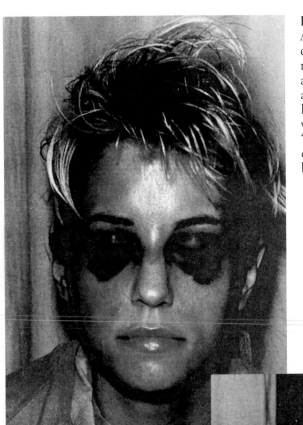

Karla Homolka—
Although she was impli-
cated in Paul Bernardo's
murders and sexual
assaults, the Canadian
authorities agreed with
Roy that Karla was a
victim, too. Her dark
"raccoon eyes" were
caused by Bernardo's
blows to her head.

Searchers also discovered a scrap of paper on Ward's dresser. Written on it were driving instructions to the Gilbreaths', plus "Baby, 1 yr. old" and "Brown Hair" and "fine looking," no doubt a physical appraisal of Mrs. Gilbreath.

Ward's employer, Jefford's Well Drilling, revealed that he had helped drill a water well on the Gilbreath property in July of 1988. The work had taken two days. Nikia had been at home. Linda Tucker recalled her daughter remarking to her and other family members in July of 1989, one month before her murder, that one of the two Jefford's employees who'd drilled the well had returned to ask if it was operating correctly.

This evidence alone connected Ray Ward to the killing of Nikia Gilbreath approximately four months before he kidnapped and raped Linda Grant.

However, "We realized that this was not a standard abduction-rape-murder thing," says John C. Bass, an investigator with the four-county Northwest Georgia Lookout Mountain Judicial Circuit. "It was much more. Ward was a danger to everybody."

His rap sheet began with two burglary counts in 1975, and then lengthened over the years with arrests for criminal trespass, receiving stolen property, more burglary charges, and one charge of stealing livestock.

Witnesses told detectives that Ward was an exhibitionist, who'd begun exposing his genitals in public at least ten years earlier, and continued to do so up to the time of his arrest. Several women in the community accused Ward of groping their breasts, of more serious sexual assaults, and of placing obscene and threatening calls to them. He was known to have stolen several purses.

His wife said she began discovering lingerie—not hers—around the house, as well as used condoms, in February of 1989. Mrs. Ward complained that her husband kept asking her to pose in the lingerie, in order for him to be sexually aroused. She said she'd generally refused his requests.

The searches of Ward's residence turned up a batch of paper slips with local women's names, addresses, and numbers written on them, apparently in the women's own handwriting. It turned out they had completed the slips as entries at a crafts fair raffle. Ward had watched as fair organizers discarded the slips, then fished them out of the trash and took them home.

The investigators also seized sheaves of newspaper articles detailing developments in the Gilbreath case, as well as other sexual crimes committed in the area, not necessarily by Ward himself.

The searches' strangest disclosure, however, was the approximately three thousand dollars' worth of women's underclothing of all sorts he had hidden in his house. There were bras, panties, slips, half-slips, swimsuits, teddies, and gowns, each individually wrapped in a clear plastic bag and labeled. Most of the undergarments had been stolen in various ways, but some had been purchased, too.

Also discovered were 2,300 or so hand-printed three-by-five notecards bearing women's names and coded physical evaluations, together with an index to the cards Ward kept in a fat spiral notebook.

There was no question that District Attorney Ralph Van Pelt, Jr., would seek the death penalty. But Van Pelt was mindful he had no eyewitnesses who could place Ward and Nikia Gilbreath together on the morning of her murder. Juries tend to favor testimony from eyewitnesses, generally not realizing how unreliable even the most convincing eyewitness can be.

Van Pelt's case, though strong, instead was built on circumstantial evidence. To ensure a capital prosecution would succeed, the district attorney wanted to paint for Ward's jury a complete portrait of the defendant's multiple deviance, an informed overview that would tie together the seemingly disparate facts of the killer's character.

"Early on I was worried that some of the stuff was just so weird that the jurors would sit there and say, 'This cannot be happening,'" Van Pelt, now a Georgia superior court judge, recalls. "'There's got to be some other explanation for all this stuff in this guy's house and for his behavior.'

"I was concerned they'd possibly think Ward might be insane, or that someone had planted the evidence."

John Bass, who had attended the FBI National Academy in 1986, immediately thought of Roy Hazelwood, his instructor in Interpersonal Violence. If anyone could make sense of Ray Ward to a jury it was Hazelwood, Bass thought.

"I told Van Pelt that I believed in the stuff they do at Quantico," Bass says, "that Roy did good work, and besides, it was free. I said we ought to give it a try, and Van Pelt said, 'Fine. Let's do it.'"

John Bass contacted Hazelwood, who agreed to testify as a prosecution expert on the connections between paraphilias, such as fetishism and exhibitionism, and deviant assaults.

Roy's experience as an expert trial witness on paraphilias dated back to a South Carolina case where deviance also figured in the defendant's criminal behavior. A fifteen-year-old girl had been found with her throat cut. She'd been raped vaginally, anally, and orally, as well as stabbed thirty-seven times and eviscerated. Her eighteen-year-old killer, John Kenneth Register, who was arrested and charged on the strength of DNA evidence, was a family friend, and had been a pallbearer at her funeral.

In a pretrial strategy discussion, Roy asked the prosecutor, Ralph Wilson, if Register had any prior arrests or a mental health history. Wilson said no.

"Nothing at all?" Roy wondered.

"Only a couple obscene phone calls when he was about fifteen," the prosecutor answered. The files were with the juvenile authorities, Wilson said, because of the defendant's age at the time of the offense, and its status as a "nuisance" crime.

Roy asked about the victims, and the content of the obscene calls.

They turned out to be a mother and daughter, each of whom had heard the teen's telephone scatology approximately a hundred times. With variations, his usual stream of invective went something like, "I'm gonna cut your goddamn throat. I'm gonna stab you till my arm gets tired. I'm gonna slit you open like a pig. And I'm gonna fuck you every way I can, and when I'm through I'm gonna use my gearshift."

Hazelwood returned to the prosecutor's office and advised him to indict Register for the phone calls.

"That's ridiculous!" Wilson said. "I'm faced with trying to convict a man for the most heinous murder this county has seen in a century, and you want me to convict this same person for obscene phone calls?"

"Yes!" Roy answered, "because he was verbalizing his fantasy. That young man was masturbating to those fantasies, which he later acted out in the murder. You can show the jury what he did, and also show them what he said he was going to do years earlier."

Roy's logic was compelling. He was telling the district attorney a way to reach into Register' mind by reaching back into the young man's behavior.

Hazelwood also interviewed two women who'd reported to the police that the defendant once had exposed himself to them.

"I asked them what he said," Roy recalls, "and they answered, 'Do you want this or my gearshift?'"

At Roy's recommendation, Wilson did indict and convict John Register for telephone scatalogia.

Hazelwood testified in the penalty phase of the Register trial.

"The autopsy was read, so the jurors knew what sort of trauma was inflicted on the victim," Roy explains. "Then the mother and daughter testified about the phone calls, and the jury could see the similarities between the two cases."

John Kenneth Register received a life sentence.

At Ray Ward's July 1991 trial for murdering Nikia Gilbreath, prosecutor Ralph Van Pelt presented to the jury all the testimony and evidence about

Ward's exhibitionism, lingerie collection, assaults, and coded card file. The district attorney also put on the record that Ward had lost his job twice in the period around the time of Nikia Gilbreath's murder, and that Ward's wife had temporarily left him, too. The jury was fully aware Ray Ward was beset with money and legal and personal worries at the time of the murder.

Then the prosecution called Hazelwood to the stand. This would be the first time such testimony ever had been accepted in a Georgia criminal court.

"What is a sexual disorder?" Van Pelt asked.

"There are two types," Roy answered.

He explained that about half the men who voluntarily seek clinical help for sexual problems are diagnosed with a paraphilia. About half those men are married.

"A type of paraphilia that you might have heard about is transvestism, a man dressed in the clothes of a woman," he said.

"Another would be exhibitionism, or flashing, exposing one's genitals to a stranger. And fetishism, the sexual attachment to objects such as jewelry or rubber or leather or lingerie—panties, teddies, that kind of thing."

"It's a kind of paraphilia?" Van Pelt asked.

"It's a kind of paraphilia," Roy answered, "the same thing as a deviation. Also, may I mention one other thing?"

"Certainly."

"When you find one paraphilia, it is commonly accepted that you will find other deviations in that same individual."

The second major type of sexual disorder is sexual dysfunction.

"You have basically three types of dysfunction," Roy explained. "Premature ejaculation, retarded or difficult ejaculation, and impotence."

John Bass sat in the gallery appreciatively taking in Hazelwood's polished exposition.

"Everyone was impressed with him," says the investigator. "He came across as really knowing what he was talking about. It was important for us to get across that Ward wasn't just some isolated crazy person. We needed Roy to educate the jury that people like Ward had been well studied."

Van Pelt asked Hazelwood what effects external stresses might have on a man with paraphilias. Ray Ward, of course, was coping with several stresses, from a disintegrating marriage to the loss of his job to the acute anxiety that any offender feels at the thought of being discovered or, in Ward's case, revealed.

"We have found that a person with paraphilias is more likely to commit one of these types of activities when he's under a great deal of stress," Roy answered.

He added that paraphilias also are reinforced when an individual's regular sex partner refuses to indulge his particular desires, just as Ray Ward's wife had refused to participate in his fantasies. The paraphiliac withdraws further into his deviance. Whatever interest he may have in conventional sexual encounters in engulfed by the paraphilia.

The prosecutor asked Hazelwood to explain erotica.

"Erotica is anything that sexually arouses or sexually stimulates a person," Roy said to the jury.

"Sometimes it's a very innocent thing, such as newspaper articles. It could be a pair of panties. It could be a movie. Different things are sexually arousing to different people."

"What does the term 'trophy' mean?" Van Pelt asked.

"We've found that quite frequently the violent sexual offender retains something which belongs to the victim," Roy replied.

"This can be something like lingerie. It can be a piece of jewelry. It can be a newspaper clipping *about* a case, concerning the investigation or the discovery of the body.

"Such items very simply represent a trophy to the offender, much as if you and I were on a baseball team and we won a trophy. They represent a victory, a conquest, something the individual can use to relive the crime and to refresh his memory of it.

"We find that he normally keeps his trophies within an area of his control. It could be his office, his garage, his work shed, or his home."

The prosecutor then produced the coded three-by-five cards and spiral notebook seized from Ray Ward's house.

Roy looked over the material and said he had carefully examined seventy-six of the cards. He told the jurors Ward had put together a highly organized cross-referenced rating system for erotic photos he clipped from men's magazines, as well as lingerie and swimsuit catalogs. The defendant favored publications featuring homemade erotica, usually nude photos submitted by men of their wives and girlfriends.

Hazelwood used this example from Ward's file:

Melissa P.   10
19
Paducah Kent.
No
Mark

Dancer
1-89 F&L

The card, he explained on the stand, described a Melissa P. from Paducah, Kentucky, who was nineteen years old, and rated a ten on Ward's zero-to-ten scale.

"No" meant she was unmarried, and "Dancer" was Melissa's occupation. "Mark" took the photo, which appeared in the "F&L" section—for Friends & Lovers—of the January 1989 issue of *Genesis*.

The spiral notebook contained a complementary classification system. A representative page contained these entries:

Gen March 88	Lacy	V.	25	No	10
	Marcy		26	Yes	8
	Jean	R.	20	Yes	8
	Ali		30	No	10

The notebook's code was the same as for the cards. The initials V. and R. represented the women's surnames, Hazelwood testified.

"Those cards and that notebook were amazing," John Bass recollects. "Ward had everything indexed, cross-referenced, and organized. He would have made a perfect file clerk."

The next topics were ritual and MO.

"Ritual," Roy said, "is that part of sexual crime that is committed to enhance the psychosexual enjoyment of the offender. It is the signature of a crime that a criminal investigative analyst looks for to link cases to one individual. The ritual remains relatively static over time.

"MO," he went on, "evolves over time as the offender matures and gains experience in committing similar crimes. The primary functions of an MO are to protect the identify of the offender, ensure control of the victim, and facilitate his escape."

Roy illustrated his points with a case from his files.

"A man breaks into a home, captures the husband and wife, and takes the wife out of the room and has her change into panty hose and high heels," Hazelwood recounted.

"Breaking into the house was MO. Tying up the husband was MO. Having the woman change into panty hose and high heels prior to the assault would be ritual."

Van Pelt's next objective was to establish with Hazelwood the behavioral links between the kidnap-rape of Laura Grant, to which Ward already had confessed, and Nikia Gilbreath's abduction-murder.

The district attorney produced an easel chart which listed on one side various features and factors of the Gilbreath case, and on the other, corresponding features and facts of the Grant case.

Examples of parallel MO, Roy testified, included the fact that no males were present at the early-morning hours of the abductions and that women with children were targeted. The presence of the kids, he explained, made their mothers more cautious, and easier to control, at least initially.

Comparable instances of ritual, Roy said, included the obvious importance of lingerie in both cases, as well as the fact that both victims were taken from their homes and driven to a second location. In both cases, that decision heightened his risk of capture, but was absolutely essential to playing out his ritual.

On cross-examination, court-appointed defense attorney Chris Townley, by reputation an able and dogged advocate, showed Hazelwood no deference.

Mocking Roy's list of case similarities, Townley archly suggested that since both women lived in Georgia and neither had gray hair, those similarities might have been included in his analysis, too.

Hazelwood allowed politely that yes, these were similarities, too.

Townley also established that possessing an item, such as a woman's purse, does not make a man a fetishist.

"It depends on why he has the purse," Hazelwood answered.

Nor does the identification of multiple paraphilias in a defendant's character prove him guilty, Townley asserted.

Hazelwood agreed again.

Townley chipped away where he could in his cross-examination, but he could not unravel the broad and distinct picture Ralph Van Pelt and Roy Hazelwood had created of Ray Ward as a troubled, deviant killer.

"Hazelwood was an excellent witness, and that helped us a lot," says the former prosecutor.

Ward's jury deliberated only briefly before voting him guilty of capital murder. In the ensuing penalty phase of the trial, members of the panel would be surprised to see Roy take the stand once again—this time as a defense witness.

Based on the detailed information provided by Laura Grant, Roy believed Ward was an essentially nonviolent power reassurance rapist. Chris Townley wanted the jury to hear Hazelwood's description of such an offender, and then make the jump in their own minds to the Gilbreath case. As they deliberated whether Ward should be executed, Townley hoped they'd consider that Ray Ward probably had not kidnapped Nikia Gilbreath with the intent of killing her. The asphyxiation had been a ghastly, tragic mistake.

With Ralph Van Pelt's and the FBI's approval, Roy agreed to testify as a defense witness.

"In the Laura Grant case, what type of offender would you be looking for?" Townley asked.

"I would classify that rapist as a power reassurance rapist," Roy replied, and then he briefly explained his typology.

"So," said Townley, "he is not trying to inflict physical pain, or trying to subject someone to physical abuse?"

"No. In the Laura Grant case, you would have seen a beating, possible cigarette burns, that type of thing."

What about the odd incident with the Christmas tree, the defense attorney asked.

"In my opinion," Roy answered, "he was trying to reinforce with her the fact that he is a nice guy. You'll recall that he dropped her off a block from her house, asked for her phone number and that sort of thing. He was trying to reinforce in her mind that he was a nice guy."

Townley also explored with Hazelwood what is known about the root causes of fetishism.

"The most prevalent and accepted theory," Roy said, "is that at some point very early in their lives fetishists come into contact with a particular object at the same time they are being sexually aroused."

At that moment, he went on, the object is believed to somehow become "imprinted" and henceforth is always associated by the fetishist with sex gratification.

In one example from the professional literature, Roy told of a large number of Englishmen who developed rubber gas mask fetishes. Research indicated that as boys during World War II, these males had been forced to wear gas masks during the German air raids, occasions when their protective mothers also held them tight to their bosoms. The experience may have sexually excited the boys, imprinting the rubber gas masks on their libidos.

Roy agreed with Townley that the fetishistic impulse can be very, very strong.

"For example," he said, "fetishists know the consequences of an illegal act, there's no question about that. But that consideration is overcome by the desire for that gratification of breaking into the house and stealing a pair of panties."

"Somehow they end up doing it anyhow?" asked Townley.

"Yes," said Roy.

Apparently, this added objective information about Ray Ward did nothing to sway the jury in his favor. On July 12, 1991, the panel voted the death penalty for him.

They did so without ever hearing Roy's most interesting contribution to the case, his speculative reconstruction of how the Gilbreath murder in fact took place.

Hazelwood believed Mrs. Gilbreath was a carefully selected victim, probably chosen when Ward helped drill the water well for the Gilbreaths.

He knew also from long experience with such offenders that Ward no doubt had fantasized a great deal about Nikia Gilbreath before committing the actual crime.

Ward's intent probably was for Nikia Gilbreath to bring to life his lingerie fetish fantasy, just as Laura Grant had been forced to do at knifepoint. Murder, however, was not on Ward's mind. Women's underwear was.

Roy surmised that Ward surveilled the Gilbreath household, and knew its rhythms. The tire tracks suggested he parked his vehicle that Thursday morning, where Nikia's mother later found the Gilbreath Cutlass partially hidden on the old logging road. He then walked the half mile to the Gilbreaths.

Ward would have watched the house from cover, knowing from his previous reconnaissance that Joe left via the back door each day at 6:30. Once Nikia's husband had rumbled away in his pickup, Ray Ward walked into the house through the back door.

Had Ward knocked on the front door, Hazelwood pointed out, Mrs. Gilbreath would have automatically pulled on a robe before opening the door.

He encountered Mrs. Gilbreath not in her bed, but on the couch in the living room, where she'd gone back to sleep after fixing Joe lunch that morning. The telephone cord was probably the first thing handy with which to bind her, and it was taken directly from the wall near the sofa.

Ward may have gained her compliance by threatening to harm the sleeping Amber. That would explain the lack of defensive wounds. The bruises discovered on her back, plus the broken ribs she also suffered from behind, most likely were caused by the 245-pound offender digging his knees into her as he hog-tied Nikia, wrist and ankle, with the blue cord, on the sofa.

Roy guessed Ward then covered Mrs. Gilbreath with the nylon bedspread and carried her out the front door to the family car, where he likely put her in the trunk. He then returned to the front porch and pulled the balky outer door closed over the new carpet, hoping to create the appearance that Mrs. Gilbreath had driven somewhere with Amber in the car.

Nikia Gilbreath, whose first concern would have been to protect Amber, probably remained silent while still in the house. Once safely away where Amber was no longer threatened, however, Nikia very likely started screaming and resisting as best she could. Everyone said Nikia was a fighter.

Roy inferred from the evidence that as Ward moved his bound and struggling victim from her car to his vehicle, he tried to muffle her screams with wads of paper towel he grabbed from her trunk and shoved down her throat. He did not realize he was asphyxiating her.

Ward must have believed Gilbreath was alive as he drove away with her; otherwise he surely would have fled immediately, leaving her dead body at the scene.

He probably did not learn what he had done until he arrived at his preappointed site for assaulting her, likely an empty or abandoned structure not too far away. The discovery would have panicked Ward.

At that moment, his motive would shift from sexual gratification to self-preservation. Roy believed the frightened killer continued driving in the direction he was headed, north, until he reached the dump, eight miles away, where Nikia Gilbreath's body was found three days later.

The dump site, Roy also believed, was selected on the spur of the moment, and was chosen only because Ward needed to quickly dispose of Mrs. Gilbreath's body lest he be discovered with it.

From the position in which she was later found, it appeared that he hastily placed her body into the dump, risking being seen and identified as he did so. The only precaution Ward took was to remove and carry home the bedspread and blue telephone cord ligatures. In his haste, he somehow grabbed the loose swimming suit bottom, too.

Either that, or as his attorney suggested, Ray Ward really could not resist a fetish object.

During his murder trial nearly two years later, a security search of Ward's cell revealed he'd secreted away a range of contraband documents and photocopies. Among the materials Ward somehow managed to procure under heavy guard was a nude autopsy photograph of Nikia Gilbreath.

SEVENTEEN ✗

Linkage Analysis

A n aberrant offender's behavior is as unique as his fingerprints, as his DNA—as a snowflake.

The challenge for the investigator is to exploit that singularity, to find the behavioral equivalent of the latent fingerprint or the electrophoretic "bar codes" of a DNA analysis that can establish an offender's identity beyond any reasonable quibble. You need to isolate the snowflake.

With serial offenders, one means of doing so is linkage analysis, a compare-and-contrast behavioral assay developed by Hazelwood and others at BSU.

This procedure looks at MO and ritual as Hazelwood did in the Gilbreath case.

"You can say that cases are linked when the number of MO characteristics and ritualistic characteristics reach a point that you have never seen in combination before," Roy explains.

"For example, an attorney may ask me in court, 'How many victims have you seen who were twenty-one years old?'

" 'Well, a lot of people.'

" 'How many of them have been white females?'

" 'A lot of them.'

" 'How many have been bitten on the breast?'

" 'Quite a few.'

" 'I see, and how many of them were struck in the face four times?'

" 'A lot of them were.'

"'Now, Mr. Hazelwood, how many cases have you seen in which the victims were all twenty-one-year-old white females who'd been bitten on the breast *and* struck in the face four times?'

"I'd have to say I'd never seen that exact combination before. Then if I saw that exact combination in another case, I could say the two cases were linked."

The offender's MO is behavior meant to ensure his success, facilitate his escape, and protect his identity. Ritual is behavior that heightens his psychosexual gratification. Sometimes, the two are not easy to tell apart.

For example, Roy has never seen an offender's method of entering a structure be anything but MO. However, the way he approaches a victim on the street, or in her bed, can be either MO or ritual.

One of the earliest and most complex cases for which Roy Hazelwood provided the police a linkage analysis was that of a Swiss serial killer.

While in Europe together on business vacation with their wives in the late 1980s, Hazelwood and Roger Depue accepted an invitation to visit Aarau, a small town about ten miles west of Zürich.

Their host in Aarau was a local police commander named Leon Borer, who took the opportunity to inquire if his guests would be curious to look over some unsolved cases in his files.

If the American agents liked, while they were consulting the criminal records, Commander Borer's officers were happy to drive Frau Hazelwood and Frau Depue on escorted motor tours of the breathtaking Swiss countryside.

Everyone immediately agreed to the idea.

Among the unsolved cases that Roy and Roger Depue reviewed for Borer in Aarau that summer was a series of child murders, mostly strangulations, which had begun in 1980. After poring over the files, Hazelwood and Depue visited various of the crime scenes, spoke to a number of the children's parents, and sketched a brief profile of the homicidal pedophile for Borer.

No progress was made toward cracking the case until August 1989, when Roy learned that a suspect named Werner Ferrari had been arrested in connection with the recent murder of a little girl in Hagendorf, close to Aarau. Ferrari, forty-two, confessed both to his homicide and to the killings of three boys, dating back to 1983.

Like Harvey Glatman three decades earlier, Werner Ferrari seemed to appear out of nowhere. Also like Glatman, Ferrari was more than just a lucky, or determined, deviant criminal. He seemed to have the same innate grasp of the successful MO: Be careful, move around, don't be seen, and don't leave any physical evidence.

Ferrari had staggered the intervals between his crimes, known and sus-pected, from between three weeks and twenty-two months. He also cannily avoided committing them one after another in a geographic cluster, so as to alarm the local populace and thus place greater pressure on the police to stop him. He finally was caught and charged with murder in August 1989 after an uncharacteristic, perhaps subconsciously intentional, lapse: Werner Ferrari left a live witness who identified him to the police.

Besides the four murders to which he confessed, investigators suspected Ferrari in six other child abductions and homicides, for which he denied any culpability.

Three of these victims (two girls, one boy) were never found, and there were no witnesses or hard physical evidence to link Ferrari to any of the three open cases where bodies were recovered. With his confessions, there was no question that Ferrari would be locked up for life. But lacking hard evidence one way or the other in their open cases, the Swiss police were loath to close them simply on their suspicion that Werner Ferrari was responsible.

That is when Commander Borer thought again of the FBI.

On the chance the Swiss authorities had missed or overlooked behavioral evidence of value either to themselves or to the courts, Borer asked Roy to re-turn to Aarau to conduct a linkage analysis.

Hazelwood flew to Switzerland on a Friday in early May, and was driven straight to Aarau, where Borer showed his FBI guest to his assigned room at the local police dormitory.

Ordinarily, Roy's routine when traveling on business is fixed and unvarying. He checks into upmarket chain hotels with big, quiet accommodations and hunkers down, leaving his room only as required. For sustenance, he relies nearly exclusively on room-service steaks (well done), American cheese sand-wiches (white bread, maybe a little butter), and the odd bowl of Campbell's tomato soup, none other.

"Do you know what's important about American cheese sandwiches on white bread?" he asks. "Wherever you go, they are *exactly* the same. I like that."

Together with the spaghetti *ajo e ojo* he first tried at the suggestion of the Mafia hood in Binghamton, plus fast-food cheeseburgers and French fries, these dishes more or less constitute Hazelwood's preferred diet in its entirety.

"It's embarrassing to order dinner with him," says Dr. Dietz.

In Aarau, Hazelwood took a deep breath as he inspected his spartan quar-ters, a small dorm room for one with no telephone and no television.

"Well, at least there won't be any distractions," Roy thought and went looking for a McDonald's.

For the next four days, investigator after investigator sat down with Hazelwood to brief him, through interpreters, on each of the ten cases.

The first victim, twelve-year-old Ruth Steinmann, lived in Wurenlos, a northeast suburb of Zürich. The slightly built brown-haired child was last seen climbing aboard her bicycle at school late in the afternoon on Friday, May 16, 1980. When Ruth did not come home, her parents went in search of her in a woods near where they lived. As they called for their daughter, both father and mother observed a jacketed young male walking toward them from the woods. When he saw the Steinmanns, he turned away, jumped on a moped, and sped off.

Not far away, Ruth's father found his little girl.

She was lying nude in the forest, on her back, under a discarded section of floor covering. Her clothes were scattered around her.

One of her socks had been stuffed down Ruth's throat, causing her death by

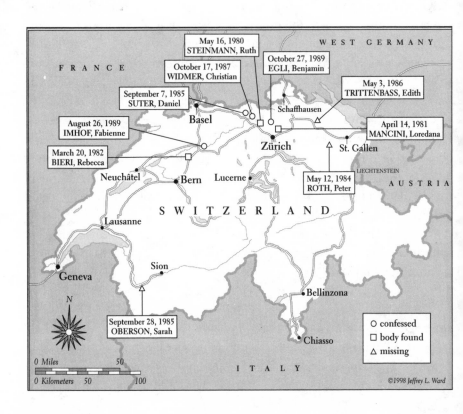

asphyxiation. The other sock was on her foot. There was a human bite mark on her left breast, and scratches on her thigh and right knee.

There were, however, no defensive wounds, and no evidence that the child had been bound. Nothing of value had been stolen, either.

Crime scene investigators retrieved a freshly broken branch nearby, and believed that the killer had inserted the limb in Ruth's vagina. He apparently had not done so violently. The girl had sustained some internal injury, including laceration to her bladder. But no seminal fluid was present, and her reproductive organs were intact and uninjured.

At the time of Ruth Steinmann's murder, Werner Ferrari lived about three miles from where she was found, a prima facie reason for suspecting he might have committed the homicide. He owned a jacket matching the description of the one the girl's parents saw the young man wearing that day. Ferrari also owned a moped identical to the one the Steinmanns described to police. He also had no alibi for his whereabouts on that Friday afternoon.

A week after the murder, Ferrari broke up with his girlfriend and moved.

The second suspected victim, eight-year-old Rebecca Bieri, lived in Niederbipp, about forty miles west of Zürich. Rebecca disappeared on her way home from school on Saturday, March 20, 1982, approximately twenty-two months after the Steinmann homicide. Bieri also was slight and had brown hair.

Her skeletonized remains were recovered in August 1982, in a wooded area. One of her stockings was found around her neck. Although neither the cause nor the manner of her death could be established to a certainty, Rebecca Bieri was believed to have been strangled with her stocking.

About a month after her disappearance, Werner Ferrari changed residences.

Loredana Mancini was a seven-year-old, also short and slight with brown hair. She lived in Rumlang, just north of Zürich. Mancini vanished late Thursday afternoon, April 18, 1983, after walking out her front door to go shopping nearby. Her skeleton was discovered about twelve miles away, in a foxhole in the woods.

Ferrari was familiar with the area where Mancini's remains were found.

The fourth case was also the earliest of the murders to which Ferrari later confessed. Like Loredana Mancini, ten-year-old Benjamin Egli of Regensberg, just west of Rumlang, had gone shopping unescorted late on a Thursday afternoon.

Ferrari told police that he'd lured the boy off the street with promises they'd play together with toys at his house. Once he had the child in his car, Ferrari drove Benjamin to a woods, where he killed him.

The boy was found, fully clothed, with no evidence that he'd been bound, beaten, or sexually assaulted. Cause of death was strangulation by ligature, which must have been done carefully, since Benjamin's hyoid bone was unharmed.

Ferrari said he murdered Egli after hearing people nearby. He said he feared being discovered with the youth.

He changed residences two weeks after the homicide.

Seven months later, on Mother's Day, Saturday, May 12, 1984, eight-year-old Peter Roth of Mogelsberg, about thirty miles east of Zürich, vanished on his way home from school. No trace of the boy was ever found.

Daniel Suter was suspected victim number six. A blond seven-year-old, just over three feet tall, Daniel visited a fair in Rumlang with his parents on Saturday night, September 7, 1985.

Ferrari later confessed that he found the boy alone at the fair and lured Daniel into his car. Witnesses told a slightly different story of seeing a child answering Daniel's description being forcibly abducted from the fairground.

Ferrari said that as they drove away together he tried to touch Daniel. The boy recoiled and tried to escape. That is when Ferrari strangled him with a curtain cord ligature—he emphasized that he did not want to touch Daniel's neck with his hands—and then bound the dead child neck-to-ankles with the cord.

He dumped Daniel Suter's body in a cornfield less than mile from where he killed him, and drove away with a keepsake, a toy ball belonging to Daniel.

Significantly, Ferrari had once been institutionalized in a juvenile home less than a half mile from where he disposed of Suter.

The boy's body was recovered where Ferrari had dumped him. Daniel was fully dressed save for his jacket, a shoe, and one sock, which were missing. Cause of death was ligature strangulation.

There was no evidence of sexual assault, although Daniel's pants were unzipped. He had not been beaten, and apparently had not struggled with Ferrari to any extent. The Suter boy suffered no defensive wounds.

Ferrari changed addresses within two months of the slaying.

Exactly three weeks later, on Saturday, September 28, 1985, Sarah Oberson, aged six, disappeared at midday on her way home from school. Sarah, who was small for her age, lived about 120 miles southwest of Zürich in a little town not far from the French border. There were no witnesses, and she was never found.

On Mother's Day, Saturday, May 3, 1986, in Wetzikon, about twenty-five miles southeast of Zürich, nine-year-old Edith Trittenbass vanished on her way to school. The small, slender child was never found.

Another seventeen months passed before it was Christian Widmer's turn.

Widmer vanished some time after 7:00 P.M. on Saturday night, October 17, 1987, in the town of Riniken, northwest of Zürich. Christian was last seen inside a Riniken gymnasium, where the ten-year-old was attending a Boy Scout fair. He was reported missing at midnight.

Ferrari in his confession to this killing said he was in the neighborhood because a girlfriend lived behind the gym.

He said he met Christian in a hallway and invited the boy to a comic book kiosk. From there, the two went to a café for a sandwich and a Coke. Ferrari then walked the Widmer boy into a nearby woods, he said.

He insisted that all he wished to do with Christian was to lay his head on the boy's body.

But Christian resisted Ferrari's advances. Angered, the killer first tried to throttle the boy with his bare hands, he told police, but Christian began to cry. So Ferrari used his belt to strangle the youngster from behind.

He also inserted a stick in the dead boy's rectum, he said, because he was angry.

Christian Widmer was neither bound nor beaten, nor did he show any defensive wounds when found. No seminal fluids were found, and his hyoid bone was undamaged.

Ferrari quit his job and broke off with his girlfriend within two months of murdering Widmer.

He final known victim in the series was Fabienne Imhof.

On August 26, 1989, a Saturday, nine-year-old Fabienne and an eight-year-old girlfriend attended a fair with Fabienne's parents in Hagendorf, about halfway between Zürich and Niederbipp, where Rebecca Bieri was killed more than seven years earlier.

The girls became separated from Fabienne's parents. While in search of them, Fabienne and her friend encountered Werner Ferrari.

He told the girls he knew where the adults were to be found, and offered to accompany Fabienne back to them, leaving her friend behind.

Ferrari led Imhof into a woods, where she began to cry, he later told police.

After slapping Fabienne, he began to strangle her, but became frightened. He then pushed her face into the ground, and continued strangling her from behind.

Ferrari removed the child's panties and took them away with him, along with some of the little girl's candy. As was true with the earlier cases, there was no indication that he beat the child or penetrated her with his penis. He did insert a stick into her vagina. Her hyoid bone was not damaged.

Ferrari later told the police he intended to quit his job following the crime. He also maintained that his motive was not sexual. All he wished to do was gain warmth from Fabienne's body, he said.

After sorting and analyzing the pertinent details of the ten cases, Hazelwood turned his attention to Werner Ferrari's personal history.

He learned from the files that Werner's mother was a drunk who bore him at age eighteen. Ferrari never met his father. Between the ages of eight and seventeen, he lived in the juvenile facility near the cornfield where Daniel Suter's body was dumped. Records show that while in the youth home Ferrari would not play with other children, refused to obey adults, stole, and was a chronic liar.

Back in his mother's custody, he committed a series of burglaries, and was sent to a reformatory, from which he escaped. In 1965, at age nineteen, Ferrari attempted to derail a passenger train by placing several large stones on the railroad tracks. A psychiatrist who interviewed him in jail at the time diagnosed Ferrari as a pedophile, likely to commit sex crimes against children once he was released.

The psychiatrist was correct. Five years later, Ferrari killed a small boy and was sentenced to fourteen years in prison. He served nine years of the term, and was released in August, 1979, approximately nine months before Ruth Steinmann's asphyxiation murder.

Ferrari's various ex-girlfriends described him as a humorless, friendless loner who eschewed physical sex with them, but enjoyed watching the women undress, and very much enjoyed resting his head on their unclothed chests or stomachs.

Hazelwood next spent four more days in deep analysis of the case material.

Besides the paramount question—which, if any, of the six unsolved murders did Roy believe Ferrari committed?—two other puzzles hung over the investigation. Why had the killer so readily conceded guilt in four of the cases, but no others? And why did he apparently prey on both boys and girls?

The police believed the answer to the first mystery was that Ferrari did not want to be known as Europe's worst-ever child killer. The most victims attributed to a single killer in Europe at the time was six. Ferrari directly told his questioners that he was not as bad as other child killers, and even held out a hope he could be cured.

Hazelwood came at this question from another perspective. He suggested that a sense of hopelessness led Ferrari to confess some of the cases. At the time of his arrest, Hazelwood pointed out, Ferrari knew he'd been positively identified, and was in serious legal jeopardy because of his previous conviction for killing a child. His personal prospects were grim, and he was aging.

"Forced sexual assault and murder is basically a young man's crime," says Hazelwood. "While nonviolent child molesters (those who rely on obtaining the voluntary compliance of their victims) may continue to operate well beyond Ferrari's age, the use of force requires a high degree of physical and emotional stamina."

Werner Ferrari may have had the stable and comparatively attractive life of an inmate in mind.

"Ferrari," Roy wrote in his report to commander Borer, "may rationally have decided that all of his problems could be resolved by confessing to a sufficient number of crimes [to] guarantee his being taken care of for life."

On the issue of victim selection, Hazelwood turned to Ken Lanning's research.

Lanning has found that pedophiles of Ferrari's type who prey on prepubescent children frequently have no gender preference. Those who prey on older children often focus on boys or girls, but not both.

The offender of Ferrari's type also often

1. was sexually abused as a child (in Ferrari's case, any sexual abuse probably occurred while he was institutionalized);
2. had limited social contacts as a teen, and little sexual interest in his age-mates;
3. makes frequent and sudden moves, often because his sexual orientation has been discovered and the offender is "run out of town";
4. has been arrested before for sexual offenses against children;
5. has multiple victims;
6. has made bold (high risk to himself) and repeated attempts to secure victims;
7. is skilled at identifying vulnerable children;
8. relates well to children on many levels;

9. easily manipulates children;
10. often dates women in order to gain access to their children;
11. frequents places and events (playgrounds, fairs) where children congregate; and
12. maintains a supply of toys and other objects of interest to children as bait.

Werner Ferrari met at least seven of the listed criteria, but because so much was known about Ferrari and his crimes, Hazelwood believed an even closer categorization was possible. Ferrari, he thought, was a member of Lanning's subtype "introverted preferential child molester," and cited four reasons for his thinking.

First, Roy wrote, the introverted molester has a preference for children, but lacks the special skills to seduce them. He therefore may resort to violence, as Ferrari apparently did on occasion.

Second, the introverted offender usually molests strangers, or victims too young to identify him.

Third, his sexual interest in children is rooted in deep-seated insecurity, as well as curiosity.

Fourth, he often cannot express anger and hostility in normal social intercourse, so he acts out against nonthreatening children.

Ferrari either lived near where the six officially unsolved cases occurred, or knew the areas from past experience. All victims whose remains were recovered were found in woods or fields. All victims were between the ages of seven and ten, and all were slightly built. Again, all but one, Imhof, was alone at the time of abduction, which occurred in all but one case (Rebecca Bieri's) in the late afternoon or evening.

Ferrari also made some sort of important life change, from relocating his residence to breaking up with a girlfriend, within two months of each child murder.

Hazelwood declined to speculate whether Ferrari killed any of the three children whose bodies were never found: Peter Roth, Sarah Oberson, and Edith Trittenbass. He lacked sufficient evidence to make the necessary linkage analysis comparisons.

Ruth Steinmann, he thinks, "very probably" was killed by Werner, an inference drawn from the extraordinary number of similarities between her death and those of the children Ferrari confessed he had murdered.

These range from MO similarities—such as abduction sites, the fact that all victims except Fabienne Imhof were alone when he accosted them, and the use of the woods as disposal sites—to shared factors that plainly spoke to Ferrari's psychosexual needs.

The children were all slightly built and prepubescent (save for Steinmann, who had slight breast development), and showed no defensive wounds or antemortem bondage. Plus there was no semen recovered from any of the bodies or clothing, nor was there any evidence of penile penetration.

To the contrary, Ferrari told police that when he was angered he placed sticks in his victims' orifices. The evidence that Ruth Steinmann was violated in that way suggests perhaps that he'd been upset by her, too, possibly because she was not completely immature sexually. Steinmann also suffered the only known bite mark, on her breast.

As for Rebecca Bieri and Loredana Mancini, both discovered as skeletons, Roy would not render a definitive opinion, except to say the cases' similarities to those of Ferrari's known victims were "interesting."

In June 1995, Werner Ferrari was sentenced to life in prison by a criminal court in Baden.

EIGHTEEN

"He Wanted to Be
My Boyfriend"

R oy's testimony as an expert in linkage analysis is especially effective
in sexual crime cases where eyewitnesses are absent, such as the
Ray Ward prosecution, or if the witnesses are less than absolutely certain, as
was the case of Kenneth Bogard, the Pacific Beach Rapist.

Molly Iverson* was his first known victim.

She lived alone in a first-floor apartment in Pacific Beach, an oceanside
family tourist destination with a large singles population, about five miles north
of downtown San Diego.

At about 11:15 on Thursday night, August 13, 1992, Iverson was awakened
from her sleep by a noise. Then she saw him, an intruder dressed only in red
Converse high tops and a ski mask.

He had entered her bedroom via the open patio door. In the dark, he appeared to be a white male in his late twenties. He held a hunting knife in one
hand. The other covered his penis.

When Iverson jumped up and began to scream, he pushed her down on
the bed and told her to be quiet. "I'm not going to hurt you," he said, pulling
her hair back.

"Who are you?" she asked.

He said his name was Johnny, and reassured her, "I'm not going to go inside you," as he instructed Iverson to remove her camisole and shorts.

"Johnny" then told the thirty-one-year-old divorcée to roll over on her stomach. He sat on her legs, stroking her back, and talked to her.

"You have a nice ass," he said, placing his hands between her legs.

Iverson resisted, pushing herself up, "Don't do it! Don't do it!" she said.

"Okay, okay, okay," he answered, and began to masturbate. In a few moments, Iverson felt his ejaculate on *HER* back.

He tried to clean himself.

"Don't wipe that shit on my blanket!" she snapped.

"Okay," he answered, and rose to leave.

"Remember to lock that door, okay?" he said on his way out.

Iverson, incensed at the assault, reported it to the police, and then began the slow process of reclaiming her life. But barely had she begun to put the incident behind her when her world again was shattered by an intruder.

The next month, at 12:30 A.M. on Friday the eighteenth, Iverson was standing in her living room when a man she believed was "Johnny" walked through her unlocked door. This time he was wearing shorts along with the red high tops and ski mask. He had a knife, too, and a bottle of massaging oil.

"I came to treat you," he said, tiptoeing toward her as he gestured with the bottle.

Iverson, surprised and furious, yelled obscenities at him until he retreated out the patio door and disappeared.

The following May, at 10:50 P.M. on Monday the tenth, Dana Holly,[*] twenty-six, also of Pacific Beach, was awakened in her bedroom, much as Molly Iverson had been. Only this time Holly noticed he was wearing a ski mask and nothing else.

She screamed. He jumped onto the bed and put his knife to her throat.

"I wouldn't," he said.

Holly went silent.

She removed her clothes as he instructed her. She asked if he had a condom.

The intruder said he did not. Did she?

No.

He said he had not had sex in six months and had been tested and was "clean."

Holly asked to go to the bathroom. He accompanied her, holding a handful of her hair. When she could not urinate, he turned on the faucet for her. Still no help.

Back in her bed, he kissed her neck and chest, working his way down to her vagina, where he performed extended cunnilingus. He said he hoped she could reach orgasm, and only stopped when she faked one.

He then tried to kiss her. When she resisted, he briefly inserted two fingers into her vagina before ordering Holly onto her stomach.

She, too, was complimented on her "nice ass."

He perched behind her as he had with Iverson, and applied some Vaseline to her back before masturbating onto it. When he finished, she directed him to a box of tissues, with which he wiped off her back.

Before leaving, he asked her to get dressed again, and covered Holly with her blanket.

"He was very calm, almost trying to be nice," she later testified.

"Good night, Darla," he said as he left, getting her name wrong. He also warned her to keep her front door locked.

Six days later, at 2:50 A.M. on a Sunday morning, Pacific Beach resident Tammy Watkins,* twenty-three, was surprised by a man in a black mask who jumped out at her from a closet as Watkins walked into her bedroom.

She screamed.

"Stop screaming or I'll hurt you," he said, holding a knife to her throat. Watkins didn't answer, and began to cry.

"I'm not going to hurt you if you do as I say," he continued, and directed her to her bed.

"Okay, now sit here like a good little girl. Don't move. I'm going to the door," he told her in a voice Watkins described in court as "sort of soft and husky . . . gentle and nice."

He didn't touch Tammy. He just left, and did not return.

Approximately eighteen hours later, just after 9:00 that Sunday night, twenty-year-old Marsha Wilson* was alone in the Pacific Beach house she rented with four other young women. She heard a knock at the door. When Wilson answered it, an arm suddenly went around her neck. She felt a knife under her chin. He pushed her to her knees and told her not to scream or she would get hurt.

As before, he guided Wilson to a bed and told her to take her clothes off. He lay down beside her, still wearing his ski mask.

Later in court, Wilson was asked if the intruder said anything.

"Like, 'relax,' you know," she said. "Just basically trying to calm me down in a really nice kind of a sort of comforting tone."

When she asked him his age he said he was twenty-four.

He fondled her and performed cunnilingus. Then as he masturbated to erection, she asked him not to sodomize her, and if he had a condom.

He answered that he did not want to hurt her, and yes, he did have a condom, which he put on before subjecting her to a very brief vaginal rape.

Afterward, he told Wilson he'd never raped anyone before and that he didn't enjoy it and wasn't going to do it again. He added that she need not worry about him returning to harm her, either. He wouldn't be coming back.

He did wait two months before striking again, this time choosing a different venue, the San Diego State University district, about five miles inland from Pacific Beach.

Victim number five was nineteen-year-old Tina Mitchell,* who awoke at 2:45 A.M. on Friday, July 16, 1993, to find the rapist's hand over her mouth. He had come through the front door and into her bedroom, ignoring a second bedroom, where her roommate slept with her boyfriend. Neither awoke during the incident.

The ski-masked intruder told Mitchell that if she did not scream she would not be hurt, and to nod if she understood him.

She nodded, and he removed his hand.

When he ordered her to undress, she protested.

He shoved her, not violently.

"He told me just follow along and I'd be okay," Mitchell testified.

She took off her nightgown and underwear and let down her hair, as instructed. He complimented Mitchell on her figure, and mentioned that she looked tense. He told her to lie on her stomach so he could give her a back rub.

He was polite and solicitous about her well-being throughout, Mitchell said.

After about five minutes of cunnilingus, he tried to kiss her, but was rebuffed. He put two fingers into her vagina, as he had with Dana Holly. But instead of simply masturbating, he stroked himself to erection, put on a condom as Mitchell requested, and vaginally raped her. The assault lasted less than three minutes.

Afterward, he pulled the covers up around her, and wished her good night as he left.

He returned to Pacific Beach for his next assault. Unlike the other victims, Kim Caldwell, thirty-two, an airline sales agent, did not care if her identity was known. In fact, she insisted on it, going to the *San Diego Union-Tribune* with the story of her physical and emotional ordeal.

"A primary reason rapists continue to rape—not why they rape, but why

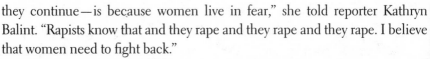

they continue—is because women live in fear," she told reporter Kathryn Balint. "Rapists know that and they rape and they rape and they rape. I believe that women need to fight back."

Later in court, Caldwell would describe how she was awakened in bed at 3:00 A.M. on Tuesday, August 17, 1993, by a man in a ski mask on top of her. He had a knife at her throat, and was saying, "Kim, wake up!"

She fought, furiously.

"Calm down, calm down, calm down," he kept saying to her. Then he began massaging her shoulders with one hand as he continued holding the knife at her throat with the other.

He told Caldwell, as he had told Molly Iverson a year earlier, that his name was Johnny. Iverson had thought him to be in his late twenties; Caldwell guessed he was thirty to thirty-five.

"Johnny" told Caldwell he had been watching her for a long time.

"He said he had watched me when I came home at nights," she testified. "He watched me when I usually got something to eat in the kitchen . . . and he watched me in the living room watching television. And he said that his favorite time to watch me was in the bedroom when I was reading. He said he did that a lot."

Her attacker told Caldwell to remove her one garment, a T-shirt, pushed her down on the bed, and began kissing her neck and breasts and performing cunnilingus. He kept telling her to relax and, over and over, that she *had* to achieve an orgasm.

He strove ardently to kiss her lips, but she clenched her teeth in refusal.

When he reached to put his fingers in her vagina, she grabbed for the knife he laid aside. He noticed her movement, and took the knife back from her. Then he placed the blade between her legs, but he did not touch her with the weapon or threaten her with it.

Finally, he pulled a condom out of a fanny pack, and put it on, only to lose his erection. "Johnny" went back to fondling and kissing her until he was hard once again, and then quickly raped Caldwell vaginally. Once finished, he removed the condom, tied a knot in it, and placed it in a Baggie back in the fanny pack.

Caldwell was shaking with fear and anger. The rapist tucked her blankets around her and then sat down on the bed to ask if she wanted him to leave.

"It was like he was trying to be nice," she'd remember. "It was like it was a date almost . . . he was apologizing the whole time."

On the way out, he called her Kim.

He found his final victim, twenty-three-year-old Jane Phillips,* back in the vicinity of San Diego State.

She was awakened at about 1:00 A.M. on Friday, October 29, 1993, by the rapist standing over her. Instead of the ski mask, he was wearing what Phillips later described as a ski cap and a Lone Ranger mask. He put his hand over her mouth and pushed her head down into her pillow.

"Don't move. Don't talk. I don't want to have to hurt you," he said.

He seemed aware that Jane shared her apartment with a roommate who was sleeping nearby.

"I'll take my hand away if you promise not to scream," he said. "We have to be quiet. We don't want to wake our roommate up."

She started crying, and jumped at the sight of his knife, which nicked her in the chin. He seemed more scared than she, Phillips later testified.

"It's okay, it's okay, you're not bleeding, see," he told her. "You have to listen to what I say and do what I say or else you're going to get hurt, because it's a very sharp knife."

He helped her sit up and remove her sweatshirt.

"He told me 'we are going to have sex,'" she testified. "Then he said the first thing he wanted to do [was] 'taste you and smell you' and he said he wanted to make me come. He wanted me to have an orgasm, and then he started to perform oral sex."

Disappointed anew that his victim did not respond as he had hoped, the rapist put on his condom and entered her vaginally. She wouldn't look at him, which further upset him.

"He would take my hands and put them on his shoulders, and then my hands would fall away. Or he'd take my legs, lift them up for deeper penetration. And my legs would fall away. He [was] continually getting soft so he would have to pull out, masturbate, harden himself up and proceed."

Phillips recollected her rapist lost his erection five or six times before he was through. Then, as before, he tucked her in and sat down to talk.

He asked how she felt and if she would now be angry at all men or just him.

"I know you didn't enjoy yourself," he said. "But I thought it could be different with you."

"It was almost like he was my boyfriend," Phillips reported. "He wanted to be my boyfriend. He was almost loving in a way."

He left by her open sliding glass door.

Next morning, Phillips discovered the spent condom where he'd discarded it, near the front of her parked car.

It would prove a vital piece of evidence.

Kenneth Bogard—"Bogey" to his friends—was well known around San Diego as a singer and lead guitarist for Dr. Chico's Island Sounds, a popular local rock group. His neighbors in the city's Hillcrest neighborhood described him as likable and outgoing.

A woman identifying herself only as Janis, who lived in the same apartment building with the thirty-six-year-old Bogard, told the *San Diego Union-Tribune*, "I've seen him lots of times in the Jacuzzi with a girlfriend, a girl with blond hair. He's very handsome, a good-looking guy. He looks like a cross between Barry Manilow and Rod Stewart."

But Bogey Bogard had a hidden personal history.

In 1980, at age twenty-three, he was convicted in his home state, New Jersey, of masturbating in public as he fondled an article of infant's clothing. Nine years later, he was charged again in California with public masturbation, but pleaded guilty to a lesser charge.

In the summer of 1993, he was caught with a video camera in the Wet Seal, a women's chain clothing store located about three miles north of Pacific Beach. Bogard had slung the camera low from his shoulder, and turned it on in an attempt to videotape under women's dresses as they shopped.

"When the police looked at the tape," says Dan Lamborn, the San Diego County deputy district attorney who would eventually prosecute Bogard as the Pacific Beach Rapist, "they found other footage of him peeking into women's apartments through blinds. He had shots of a woman undressing, another woman having sex, and another of a woman sunbathing, focusing in tight on her crotch."

In 1992, Bogard also was caught masturbating outside a coed's apartment in the San Diego State area. The same neighborhood had been plagued previously by a flasher nicknamed Zorro, for the mask he habitually wore.

On a second occasion, police responding to a report of a masked man masturbating discovered Bogard in the vicinity with Vaseline on his hand. They later recovered a Zorro mask nearby.

"They detained him, but didn't file a case because they didn't actually see him masturbating," says Lamborn.

The two incidents persuaded the police they should take a closer look at Bogard. In December, they obtained a court order to take tissue samples, which proved a match for the semen in the condom discarded near the front of Jane Phillips's car in October, as well as other specimens recovered from the various Pacific Beach Rapist crimes scenes.

Bogard was arrested in January 1994.

In all, Lamborn had DNA evidence that directly implicated Bogard in only one of the assaults. Bogard vehemently denied all guilt. And after viewing Bogard in a lineup, only one of his victims, Dana Holly, was able to identify him as her attacker, and then only indirectly, by his voice.

There were no eyewitnesses to any of the assaults. What is more, there was no fingerprint evidence.

It was going to be an uphill prosecution, but for two key factors. One, the judge let in Bogard's videotape, which the deputy district attorney was pleased to show the jury.

"The videotape clearly shows he was a pervert, and that of course was fifty percent of the battle in front of a jury," says Lamborn.

Lamborn's other weapon was Roy Hazelwood.

Lacking any solid eyewitness identifications, the prosecutor needed to tie the crimes together in a way the jury could follow. So as he prepared for trial, Lamborn contacted Hazelwood, who had just retired, and hired Roy to conduct a linkage analysis.

Bogard's trial was held in May 1995, in San Diego's seven-story county courthouse, a plain and architecturally undistinguished box erected downtown in the 1960s.

Inside superior court judge John Thompson's windowless, fluorescent-lit third-floor courtroom, Hazelwood took the stand, turned to the jury, and began to testify. Dan Lamborn remembers he had little to do except to occasionally interject a question or ask for amplification.

"Roy," says Lamborn, "was the star of the show."

Hazelwood explained to the jury his rapist typology, the motivational roles of power and anger in rape, the difference between MO and ritual, and how, if enough behavioral evidence is available for him to study, he can say with expert assurance whether a single criminal or multiple offenders committed a given set of deviant crimes, such as serial rape.

Among the Pacific Beach Rapist cases he reviewed, Roy said, he believed the same man assaulted Iverson, Holly, Wilson, Mitchell, Caldwell, and Phillips. He said there was not enough behavioral evidence to confidently link that offender to Tammy Watkins or to say with certainty that Molly Iverson's second intruder was also her assailant.

"I noticed that all of the attacks were in the victims' residences," said Hazelwood. "And I noticed that each of the entries were made through an unlocked window or door.

"I noticed the offender was armed with a knife, a weapon of choice, and he brought it with him. He took the weapon with him when he left.

"He attempted to protect his identity by wearing a mask in each of the crimes. He took nothing at all with him.

"The two neighborhoods were very similar as to the age of their residents and the local socioeconomics, and they were within five or six miles of each other."

Hazelwood noted all the crime occurred late at night, and that the UNSUB endeavored in most of them to deny the police scientific evidence. Either he wiped himself when he was through or he used condoms.

"I then considered the ritualistic similarities," Roy continued. "I looked for the theme running through these assaults.

"First, all the victims were white females from age eighteen to thirty-two, with an average age of twenty-five. He used the surprise approach in every instance, and there was no injurious force. He preselected the victims either through peeping in their windows or through surveillance.

"The method used for control was strikingly similar, too. He had a knife, but he primarily controlled his victims verbally.

"Then I looked at his reaction to resistance. Each of the victims did in fact resist. Two of them, I believe, screamed. Two of them jumped out of bed. According to their descriptions, even though he had a knife, he did not respond with violence."

Roy next examined the UNSUB's sexual behavior, pointing out the rapist's insistence that the victims remove their own clothing, as well as the persistent fondling, kissing, rubbing, and cunnilingus he performed.

He was a power reassurance rapist, no doubt.

"The theme running through the sexual behavior was attempts to bring his fantasy of a consenting relationship to reality," said Hazelwood.

Moving on to the UNSUB's verbal behavior, "the theme was nonviolence," Roy said. He added that the rapist tried in every case to reassure the woman she would not be hurt.

"Ms. Holly said, 'He was very calm, almost trying to be nice.' Ms. Wilson said, 'He had a really nice kind of a sort of comforting tone.' Ms. Phillips said, 'He was almost loving in a way.'"

If Roy missed anything, the jurors apparently didn't notice.

"His testimony was very useful," says Lamborn. "In some of the cases we had the DNA evidence, but on one or two of them all we had was MO. Hazelwood could combine them all as a series.

"He had a nice, gentle approach to the jury that doesn't try to overstate his testimony. He's down to earth. When you listen to him you say, 'That makes a lot of sense.' And if it makes a lot of sense to a jury, they'll retain it when they deliberate."

Kenneth Bogard was found guilty on all counts, and then stood up in court to confess his guilt, calling himself a sex addict. He said he'd found God in jail while awaiting trial.

Kim Caldwell was having none of it.

"It's over for you," she said in the wood-paneled court. "This is your funeral. You're dirty and perverted because you don't accept or take responsibility for what has been determined to be your guilt. This is not your celebration today. This is my celebration."

Judge John Thompson sentenced Bogard to ninety-six years in prison. He must serve half that time before being considered for parole.

NINETEEN

Pseudovictims

I t was a vulgar spectacle played out among the tired old river towns of the lower Hudson Valley, a notorious, cynical, race-baiting hoax sparked by a troubled teen's false—and confused—accusations of kidnap and rape.

Under a pale autumn sun early on November 24, 1987—the Tuesday before Thanksgiving—fifteen-year-old Tawana Brawley of Wappinger Falls, New York, left her home, ostensibly headed for school. Instead, Brawley took a bus thirty miles west across the Hudson to see a former boyfriend, Todd Buxton, then resident in the Orange County Jail in the city of Goshen, New York.

After visiting the young man, she boarded an eastbound bus in the company of Buxton's mother, Geneva, and rode twenty miles to Newburgh, where Geneva Buxton lived.

The next bus back across the Hudson from Newburgh to Wappinger Falls departed at six, but Tawana Brawley was reluctant to board it.

She told Mrs. Buxton she was having trouble at home with Ralph King, her mother's companion. He'd recently grounded her, she said, for staying out until five in the morning.

King kept going "on and on" about it, and "wouldn't let go" of the matter, Brawley complained.

This was not an isolated incident in the King-Brawley household.

Glenda Brawley, thirty-one, had on numerous occasions disciplined her daughter for running away or spending the night with boys. "And there were numerous reports of fights specifically between Mr. King and Miss Brawley," *The New York Times* later reported. "When [Tawana] was arrested on shoplifting charges the previous May, the police had to intervene to prevent Mr. King from beating her at the police station."

Ralph King's personal history of violence predated his acquaintance with Glenda Brawley. In 1969, King was accused of stabbing his then-wife multiple times. While awaiting trial for the assault, King shot her to death. He spent seven years in prison for the crimes.

The grand jury impaneled to take testimony in the Brawley case would hear abundant testimony of what the *Times* called "strains" between Tawana and King.

"One witness said Mr. King 'would watch her exercise' and talked about the girl 'in a real sexual way,' sometimes describing her as 'a fine fox,'" the paper reported. "Another witness said Miss Brawley referred to Mr. King as 'a filthy pervert.'"

At about 8:00 P.M. on the twenty-fourth, Tawana Brawley finally did board a bus in Newburgh. She asked the driver, with whom she was acquainted, to drop her in Wappinger Falls. He explained that the town was not on his route at that hour. The best he could do was nearby Wappinger.

As it happened, Tawana was familiar with Wappinger. Her family had lived in the former mill town until earlier that month, when they were evicted from their town house at the Pavilion Condominiums, 19A Carnaby Street. Tawana still had a key to the vacated unit.

The truth of what else happened to Tawana Brawley on the night of the twenty-fourth may never be publicly known. She declined to appear before the grand jury, which was left to piece together a summary of her account from what she told authorities over the course of three brief interviews.

According to the summary, the last reliable report of Brawley's whereabouts on the night of the twenty-fourth was as she stepped down from the bus in front of a Mobil station in Wappinger.

Then, according to the grand jury's summary of the teenager's version of events, "a dark, four-door car with two men inside approached, and a white man wearing a black jacket with a silver badge hit her, pulled her by the hair into the back seat and got into the back seat himself.

"Ms. Brawley was lying down on the seat and did not see what the driver looked like. She recalled being at a place where there were three men dressed in dark clothes, but did not know where she was, although she thought she was in the woods. She was struck again on the head by the man who had previously hit her. One of the men was tall with blond hair and a mustache. He was also wearing a shoulder holster. She recalled feeling cold. The men urinated on her and in her mouth. Ms. Brawley had no recollection of what happened after that, nor of what happened to her on Wednesday, Thursday, Friday, or Saturday."

The grand jury noted it was never clear from Tawana Brawley's few contacts with authorities, or from comments attributed to her by relatives and other witnesses, exactly what sort of sexual assaults she claimed to have suffered. At various times she seemed both to allege and to deny that she had been vaginally raped and forced to fellate her assailants. She never could locate for police the woods where the alleged assaults took place.

There was considerable physical evidence that connected Tawana Brawley to the interior of her family's deserted condominium for the period November 25–28, the days for which she claimed no memory. The heat had been turned on in the apartment. The denim jacket she was wearing November 24 was discovered in the apartment washing machine. Fibers indistinguishable from those of the apartment carpet were found on her person. An insulating material called Hollofil, recovered from combings of her pubic hair, matched the Hollofil found in a pair of white boots inside the apartment.

Moreover, between November 26 and November 28, neighbors reported they periodically saw a young woman answering Tawana Brawley's description in and around the Pavilion complex.

Brawley's family apparently began searching for her on the night of the twenty-fourth, although she was not officially reported missing for another four days. Sometime that evening, a black female identifying herself as Brawley's aunt appeared at the Newburgh Police Department to report her niece had run away. She said Tawana was believed to be in Newburgh. On the twenty-seventh, Friday, another member of the family personally accused Todd Buxton's sister of kidnapping Tawana.

At approximately 2:00 P.M. on Saturday the twenty-eighth, after visiting the Pavilion apartments on what she said was an errand to pick up the family mail, Glenda Brawley drove to the Wappinger Falls Police Department to file a missing person report on her daughter.

Asked by a desk officer why she waited four days, Glenda Brawley said that she worked nights, and did not have a car.

According to the grand jury report, about the same time Glenda Brawley was seen at the Pavilion complex that Saturday, an unnamed resident looked out her sliding glass door "and observed Tawana Brawley in a squatting position . . . a few feet from her family's former apartment at 19A. There was no one else in the area.

"According to this witness, Miss Brawley, after looking around for a couple seconds, stepped into a large plastic garbage bag and pulled it up to her neck. She remained stationary for another couple of seconds and continued to look around. She then hopped two times and lay down on the swampy ground beneath an air conditioner. . . . When she did not move, the neighbor called the sheriff."

The *Times* reported that Eric Thurston, the responding Dutchess County sheriff's deputy, found Brawley "smeared with feces and seemingly dazed; her jeans were scorched and torn, and racial slurs, including 'Nigger' and 'KKK' had been written on her body."

Forensic tests would trace the excrement to a neighborhood collie named Remi, who was also the source of the feces discovered within a pair of denim pants found inside apartment 19A. Small wads of Hollofil were found in Brawley's nose and ears, an apparent attempt to protect the orifices from the dog droppings.

At about the time Glenda Brawley was reporting her missing, Tawana Brawley was being taken by ambulance to a local hospital. There, emergency-room personnel found "KKK," "Nigg," "ETE SHI," "NIGGER," and "BITCH" written on her chest and torso with a black substance resembling charcoal. Traces of it were detected under Brawley's fingernails.

Her hair was matted and jagged, as if someone had randomly sheared off clumps of it.

The only evidence of physical injury that physicians discovered, however, was an old quarter-size bruise behind the teen's left ear, plus some swelling in Brawley's left arm, where an IV had been inserted by ambulance paramedics on her way to the hospital.

No sticks or leaves or dirt or other detritus consistent with Tawana Brawley having spent a considerable time being sexually assaulted in the woods were discovered about her, in her, or on her clothing, either.

A rape kit examination disclosed no evidence of sexual assault or sexual intercourse. Brawley was discharged from the hospital at about 10:00 P.M. that Saturday night.

False accusers are a small fraction of the hundreds of thousands of women who report stranger rapes each year, somewhere between 4 and 7 percent of the total, according to Hazelwood, who has studied the behavior of hundreds of what he calls pseudovictims.

Roy frequently consults in rape and assault cases where a false accusation is suspected, so it was no surprise that immediately after the Brawley case broke, Hazelwood received a telephone call from J. J. Thompson, a Dutchess County investigator.

Thompson wanted Roy's opinion of Tawana Brawley's truthfulness. Hazelwood in turn routinely asked for FBI clearance to offer his help. But the Bureau, concerned with the incendiary nature of the case, told Hazelwood not to have any official involvement in the investigation.

So Roy assisted unofficially. He reviewed the case for Thompson, and then served as an informal consultant to the ensuing official investigation.

Although the evidence would show there was no substantive reason to believe Brawley's allegations—which under normal circumstances should have quickly faded away—reasonableness soon was the scarcest commodity in Dutchess County, where the investigation took place.

Two lawyers, Alton H. Maddox, Jr., and C. Vernon Mason, together with the Reverend Al Sharpton, an activist preacher from Brooklyn, appeared together on the scene as Tawana Brawley's "advisers." This "trickster trio," as reporter Steve Dunleavy described them in the New York Post, proceeded to promote an epic hoax based on a single, bogus allegation of conspiracy.

A short while after Brawley reported her story, a part-time white local police officer named Harry Crist, Jr., committed suicide, apparently as a consequence of career and personal problems.

Because of Brawley's accusations, Crist's movements at the time of her alleged abduction were of understandable interest to investigators. However, Steven A. Pagones, a Dutchess County assistant district attorney, came forth to say that he and Crist were friends, and that they had been together with a third white male, a state trooper named Scott Patterson, at the time of the alleged assault on Tawana Brawley.

Although no evidence connecting Crist, Pagones, or Patterson with Brawley has ever surfaced, her three black advisers seized on Pagones's information as evidence of a cover-up.

"Mr. Pagones and his organized crime cronies are suspects," Sharpton said on Geraldo Rivera's television program. Sharpton repeated the accusation in several other venues.

"He was one of the attackers, yes," Alton Maddox, Jr., said in a televised press conference, adding, "If I didn't have direct evidence, I wouldn't be sitting here saying that."

One theory that Brawley's three advisers floated had Pagones and Patterson actually killing Crist, staging the crime as a suicide.

Pagones finally filed a $395 million defamation suit against the three advisers and Tawana Brawley in 1988.

As the contrived controversy gained momentum, and national attention, New York governor Mario Cuomo named Bob Abrams, the state attorney general, as a special prosecutor.

Sharpton responded by comparing Cuomo and Abrams to Klan members. At one event, Maddox swore indignantly, "Robert Abrams, you are no longer going to masturbate looking at Tawana Brawley's picture!"

Public opinion polls indicated that most New Yorkers, white and black, disbelieved Brawley's account. Nevertheless, the comedian Bill Cosby put up a twenty-five-thousand-dollar reward for information. Boxer Mike Tyson gave Brawley his Rolex, and talk-show host Phil Donahue took his show to Dutchess County, where he broadcast live from a rally of Brawley supporters.

To a degree, Sharpton, Mason, and Maddox succeeded in making the truth of the case irrelevant. They promulgated a "could have been" theory that had resonance for many blacks distrustful of white authority.

Lateef Islam, a local activist who marched frequently in support of Brawley, told *Washington Post* reporter Dale Russakoff that at the time of the hoax he refused to dwell on the issues of truth.

"I was working on the fact that it could have happened," Islam explained, a position Islam shared with many of Brawley's supporters. "I've known incidents like that that happened, and I was angry at people who said it couldn't have happened."

Such crimes of course do occur. But there were two major reasons to conclude that this purported incident could not have happened in the way Tawana Brawley claimed. One, there wasn't a scintilla of corroborative physical evidence, when there should have been a great deal of it. To the contrary, the physical evidence all pointed away from Brawley's version of events. Secondly, as Roy would explain in his informal consultations with the task force, it was clear from the behavioral evidence that Tawana Brawley's allegations were unsupported.

There are several routinely observed factors in false accusations of rape— although none should be taken as absolute proof that a self-described victim is lying. Many occur in truthfully reported cases as well.

Pseudovictims range in age from young girls to mature men and women, and come from all socioeconomic backgrounds.

In Roy's experience, the motivation for falsely reporting a stranger rape often is a desperate need for attention. Many pseudovictims also are highly self-destructive, and in the past have tried less dramatic means of gaining attention, most commonly feigning illness.

When a police department questions a victim's allegations, as in the Brawley case, Roy advises them to check for recent stresses in his or her life, emotionally upsetting incidents such as Tawana Brawley's clashes with her family.

Pseudovictims sometimes have a history of making similar accusations, and that history may be a long one, too. In the most extreme case Roy knows of, a woman made two identical false rape allegations twenty-seven years apart.

False allegations of rape also may follow similar incidents of which the pseudovictim is personally aware, or learns about in media reports, or sees portrayed in the movies, on television, or in popular fiction.

In one example of this copycatting, a woman walked into a police station to report she had been stopped on the highway at 1:00 A.M. by a black police officer, who raped her at gunpoint. She described him as six two, with a black patch over his left eye. He was missing three fingers from his gun hand, too, she said.

The city police suspected an impersonation rape, and issued a composite sketch, along with a warning, to the public.

A week later, the woman admitted she'd made up the whole thing.

Two weeks after that, two women came forward to say that they, too, had been driving on the beltway and had been stopped and raped at gunpoint by the same assailant.

Informed that the previously publicized allegations were false, the women turned and wordlessly departed the police station.

A short while before Tawana Brawley made her accusations, a former classmate, also a black girl, reported that two white men had abducted and raped her. She recanted the story.

Geneva Buxton later told the grand jury that on the afternoon of November 24, after visiting her jailed son she and Tawana Brawley were passed on a Goshen street by two white men in a vehicle. She said the pickup slowed and made a U-turn, then drove by again, slowly, as the occupants looked "real hard" at Brawley.

In the weeks following her accusations, three more black females, one in New Jersey and two in New York, also falsely reported they'd been sexually assaulted and smeared with feces by groups of white males.

In an illustrative case, an imaginative sixteen-year-old girl told police she'd been attacked and raped in a service station rest room on a day that she skipped school.

According to her story, the girl consumed a half bottle of vodka, and had stopped to use the rest room when a razor-wielding assailant followed her inside.

They struggled. She suffered three superficial scratches on her neck, as well as single cuts, ostensible defensive injuries, lengthwise on both her palms.

She said that after raping her, the man carved "Don't forget" into her lower abdomen, bracketing the words with acute diagonals similar to the > "greater than" and < "less than" symbols on a computer keyboard.

The teenager later admitted fabricating the story.

While pseudovictims tend to avoid injuring sensitive areas of their anatomy, one woman in Roy's casebook required surgery for removal of a tree branch she'd inserted into her vagina.

Typically, the pseudovictim's report will be either extremely vague or lavishly detailed. Roy once served as a consultant to authorities in a British serial rape case where the suspect was alleged to have assaulted seventeen victims. Hazelwood reviewed the statements from all seventeen women, noting that each, except for one, was able to tell her story in three to five pages of text. The exception's account ran to twenty-seven pages. She finally came to the alleged rape itself in the middle of page 26.

Hazelwood told prosecutors that he found this victim's story suspicious. The next day, the defendant in the case abruptly confessed to sixteen of the rapes, but adamantly insisted he knew nothing of the elaborately narrated story that Roy questioned.

A pseudovictim will stress his or her powerlessness to repulse the attack as a face-saving factor, and the rape will be described as both violent and degrading.

As the investigation continues, the pseudovictim may evince scant interest in actually identifying his or her attacker. Tawana Brawley did not speak to investigators after November 30.

Pseudovictims also may exhibit features of borderline personality disorder, the mental warp portrayed with icy brilliance by actress Glenn Close as the depraved Alex Forrest in the movie *Fatal Attraction*.

Like Forrest, they can be impulsive, moody, histrionic, reckless, and highly unstable in their relationships.

Their romantic attachments especially can be obsessive, and a not uncommon object is the detective assigned to their case.

Roy's advice to the incautious rape investigator contemplating such an affair is simple: Don't do it. "Remember the rabbit in the pot," he says.

Both the most interesting and unique false allegation he's ever encountered was made by a twenty-seven-year-old woman, mother of an eight-year-old child.

She was found lying on the ground, comatose and close to death, with her throat slashed. Examination with a rape kit revealed pubic hairs of unknown origin around her vaginal area, and seminal fluid in her vaginal tract. Only a medical "miracle" at the hospital saved her life.

The whole scene had been staged.

She was a drug addict who supported her habit by working as a prostitute. Despairing of her existence — but unwilling to have her child grow up knowing that Mom killed herself — she faked what looked like an assault and rape.

The pubic hairs, for example, were taken from one customer. From another, she obtained the semen specimen found in her vagina. She chemically induced unconsciousness, and slit her own throat with a razor blade, which she managed to dispose of before slumping to the spot where she collapsed, was discovered, and then rescued.

Because he played no official role in the Brawley investigation, Roy did not testify before the grand jury. However, his colleague and research partner, Park Dietz, did.

The forensic psychiatrist testified to many of the behavioral clues that point to pseudovictimization, including offender behavior which could be inferred from the victim's report.

As the grand jury reported in its published notes, Dietz and Hazelwood and Dr. Janet Warren were then conducting research into sexual offenders who degrade their victims, as Tawana Brawley alleged that she had been degraded by her attackers.

"There are two principal reasons that offenders degrade their victims," the grand jury notes report of Dietz's testimony. "The first reason is anger. Angry rapists often punch their victims in the face, and the face is a significant target. There were no injuries at all to Ms. Brawley's face. Even the fecal smearing avoided the face.

"An angry rapist who chooses to smear feces on a woman would smear the face, and probably attempt to put the feces in her mouth. More important, however, angry rapists are not known to smear their victims with feces.

"The other motive for degradation is sexual sadism. Sexually sadistic offenders can hold their victims for periods of time and degrade and humiliate them. They will torture their victims with physical means that leave scars and often kill them.

"Most sexually sadistic offenders operate alone, according to Dr. Dietz. A significant number operate with a partner, but not in a group of three or more.

"Dr. Dietz did not see any reason that an offender would put cotton-like material into Ms. Brawley's nose and ears [but] did see reasons why Ms. Brawley might do so.

"The cut hair, if it was cut, the wearing of burned clothing and the fecal smearing can all be seen as non-permanent degradation of oneself.

"Dr. Dietz concluded that Tawana Brawley's physical appearance when she was found is consistent with self-infliction and a false allegation. It is inconsistent with known patterns of offender behavior."

The grand jury concluded in its 170-page report that Tawana Brawley had made up the whole story, and dismissed each of her "advisers'" allegations.

Hazelwood received a letter of commendation from Robert Abrams for his assistance to the investigation. As an informal member of the Brawley task force, he also received a special T-shirt designed and printed as a commemorative souvenir of the experience.

The front of the T-shirt features a sketch of the Poughkeepsie armory, where the task force was headquartered. Lettering on the back reads: "Brawley Task Force — 244 days of fact, fiction and feces."

Alton Maddox later was suspended from practicing law for five years after refusing to cooperate with a lawyers' disciplinary committee investigating his conduct during the Brawley affair.

C. Vernon Mason was disbarred for seven years by the New York State Supreme Court for price gouging his poorer clients. He entered the New York Theological Seminary as a student.

In 1991, the Reverend Al Sharpton was stabbed and superficially injured by a white man during an outdoor rally.

He has since entered politics. He has run unsuccessfully for the U.S. Senate from New York. In 1997, Sharpton placed a close second in the New York City Democratic mayoral primary.

Tawana Brawley, who never testified before the grand jury and was never charged in the case, subsequently moved to Virginia with her mother and Ralph King, and later attended Howard University. She left the university in 1992 and became a Muslim. Now Maryam Muhammad, she lives in Temple Hills, Maryland, and reportedly has worked in a Washington-area hospital.

In November 1997, Steven Pagones's $395 million defamation suit, filed nine years earlier against Brawley and her advisers, finally came to trial in Poughkeepsie.

On July 13, 1998, after eight months of protracted and acrimonious legal wrangling, a six-person jury decided that Sharpton, Mason, and Maddox indeed had defamed Pagones. Sixteen days later, they assessed Sharpton $65,000 in damages, Maddox $95,000, and Mason $185,000. Altogether, the awards roughly matched the amount of money Steven Pagones reportedly spent in waging the legal battle against his accusers.

Tawana Brawley did not testify in the trial.

TWENTY

"I Felt I Was
Rehearsing for My
Own Death"

Gray daylight spread slowly over Kingston, Ontario, as Roy Hazelwood awoke Tuesday morning, August 13, 1996.

Summer had deserted eastern Canada. A drizzle was falling. It was going to be a dreary day.

But as he glanced out his window, Hazelwood hardly noticed the rain and ragged, lowering clouds.

His thoughts instead were of the radiantly winsome inmate awaiting him in the nearby Prison for Women. Bracing himself against the emotional ordeal he knew lay ahead that day, and the next, Roy exhaled abruptly, punched up CNN on the bedside remote, and headed for the shower.

For this excursion to Kingston, just across the headwaters of the St. Lawrence Seaway from upstate New York, lodgings had been arranged by Inspector Ron Mackay, head of the Royal Canadian Mounted Police's Violent Crimes Analysis Branch.

Mackay is Roy's former pupil. In 1989 and 1990 the RCMP inspector was a police fellow at the BSU, where he learned profiling from Hazelwood.

"He's the best teacher, bar none," says Mackay. "A lot of people read a few books and think they grasp it, but don't. Roy just has this special way of making the subject understandable."

Familiar as he was with Hazelwood, Mackay was unaware of Roy's rigid rules of the road, and unwittingly booked his famous mentor into a Victorian bed-and-breakfast at Kingston.

Hazelwood was deeply skeptical. However, once established in his taste-fully appointed room with its four-poster bed—and after a steak dinner in a local restaurant with Mackay—he slept well and awakened keen for his morning interview with Karla Homolka.

She would be the eighteenth of twenty subjects in Hazelwood's survey of what he calls the "compliant victims" of sexual sadists. Rare and anomalous even in the realms of the aberrant, these women frequently are complicit in their husbands' and/or boyfriends' criminal acts, including sexual assaults, torture, and murder. That's why many of them were in prison at the time Roy interviewed them.

Yet they are victims, too, compliant also in their own horrific abuse.

"Interviewing these women has been emotionally draining," he says. "They bother me. They are so vulnerable, so childlike in many respects. They've been so easily manipulated."

The compliant victim's traits and characteristics that, in combination, make her so vulnerable to a sexual sadist include passivity, low self-esteem, and a pervasive fear of abandonment.

Some exhibit features of dependent personality disorder, characterized by an inability to think or act for themselves. They are willing to be controlled in order to please.

Hazelwood expected his interview subjects would be homely, ill-kempt, slow-normal slovens, probably dependent on one or more controlled substances.

"In other words," he says, "all the biases you can imagine."

Just the opposite was true. They tended to be intelligent (if naive), attractive, and respectable—exactly what should be expected in light of their victimizers' needs.

A sexual sadist differs from the far more common wife batterer in that his sexual partner's pain and degradation are necessary components of the sex act for him. He feels no remorse for something he enjoys. Also unlike most batterers, the sexual sadist is untreatable.

"Unless he is homosexual, the sexual sadist *hates* women," explains Hazelwood. "To him, *all* women are bitches, whores, and sluts. This means *all* women; his mother, his sister, his wife, his Sunday school teacher, Mother Teresa.

"He believes that if he pushes the right buttons, he'll find this to be true of all women. And to prove this belief, he takes a nice middle-class woman and tears her down. He tries to create a slut, thus proving his theory. Then he punishes her for being like that."

Sexual sadists are amazingly alike in their sexual requirements and the demands they make upon their victims. "It's like they all studied in the same schoolroom," says Hazelwood. "They have the same motivation, the same fantasies. And they act out in very similar ways."

They easily are the most destructive of predatory criminals, as well. The twenty-six felons in John Douglas and Bob Ressler's serial killer survey committed 127 known murders. Of the thirty sexual sadists Roy has surveyed, the twenty-two who also were killers committed at least 187 murders.

They differ from other sexual criminals in another way, too.

A criminal sexual sadist may capture his intended prey using a simple con. Typically, he will then assault and discard her, dead or alive, in a matter of hours or days.

But when he's hunting for a companion, he is deliberate, patient, and infinitely resourceful. In the first instance, he's focused on his goal. In the latter, the process matters. Although he never loses sight of his objective, to dominate and emotionally destroy the woman he selects for a companion, half the fun for him is getting there.

Roy's first interview subject in the compliant companion survey had helped her husband capture one girl, whom he killed while trying to cut her vocal cords, and then another victim, who was kept for several years as a sex slave.

For a large part of that time, the girl was kept in a box in the couple's basement. Later, she slept at night in a coffinlike wooden container beneath their water bed.

Another young wife was enlisted by her husband to lure his selected victims from shopping malls and country fairs to his vehicle.

Roy consulted in one case where a sadistic killer kept several women in his thrall at once. James Ray Slaughter of Oklahoma City—married with three children—maintained extramarital liaisons with four other women, three nurses and a psychiatrist.

All became pregnant by Slaughter, and all but one acceded to his demand that their fetuses be aborted. Slaughter insisted that only his wife, Nikki, would bear his children.

Then one of the women, a nurse named Melody Wuertz, defied Slaughter and bore a daughter by him. When he learned of Wuertz's decision, he coolly plotted her death, recruiting one of his other mistresses, Cecilia Johnson, into his plan.

At Slaughter's order, Johnson supplied him with evidence to help stage Wuertz's murder scene. She collected a set of soiled men's undershorts from a patient on her hospital ward, as well as the patient's head hair, and mailed them to her master. Slaughter in turn planted the hair and soiled underwear in Wuertz's residence, and then shot to death both Melody Wuertz and his one-year-old daughter, Jessica. He then mutilated both bodies to make the crime appear to have been a satanic, ritualistic murder.

The double murder went unpunished for two years until Cecilia Johnson broke down, admitted her role in the plot to a grand jury, and then committed suicide.

All twenty women in Hazelwood's survey shared their remarkably similar hidden hells with him. But each woman's story is uniquely heartbreaking.

Debra Davis, the youngest of six sisters in a working-class family, was born in November, 1957, in Talahoma, Tennessee. She was raised from the age of four in Houston.

"I was very quiet and very shy, a real loner," Debra recalls of her girlhood. "I was sick quite a bit."

Debra was sexually molested at age six by an eighteen-year-old neighbor boy. Although the boy and his family moved away a week later, Debra's world did not grow any sunnier. "I kind of faded into the woodwork," she recalls.

Depression, a common consequence of sexual molestation, became her intermittent burden. She was given to mood swings—"feeling out of control," as Debra describes it—plus bouts with low self-esteem and guilt. Whatever went wrong, Debra tended to blame herself for it.

A pretty girl, just four feet nine inches tall, Debra discovered herself pregnant at age seventeen in 1975, and left home to marry the child's father, her high school sweetheart.

Their first son was born later that year. A little brother came along in 1978, followed in 1981 by Debra's third and last child, a daughter.

In 1983, Debra suffered a major depression, and made a serious attempt at suicide using pills. That same year, life with her husband, Jimmy, fell apart. Too broke to divorce and set up separate households, Debra and Jimmy decided to go on sharing the same residence, if not the same bed.

Then Robert Ben "Dusty" Rhoades came into her life.

She met the thirty-eight-year-old Rhoades, a tall ex-marine, at a Houston nightclub. He was wearing an airline pilot's uniform. They danced a few times that night.

Rhoades reappeared a week later at the same club, this time in western wear. Debra liked his easy, reassuring manner. They danced some more and had a few drinks. She found it all very pleasant. Debra started calling him Bob in the familiar way she might refer to an uncle.

She had no thought of falling in love with him. It didn't even occur to her that she might. To Debra, the relationship simply was a welcome change of pace from the stresses of her split household.

"We talked all the time," she remembers. "He was my best friend. I told him everything."

Bob spoke little of himself.

"He only told me what he wanted me to know, and that was very limited, no details," Debra says.

Rhoades admitted he was a truck driver, not a pilot, which hardly mattered to her. He also told Debra of growing up in Council Bluffs, Iowa, where his father, Ben Rhoades, was arrested twice for molesting Bob's cousins, one boy and one girl. Ben Rhoades later committed suicide.

Bob intimated that he, too, might have been molested as a youngster.

"He had a real rough time of it," says Debra.

Gradually, Rhoades began to win Debra's trust. He contributed paychecks to the beleaguered family exchequer, counseled with Debra, sent her flowers, and took her out to dinner.

Still, they remained just friends in Debra's mind until one night when Bob called from the road.

"I gotta tell you something," he said. "I really love you."

Rhoades's timing was exquisite. The sudden, dramatic profession of love jolted Debra, disconcerted her. But it was not wholly unwelcome.

Debra was vulnerable.

When he returned to Houston, Bob took her out to a romantic candlelit dinner, and then later that night made passionate love to Debra. The moment was spectacular for her, and the comfortable friendship soon deepened into something much more serious.

She was hooked.

"I felt I was the only thing that mattered to him," Debra says. "He did anything and everything I wanted. I felt like I was a queen."

Rhoades even welcomed Debra and her three kids to come live with him. She recalls that they all got along fine.

Nor did Bob's attentions flag.

"When we went out I was like his paper doll," she says. "He dressed me just the way he wanted. I'm a jeans and T-shirt girl. He wanted the garters, the panties, all the nice stuff, things I would not normally wear."

Bob also contributed ideas about the type of makeup Debra wore, and how to apply it.

The first hint of a hidden objective came on a date one night in his car outside a dance joint when he clapped a handcuff on Debra's wrist. The gesture was not overtly hostile, but it unsettled her. Debra told him she was not amused, and he removed it.

Far less ambiguous was the Saturday night that Rhoades took Debra to a swingers' club in Houston. She had assumed when he said swingers he meant swingers in the country music sense of the word. She learned otherwise when a woman at the club slipped her hand up Debra's leg.

"I got mad at him and slapped him and said, 'Let's leave!' Afterward he told me how closed-minded and naive I was."

Rhoades eventually coaxed Debra back to the club and the spouse-swapping scene in Houston, with which he seemed very familiar.

"I remember he got me totally wasted one night and we went to this couple's house. This guy was dragging me into the bedroom and Bob's got the woman in the living room.

"I said, 'I'm leaving. I am not comfortable with this.'

"Well, Bob takes me into the living room where this girl is totally passed out and he's trying to make love to her. I got really upset, and we left."

Eventually, Debra did acquiesce to Rhoades's insistence that they try group sex. "He was my Prince Charming," she explains. "He rescued me. He was going to fix everything, and make it okay. My whole life had been a disaster. I was willing to do this for him."

There were limits, however.

She agreed one Halloween to attend a costume party as a dominatrix, leading Bob, her collared sex slave, on a chain.

"We won first place," she says.

But she vehemently refused any more radical sexual experimentation. Bob wanted to introduce bondage into their sex life, and sadomasochistic devices, such as nipple clamps.

"He'd bring those things home and I'd tell him to get them out of my damn house."

One day, an odd-looking stranger appeared at the front door and announced that he was the love slave Bob had ordered for her. Debra hardly knew how to respond, except to shove her visitor back out the door, telling him there'd been some sort of mistake.

Bob read a lot of books and magazines, much of it violent pornography, which Debra found hidden around the house, along with the enormous phone-sex bills that Rhoades ran up.

She also began to sense that Rhoades connected sex to violence and pain in ways she could not previously have guessed. When she developed sick headaches, he sometimes would lie down with her, just to watch Debra suffer. When she was diagnosed with lupus and hospitalized, her evident pain and discomfort sexually aroused him. Once, Rhoades climbed into Debra's hospital bed to have sex with her.

Her first halfhearted attempt to break free came in late 1986, when Bob was on the road in his rig for three straight months. "I found out that I could make it on my own," she says. "I didn't need any help."

She began to signal her independence during phone calls with Bob, sounding less meek and more self-assured. Not coincidentally, Debra believes, an avalanche of love letters started arriving from Rhoades.

Bob was highly sensitive to her moods when he chose to be.

"It's true there are other things in my life," read one letter he sent from the road, "but for the life of me I can no longer find any value in them without your warmth; the nights are dark without your fire."

"I guess he felt like he was losing me," says Debra. "He came home and we got married in two days, on Valentine's."

She stayed with him for two and half more years.

"His thing was control. It drove me nuts. Even when we had sex he never lost control. He could drink all night and never get drunk. He *never* lost control."

Rhoades spent a year off the road, recovering from bone graft surgery to repair an arm he'd broken in an industrial accident.

Debra remembers him coming out of surgery, groggy from anesthesia, but collected enough to yank the IV tube from his arm.

"I had to sit with him in the hospital to make sure he didn't do it again," she recalls.

"He refused even to take pain medicine, because he was afraid of losing control."

It was a night in October 1989 when Rhoades finally stepped over the line. Bob demanded anal sex. Debra refused him. So he raped her.

"He really lost it," Debra says. "He beat the hell out of me."

"I got up and looked him in the eye and said, 'Are you through?'"

"He said, 'Yeah,' and went in the living room.

"I'd been sleeping with a baseball bat underneath my bed for a while. I went and got it and walked out and hit him in the arm.

"Then I said, 'Now I'm through,' and I packed my bags and left. After I slammed the door, I could hear him breaking things in the house."

Debra believed she'd cut the cord, hardly realizing that in some ways her trials hadn't yet begun.

About a year later there came a telephone call from Arizona. It was Bob. As Debra would learn, her ex-husband had been parked in his rig on the shoulder of Interstate 10 in Casa Grande, south of Phoenix, when a patrol officer happened along. Concerned that the big truck was stopped too close to traffic, the policeman pulled out his flashlight and climbed up to the cab, expecting to find the trucker asleep.

Instead, he discovered Bob Rhoades in the rig's sleeping compartment with a young girl, who was nude and crying uncontrollably. There was a horse bridle strapped to her neck, with a long chain attached to the bit. The hysterical teenager was handcuffed, too, and there were red whip marks on her back. When she saw the policemen, she burst into screams.

This incident was going to cost Rhoades six years or more in an Arizona prison. But much more serious jeopardy prompted his call to Debra. He asked her to rush to his Houston apartment and clean the place up, throw everything out.

The authorities, however, beat her to it. They already had tossed Bob's place, where they discovered evidence suggesting that the incident in Arizona was not isolated.

Far from it.

They found women's underwear, articles of clothing and shoes and jewelry, violent pornography, and a giant dildo. The police recovered a single handcuff, too, an ominous mystery. How had it been snapped from its mate?

Rhoades obviously had been busy. There was a bondage rack in the apartment, too, and nearby a white towel drenched in blood.

Also recovered in Rhoades's apartment were several sets of photographs of a young girl, who turned out to be Regina Kay Walters of Houston. Walters had vanished in February 1990, several months after Debra walked out on Rhoades.

The teenager's desiccated remains were found in late September 1990, hundreds of miles away in an old barn near Greenfield, Illinois. She'd been strangled with a piece of wire twisted around her neck fourteen times, one twist for every year of her life.

Rhoades's photos sorted into several groups. The first pictures were nudes of Regina. She was chained inside his truck cab. Her hair had been cut, and she was handcuffed. There was a choke chain around her neck. He had shaved Regina's pubic hair, too, and pierced her clitoris with a ring, also attached to a chain.

The second group of photos, taken out of doors, depicted the girl, both dressed and undressed, in a variety of poses. Her fingernails and toenails were painted bright red, and she was wearing bright red lipstick, too.

In the final set of pictures, evidently taken in the old barn just before he murdered her, Regina's eyes express exactly the same silent, frozen terror that Harvey Glatman's victims had in his photos more than thirty years before.

Like Glatman, Bob Rhoades scared his victim half to death, then killed her.

He was extradited from Arizona to Illinois, where Rhoades pleaded guilty to the Walters murder. He was given a life sentence in Illinois, and is a suspect in a number of other abduction-murders in other states as well.

In the aftermath of her experience with Rhoades and the disclosure of his crimes, Debra fell into a disastrous third marriage, and attempted suicide for a second time.

"I was having a real rough time with it," she says. "I was feeling lots and lots of guilt. My way of thinking at the time was that if I'd just stayed with Bob, that young girl would not be dead. It would have been better if I had died. I felt that if I loved this evil man, then *I* must be an evil person, too."

As she recovered, she heard from local FBI agent Mark Young that Roy Hazelwood would like to speak with her for a survey he was conducting. Debra agreed to cooperate, and told Hazelwood her story.

"Roy had this big book of questions," she recollects, "and he started asking me questions about childhood and about my family. It seemed that once I started talking to him, I finally could talk about it. No one ever wanted to listen before.

"And the whole time he kept reassuring me that I was a victim, that it wasn't my fault, that I didn't do anything wrong. The more he made me understand, the better I felt.

"It was so important for me to hear that from him. Roy made me realize what really had gone on, that I wasn't a bad person just because I loved a bad man. Roy gave me the courage to take control of my life."

Debra regularly speaks on spousal abuse to audiences in the Houston area. She also counsels physically and sexually abused women. The last thing she heard about Bob Rhoades was that he'd developed colon cancer.

"And when I heard that I just busted up laughing," she remembers. "Mark Young asked me, 'Debbie, are you all right?'

"I said, 'Yeah, I'm fine!'

"Why are you laughing?'

"'Well, after all these years, I couldn't get him, but God did. I hope he has a long, painful time. He deserves it.'"

Michelle Townsend* wishes her tormentor agony in equal measure, but lives in constant dread of him.

Her story begins in the autumn of her senior year in high school, when Michelle, seventeen, was a slender, green-eyed schoolgirl.

Jack* was thirty-five, a Vietnam vet who managed the business where one of her sisters worked.

Michelle at the time was unhappy and confused, still mourning an older sister who'd died in a car accident, and perplexed over her sexual orientation.

"I didn't have much experience with men at all," she explains. "I found him both intriguing and mysterious. He was charismatic and attentive. Four days after we met, he proposed.

"I wasn't in love, but I saw this as a way to escape my problems. I thought I could eventually fall in love with him, and rid myself of feelings for other women."

Self-destructive emotional currents guided her thoughts as well.

"I have problems with boundaries and saying no," she says. "I feel guilty when I say no, like there's something wrong with me."

Approximately six weeks after he proposed, and one day after her eighteenth birthday, Jack and Michelle were married by a justice of the peace.

"He was real attentive at first. I was like on a pedestal. I was his showpiece. He picked out and bought my clothes. He had me change my hair to blond, and grow it out. He had me start wearing makeup. He put me in mostly high heels and boots."

Jack, who was large, over six feet, demanded total power over her.

"He controlled *everything*," she says, "everything that came out of my mouth, every thought I had.

"He said I was like a new book, and he was going to write all the pages."

Jack and Michelle spent a trouble-free first three months of marriage in the old farmhouse he was renting. Then one day she decided to clean and straighten Jack's "War Room."

"It was his personal shrine to two tours of duty in Vietnam," she says. "The walls were covered with certificates, maps, guns, ammunition belts, knives, and photographs of dead Vietnamese soldiers."

As Michelle was cleaning, she came upon a ratty old reddish pink suitcase in a closet. She opened it to find it stuffed with sadomasochistic pornography, most of it depicting women being sexually brutalized. She found Ace bandage rolls and scalpels in the worn suitcase, too. There also were broken arrows. She'd soon learn their use.

Her new husband walked into the room at just that moment—it might not have been a coincidence—and exploded in a rage. Jack roared that Michelle had violated his privacy. He demanded an immediate divorce.

Michelle pleaded that she'd made an innocent mistake, and begged Jack for another chance.

Suddenly he seemed to reconsider, and presented to Michelle what she took to be a nonnegotiable demand. She could redeem herself by helping him act out certain fantasies suggested by the materials Michelle had discovered. Or he'd find another woman who would.

Michelle agreed to cooperate.

"I was told that what I'd discovered was practiced by all married couples, only not talked about," she says. "He told me that all normal people do these things, and he wanted to teach me all about it. He said it was a need of his that must be fulfilled every once in a while so that he could control his temper.

"I wasn't into it, and I didn't understand it, and I couldn't imagine being turned on by what appeared to be hurting one another. I felt there was something wrong with me, however. I didn't want to fail him as his wife.

"He assured me it was only a game, and that no one really gets hurt."

Jack explained what he required in detail. He called his fantasy "the Games," and said they unfolded in five episodes: (1) Capture, (2) Struggle, (3) Torture, (4) the Final Kill, and (5) Postmortem Rape.

The moment he began describing what he wished for her to do, Michelle had the feeling that Jack had done this many times in the past—that "the Games" were really a reenactment.

"I always felt deep in my heart that he'd done this before, that he'd killed women," she says. "I felt I was rehearsing for my own death."

In part one, "Capture," Michelle was to costume herself in loose-fitting garments, such as an old dress, that would be easy for Jack to tear from her body. She was then to assume some sort of preoccupied pose, such as combing her hair, or dancing in a room by herself.

As she did so, Jack would creep up from behind—*always* from behind—and violently grab Michelle, one hand over her mouth, the other around her neck, and pull her face to one side.

Then came "Struggle."

Michelle was to respond in terror, communicating that fright with her eyes as she struggled with him, before falling into unconsciousness. Sometimes she was told to add verisimilitude to "Struggle" by going outside and smudging her face and arms with dirt.

They rehearsed the scene again and again, often working on it all day. Sometimes Jack would have Michelle smoke a joint to relax. Sometimes they'd watch slasher movies together. Michelle was instructed to carefully study the female victims for tips on how she was to behave.

Sometimes "the Games" were played under strobe lights to the accompaniment of sixties-era hard rock. Michelle remembers hearing Iron Butterfly's "In-A-Gadda-Da-Vida" on the stereo again and again and again.

In the midst of "Struggle," Jack tested Michelle for limpness, lifting and dropping her arms and legs and rolling her from side to side. The more lifeless she seemed, the better. Next, she was to regain consciousness and beg for mercy. Often, Jack would demand fellatio at this stage. After she again begged for her life—"Please, don't kill me, master! I'll do anything!" according to the script she memorized—Jack would throttle her. Michelle was to feign asphyxiation, and fall unconscious again.

Then "Torture" began. Jack inserted the broken arrows so it would appear they'd been brutally jammed into her anus. Then he'd carefully photograph her.

On one occasion, he purchased a plastic child's sword and modified the toy using a coat hanger so that it would appear Michelle had been run through with an actual weapon. This Jack photographed as well.

Other times he placed his hunting knife between her legs and ordered Michelle to grasp and hold its blade with her buttock muscles.

After removing it, slowly, Jack ran the sharp blade over Michelle's body, urging her to quiver and jerk as he did so, sometimes heightening the experience for him by smearing her and the weapon with theatrical blood.

Michelle recalls that this routine occasionally was varied with threats to "roast me like a pig." Jack would insert a cold metal rod into her so that she resembled an animal to be roasted on a spit, and he'd talk of how "tender and juicy" she was.

At last came "the Final Kill" and "Postmortem Rape," in which Jack would pretend either to stab or to strangle Michelle to death, usually as she hung nude from pullies over their bed, or from a large metal hook he'd installed in the living-room ceiling. This scene also was rehearsed repeatedly.

Michelle once more was to beg him for her life, wide-eyed with terror. Then she was to expire at his hands, realistically "gurgling, begging, jerking, and quivering," she says.

Although Jack at first said "the Games" would be an infrequent thing, in time they became nearly constant.

The only interruption occurred when Michelle conceived. Although Jack was unhappy about the pregnancy, for the period of time Michelle carried Sarah* he was marginally less abusive. "He pushed me around, but he wasn't as physical, as rough," Michelle recalls.

At about this time, according to Michelle, Jack quit his job, or was fired — he never made it clear to Michelle — and turned to dealing drugs. Once in a while, he allowed her to take jobs, but only temporarily.

He introduced her to group sex with other women.

"We'd find them in bars, truck stops, once in a restaurant," she says. Most of their recruits were young girls, to whom he'd introduce himself as Bill.

Some were brought home. Others were taken to motels. Jack's ultimate fantasy, he told Michelle, was to kill one of the girls. Only one of them.

"He used to try to talk me into picking up a female hitchhiker and having our way with her. He explained that when we were done, we would dispose of her body along the roadway. I always refused."

Jack also mentioned from time to time his interest in providing Michelle with a sex slave, whose tasks would include serving as her surrogate during "the Games."

Like his fantasies of committing joint murder, her husband never acted on this impulse, she says.

Michelle, like Debra, did try to break away. Once, after a particularly brutal beating, she went to the local police, a very small agency, with her story. The officer who interviewed her turned out to be a Vietnam vet, just like Jack. After listening to her story, he advised Michelle to return to her marriage.

She learned to cope with Jack's physical abuse by dissociating, pushing her mind anywhere but the here and now as he whipped her, beat her, kicked her, pulled her hair, and threw her around the room. By this time, six years or more into their marriage, Michelle had been completely broken down. Jack had destroyed her will. She didn't care what happened.

Then came a transforming moment. One day, Jack began punching and slapping Michelle as Sarah, then a toddler of about three, sat on the couch. Michelle could absorb the punishment, but she feared now for her little girl.

Jack turned for a moment, and suddenly, Michelle found herself pointing his loaded shotgun at the back of his head. He was totally unaware of the instant oblivion to which his compliant companion was about to consign him.

But she couldn't pull the trigger.

Michelle lowered the gun, realizing that nothing could drive her to homicide. But seeing her baby in peril nevertheless had galvanized her. She had felt a force, mother love, that was even stronger than her fear of her husband. If Michelle couldn't escape from Jack for her own sake, she could for the child's.

She left in the night, taking with her only Sarah and some clothing. Ironically, Michelle fled to one of the very social contacts Jack had ever allowed her, a loose-knit group of wives of other Vietnam vets. These women saved her.

Mother and daughter spent weeks on the run, moving from house to house, shelter to shelter, sometimes with her enraged husband, who vowed to kill her, very close behind. Finally, Michelle returned to the doubtful security of her parents' house, where Jack need not even approach her to keep Michelle in perpetual fear.

"In the beginning," she writes in her personal history,

> I was so terrified that I couldn't ride sitting up in a car. I just knew he would shoot me. If anyone walked behind me, cold chills went up my spine. I had to see in all directions, and worry that he might be hiding nearby. So many little things through the day kept me in a state of panic: sounds, sights, smells. I kept the drapes pulled, and wouldn't turn my back on an open window. Every man that I saw looked like him. I was very paranoid, and in fear for my life . . . . He lived in my dreams . . . . My eyes would open, but I couldn't wake up. I would run upstairs, turn a light on, and sit. But my feet were still moving beneath my chair.

Michelle suffered depressions as black as Debra's, and was hospitalized four times. Like Debra and the self-destructive third marriage she entered after discovering Bob was a killer, Michelle also plunged into a disastrous relationship with a married woman, which compounded her emotional turmoil.

But also like Debra, Michelle met with Roy Hazelwood and told him her story, the first step toward healing, and reclaiming her life.

Slowly, she put Jack, and most of the rest of her troubles, in the back of her mind. She went to college, where she did well and discovered her first small sense of self-esteem.

Although by no means fully recovered, Michelle is holding tight to her daughter, and to hope.

"I'm learning how to live all over again," she says. "I'm attempting to take control of my life, one step at a time. With determination in my heart, I know I will make it."

TWENTY-ONE ⚡

Ken and Barbie

Karla Homolka is an enigma.

Bright, intensely feminine, and outwardly well adjusted, the twenty-two-year-old veterinarian's assistant stunned Canadian lawmen in 1993 when she confessed her active role in a sadistic husband-and-wife killing spree.

To their neighbors in suburban Port Dalhousie, Ontario, the winsome Karla and her curly-headed husband, Paul Bernardo, seemed like a perky pair of well-scrubbed yuppies sprung straight to the headlines from a Mattel catalog.

They were jokingly known as Ken and Barbie.

Together, their abduction-murder victims included at least two teenage girls, both strangled with an electrical cord, plus Karla's own little sister, Tammy, whom Bernardo had demanded as a Christmas 1990 "gift."

Karla obliged him, providing the Halcion with which Tammy was surreptitiously sedated in her parents' basement on Christmas Eve. Karla also brought from her job at a veterinary clinic a liquid anesthetic for animals, which she poured into a cloth and held over her sleeping sister's mouth. Karla looked on as Bernardo raped the comatose teen, while the rest of the Homolka family slept upstairs.

Later that Christmas Eve, Tammy drowned in her own vomit.

Bernardo's secret videos of the assaults included scenes of Karla performing, at Paul's direction, various sexual acts on the victims, including oral and digital sex on her unconscious sister.

224

To a horror-struck public, it seemed as if some gigantic disconnect had occurred. Karla and Paul were as unlikely-looking a pair of deviant felons as Ted
Bundy had been a serial sex killer.

To Hazelwood, however, Paul Bernardo was a textbook sexual sadist.

Of the thirteen blitz-style sexual assaults he later admitted committing as
the so-called Scarborough Rapist, the first occurred about five months before
he met Karla Homolka. Bernardo at the time was living with his parents in
Scarborough, a blue-collar Toronto suburb of strip malls and car dealerships,
known in tonier sections of the city as Scarberia.

Bernardo was about to graduate with an accounting degree from the local
campus of Toronto University. He also was a small-potato scam artist, a member of a gang who stole and peddled hot computers and other big-ticket con-
sumer items.

At about 1:00 A.M. on May 4, 1987 (coincidentally, Karla's birthday),
the handsome twenty-three-year-old Bernardo followed a twenty-one-year-old
woman from her bus stop to her front lawn in Scarborough. There, Bernardo
threw the girl to the ground and raped her both vaginally and anally. He also
pummeled the victim's face, arms, and breasts.

Nine days later, in similar circumstances in the same community and using
the same bus stop MO, Bernardo attacked a nineteen-year-old female, beating
her with his fists and dragging her into her backyard, where he bound the
young woman's wrists and lashed her by her neck to a fence, using her belt.
This time, he also produced a knife, and said he'd slit her throat if she made a
sound.

As far as is known, Bernardo did not strike out again as the Scarborough Rapist until December 1987. In the meantime—mid-October—he met
seventeen-year-old Karla Homolka, a high school senior from St. Catharines,
Ontario, near Niagara Falls, who was visiting Toronto with a girlfriend.

Bernardo was trolling for girls with a buddy when he encountered Homolka in a Howard Johnson hotel restaurant. Within an hour they were in bed
together in her room, heedless of her girlfriend and his male friend, sitting only
a few uncomfortable feet away.

Later, those who believed that Karla, like Paul, should spend the rest of her
life in prison, argued that a relationship so instantly and intensely sexual suggested to them that the comely schoolgirl from St. Catharines had a wanton
side, and was far less a victim, and much more a willing victimizer, than she appeared.

Karla, who had a reputation among her friends as a free spirit before meeting Bernardo, seemed awestruck by him, they said, overwhelmed, unwilling and unable to resist him. The transformation was abrupt and dramatic and complete.

Among the explanations advanced for her behavior was that Karla was sexually excited by the menace she sensed in Paul.

John Money, a Johns Hopkins University sex researcher, describes such a paraphilia, which he calls "hybristophilia" in his book *Love Maps*.

According to Money, the hybristophile (from the Greek, *hybrizein*, "to commit an outrage against someone," plus *philia*) is sexually aroused by the knowledge her partner has committed a violent act, such as rape or murder or bank robbery.

Money says one of the purest expressions of hybristophilia is actress Faye Dunaway's behavior as outlaw Bonnie Parker in the opening scenes of the movie *Bonnie and Clyde*.

As Dunaway plays her, the libidinous Parker joins the handsome Warren Beatty as Clyde Barrow on a bank robbery and subsequent car chase. Parker is so erotically stimulated by the gunplay and danger that she impulsively gropes Barrow, and attempts to disrobe the surprised outlaw in the front seat of their stolen getaway car.

As Money explains it, the hybristophile's behavior is not compliant, but collusive. "Compliancy means you follow instructions," he says. "Collusion means you fit yourself in to become the other person's counterpart."

By late 1987, Karla was seeing Paul almost every weekend, and spending as much as two hundred dollars a month on telephone calls to him from her parents' house in St. Catharines. Karla decorated her bedroom mirror with Paul's photos, and doodled his name in her high school notebooks. Paul also called Karla nearly daily, sent flowers, and took the schoolgirl to expensive restaurants on weekends.

On December 16, 1987, the Scarborough Rapist attacked his third known victim, a fifteen-year-old girl, at about 8:30 P.M. as she was walking home from her bus stop.

"It was a repetition of the other attacks involving vaginal and anal intercourse while the victim's head was pushed into the ground," wrote retired Canadian appeals judge Patrick T. Galligan in his subsequent review of the case.

> He ran his knife along the victim's back, then grabbed her by the hair and pounded her head against the ground. He forced her to perform fellatio, then to lick his penis and say that she loved it. He

made her wish his penis a Merry Christmas. The assault lasted an hour. . . . Medical examination disclosed a torn hymen, two tears in her anus, plus a number of abrasions on other parts of her body.

Throughout 1988, Bernardo continued his periodic sexual assaults as the Scarborough Rapist, while gradually metamorphosing, according to Karla Homolka's later account, from her caring and attentive lover into a cruel and violent master.

Soon after Christmas 1987, Judge Galligan reports,

> [h]is treatment of her began to change subtly and very gradually. . . . He began telling her what to wear and how to style her hair. He told her where she could go, and where she could not go. He began to encourage her to disassociate herself from her friends because they were immature and stupid. He began encouraging her to drink more and more alcohol.

The judge recounts in some detail how Bernardo began insisting on fellatio, then anal sex, by late spring 1988. Karla obliged him. Also to please Bernardo, she wore a dog collar during sex and would repeat at his direction: "My name is Karla. I am seventeen years old. I am your little cocksucker. I am your little cunt. I am your little slut."

As he progressively reduced the once-lively Homolka into an obedient sex chattel, Bernardo also intensified the violence he inflicted as the Scarborough Rapist. By autumn 1988, he'd committed at least eight rapes. In November, stumped Metro Toronto police detectives sent the Scarborough Rapist file to the BSU, where newly arrived agent Gregg McCrary was assigned to do the profile.

When it was completed, McCrary and then unit chief John Douglas traveled together to Toronto as a team to consult with local authorities. Roy did not directly assist in their analysis, or in the police investigation.

McCrary correctly pegged the UNSUB's age as early twenties, and was accurate as well in surmising that the Scarborough Rapist lived at home with his parents. He also believed that the violence would lead inexorably to murder.

It did, although in retrospect Bernardo's depredations could have been curtailed. After a composite sketch of the Scarborough Rapist was published in Toronto in late May 1990, a female acquaintance tipped the Metro police that Paul Bernardo bore a close resemblance to the drawing.

In November, Bernardo was interviewed by the police, and voluntarily provided samples of saliva, blood, and hair for DNA fingerprinting. Not until February 1993, however, were the police informed by the Toronto Center of Forensic Sciences that Bernardo and the Scarborough Rapist were one and the same person.

In an official review of the Bernardo investigation, Ontario justice Archie Campbell pointed out that had the collected specimens been tested within ninety days as they should have, "it is clear these rapes and murders could have been prevented."

Certainly Leslie Mahaffy and Kristen French might have been spared.

On June 15, 1991, Bernardo abducted the fourteen-year-old Mahaffy and took her to the Port Dalhousie house he shared with Homolka. Both Paul and Karla sexually assaulted the teen. Bernardo then strangled Mahaffy.

The next day in his basement workshop, Paul dismembered Leslie and partially encased her severed remains in molds of Kwik Mix concrete. He then enlisted Karla's assistance in disposing of the weighted parts in Lake Gibson, near the Homolka family residence in St. Catharines.

Canoeists discovered Bernardo's grisly handiwork on Saturday, June 29. On the same day just a few miles away, Paul and Karla were married in the village of Niagara-on-the-Lake.

On Thursday afternoon, April 16, 1992, Ken and Barbie kidnapped fifteen-year-old Kristen French from a church school parking lot, and drove her to their house at 57 Bayview Drive in Port Dalhousie, just as Paul had brought Leslie Mahaffy home.

The girl was kept for four days and subjected to a marathon of physical, sexual, and emotional abuse before Bernardo strangled her. Karla bathed and douched Kristen's broken body. Then she and Paul drove in the night to nearby Burlington, Ontario, where they dumped Kristen along a roadside drainage ditch not far from where Leslie Mahaffy was buried.

"He told me that he decided that he wanted to put the body in Burlington close to where Leslie was buried," Karla later testified, "because he wanted to confuse the police into believing the killer came from Burlington."

Fearing finally for her own life, Karla Homolka broke away from Paul Bernardo in January 1993 and went to the authorities with her story. A plea bargain was arranged. Karla would testify against Paul, and would serve two concurrent twelve-year sentences for manslaughter. One explicitly worded condition of the agreement firmly prohibits Homolka from discussing her case with the media on pain of having the deal revoked.

Paul Bernardo was arrested in February 1993.

Since there was almost nothing to tie Bernardo to the three homicides except for Homolka's testimony, the police realized that their search of the house in Port Dalhousie would be critical to uncovering whatever physical evidence of the murders might remain. And since any items seized in such searches generally must be specified in the warrant itself—or they can't be used in court against the defendant—the local authorities wanted expert advice on the types of physical evidence that sexual sadists might keep around the house.

They again contacted Gregg McCrary, who recommended to the Canadians' attention "The Sexually Sadistic Criminal and His Offenses," a report on the survey of thirty criminal sexual sadists Roy had undertaken with Dr. Dietz and Janet Warren of the Department of Behavioral Medicine and Psychiatry at the University of Virginia.

One of the study's key findings was how meticulously some sexual sadists maintain records.

Of the thirty sadistic offenders included in the survey, more than half kept records of their crimes as a means of reliving them. "Although some have shared these records with crime partners," wrote Hazelwood and his coauthors, "they are otherwise their most secret possessions, intended to be seen by no one else."

Easily the cleverest of the record-keeping sexual sadists Hazelwood studied was Gerard John Schaefer, a onetime Florida policeman suspected of at least twenty-nine gruesome slayings. The Florida newspapers called him the "Sex Beast."

Schaefer wrote that he kidnapped hitchhikers, whom he drove to remote, selected locations deep within the Florida swamps. There, he'd set up a stepladder under a tree limb, and direct the girls and women at gunpoint to mount the ladder, nude. In this humiliating posture, they were told to drink beer and urinate, which Schaefer enjoyed watching.

(Paul Bernardo videotaped his victims as they urinated, too.)

Shaefer placed a noose over the victim's neck, threw the rope over the tree limb, attached the other end to his car's front bumper, put the vehicle in reverse, and backed away slowly until the noose lifted the woman from the ladder and she was hanged to death, asphyxiated by the noose.

He'd have sex with her dead body, then bury her nearby. He'd also repeatedly return to the scene, disinter the victim, and have sex with her corpse.

Schaefer's innovative scheme for capturing the experience, and legally protecting his record of it, began with a visit a psychiatrist. He confided to the doctor he was having horrible fantasies of hanging women and then having sex with them. As Schaefer hoped, the doctor decided it would be therapeutic if he wrote out his fantasies, which he delightedly did in detail.

The resulting documents—later discovered in his possessions—richly recounted Schaefer's deviant adventures, but were covered by doctor-patient confidentiality. They could never be used as legal evidence against him. Schaefer, who went to prison for a noncapital shooting homicide, was murdered there by another inmate.

As detailed as a sexual sadist's audiotaped, videotaped, photographed, and written records are, rarely do they depict his victim's actual murder. Hazelwood believes the omission is conscious. "The act never completely fulfills the fantasy," he says. "If the guy shows the killing, it might spoil the fantasy, and fantasies always are perfect."

In an investigative application of this rule, Hazelwood once was called by a West Coast police department to consult on a highly unusual case.

A businessman had collapsed and died during a convention. Toxicological tests determined his cause of death was an overdose of PCP, or angel dust. A search of the man's hotel room turned up a forty-five-minute audiocassette in which he described in detail the gruesome murder of two unnamed teenage couples. The question police put to Roy Hazelwood was simple: Was this story on the tape fact or fantasy?

"On the tape he says he quickly killed the females in both crimes," says Hazelwood. "So it's obvious his orientation was toward the males. He says, 'When I had Jack on the bed I wish I'd put a plastic sheet beneath his body, because when I cut his throat his blood saturated and ruined the sheets and pillows.'

"With the other male victim it was, 'I wished I'd stabbed him in the kidney, rather than the throat, because he died too quickly.'

"Fantasies are always perfect. This wasn't perfect. I told the police department that in my opinion this was not a fantasy tape."

Although the Toronto police inserted the appropriate language into their search warrant for the Port Dalhousie house—and Karla told them repeatedly of the videotapes Paul had made and how she was sure he'd kept them—repeated searches of the residence failed to find them. As it turned out, Bernardo's lawyer, acting on his client's directions, retrieved the cassettes in early May 1993, and didn't produce them until September 1994.

Between Karla Homolka's January 1993 break with her husband and Bernardo's arrest in February, Inspector Ron Mackay of the RCMP was summoned from Ottawa to Toronto. In a case so obviously outside the bounds of customary criminal behavior, local investigators wanted input from an expert in aberrant offenders.

Mackay had recently received from Hazelwood a draft of his compliant victim survey, which Roy was preparing for publication that spring with coauthors Dietz and Warren.

When he arrived in Toronto and learned why he'd been summoned, Mackay immediately thought of Hazelwood's unpublished study.

"I could see the application in this case," Mackay recalls. "I tracked Roy down in Tennessee and got his permission to share that unpublished paper with the investigation, because of their operational needs, so they could better understand what they were dealing with."

Mackay also recommended the investigation reach out to Peter Collins of Toronto's Clarke Institute of Psychiatry, a consulting forensic psychiatrist to the RCMP's Violent Crimes Analysis Branch, who'd also worked cases with Hazelwood. Collins, too, had just read a draft of "Compliant Victims of the Sexual Sadist," and agreed that the paper would shed light on Karla Homolka's puzzling relationship with Paul Bernardo.

The study would play a pivotal role in persuading the police (and later, prosecutors) that while Karla Homolka was hardly an innocent, her husband was the motive force behind their crimes. "It was thought," says Collins, "after everyone acquainted themselves with Roy's work, that had Homolka never met Bernardo at that Howard Johnson she never would have played a part in any such crimes. She was his perfect victim."

Hazelwood later also informally advised Bernardo's prosecutors via their lead forensic psychiatrist, Steve Hucker. "We were talking one day and he said, 'Guess what?'" Hucker remembers. "'There's another case just like yours that happened in Kentucky, and there's just been a book published about it.'"

Mel Ignatow (pronounced Ig-NAH-toe), aged fifty, was a salesman for an import-export company in Louisville, Kentucky. Pretty, brown-eyed Brenda Sue Shaefer, thirty-six, was his fiancée.

In late September 1988, Shaefer's four-year-old Buick Regal was found abandoned along a stretch of Interstate 64 in St. Matthews, a district within the urban Louisville area.

There was no sign of a struggle in the car, and police discounted the possibility of a random attack. Yet they also could not find the victim, who was presumed dead. Nor could they generate a case against their prime suspect, Ignatow himself.

Then in January 1990, Ignatow's former girlfriend, Mary Ann Shore, came forth to say Brenda Shaefer had been murdered, and that Shore knew all about it because the killing had occurred in Shore's house, and she'd been there when it happened.

After agreeing, as had Karla Homolka, to a reduced charge and limited prison time in exchange for her testimony, Shore told investigators how Ignatow had brought the highly inhibited Shaefer to her house for a "sex therapy" session. As Ignatow alternated with Shore at his 35mm camera, recording each step, Shaefer was made to pose in a series of progressively more demeaning postures, from full-frontal upright to her knees, head bent to the floor.

Then the entire sequence of photos was exactly repeated in the nude.

Shaefer next was tied to the coffee table, where Ignatow raped her anally. Then she was taken to Shore's bed, tied again, and raped again, repeatedly. Ignatow finally killed her with chloroform administered to her mouth with a cloth, just as Karla Homolka, at Paul Bernardo's instruction, had dosed her sister Tammy with the animal anesthetic.

Although Mary Ann Shore bolstered the credibility of her story by leading investigators to Brenda's grave behind her house (which she said Ignatow had dug in advance of Shaefer's "sex therapy"), the photos she and Ignatow took did not surface, and a jury in December of 1991 chose not to believe her testimony.

Ignatow went free.

The next month, local U.S. attorney Alan Sears hit on a new scheme for bringing the killer to justice. Sears couldn't charge Ignatow with murder again, because of the constitutional protection against double jeopardy. But Ignatow earlier had sworn to a federal grand jury that he was innocent of murdering Brenda Shaefer. If a federal jury could be persuaded that he in fact was guilty, then perjury charges might stick.

In January 1992, a three-count federal perjury indictment was handed up against Ignatow.

In March of that year, Roy Hazelwood and BSU colleague Steve Mardigian were invited to Louisville to review the evidence, conduct a tutorial on sexual sadism for the federal prosecutors, and offer both investigative and trial strategies.

They suggested some forty leads that authorities might pursue, especially emphasizing the importance of locating and interviewing Ignatow's previous wife and any girlfriends. Hazelwood believed they would have been forced to submit to the same degradations Shore reported.

Another recommendation was to keep searching for those pictures, because Ignatow surely had them hidden somewhere. Never mind that the house he occupied at the time of the murder had been thoroughly searched, the second time by a team of eleven highly trained search specialists. Hazelwood was adamant.

"Sexual sadists and pedophiles," he told the lawmen, "have their own little ways of hiding things."

Among the more creative at it was Mike DeBardeleben, the Mall Passer, who artfully secreted handguns in the walls of his house by hanging them from twine secured to boards in his attic.

In mid-October 1992, just five days before Ignatow's perjury trial was to commence, Hazelwood's admonition was borne out.

Ignatow by this time had sold his house, and the new owners of Ignatow's prior residence were installing new hallway carpet. As workers took up the old carpet, they discovered beneath it a four-by-ten-inch covered heat duct. Inside, they found a Ziploc bag, taped to the side of the duct with gray duct tape. Within the Ziploc were a ring and diamond bracelet Mel Ignatow had given Brenda Shaefer, a lucky five-dollar gold piece from her father, plus three canisters of undeveloped 35mm film.

An FBI forensic photographer opined that exposed but undeveloped film stored four years in a furnace duct would be destroyed by the heat. Luckily for Ignatow's prosecutors, he was wrong.

"The photos came out perfectly," says Hazelwood. "Plus the duct tape matched that found binding Brenda in her grave. That is why I title this case 'There Is a God.'"

Confronted with the unequivocal evidence against him, Mel Ignatow pleaded guilty and received a ninety-seven-month federal sentence for perjury. He was released on Halloween, 1997, only to be reindicted, again for perjury, and for being a persistent felon by a state grand jury in Louisville.

Paul Bernardo's "own little way of hiding things" was to secrete the six highly incriminating videocassettes of his assaults inside an upstairs bathroom light fixture at the Port Dalhousie residence.

The videos also implicated Karla, who by that time had plea-bargained with the Canadian authorities and already had begun to serve her twelve years, waiting to testify against Bernardo.

With that testimony no longer so vital—the videos were explicit and damning—Karla's plea bargain and relatively mild sentence came under withering public criticism. Even Crown attorney Ray Houlahan, who'd questioned Homolka as his own witness during the Bernardo prosecution, publicly denounced her in his August 1995 closing arguments. Had the videos been found before Homolka's confession, Houlahan told a Toronto jury, Karla would have been charged with murder, as well.

"She implicated herself in first-degree murder as surely as her accomplice," said Houlahan, who described Homolka as "definitely, definitely not a victim."

On one level, the deal was entirely defensible. "The bottom line was that when she came forward they didn't have any evidence against Bernardo," says prosecution psychiatrist Steve Hucker.

"You might look back at it and say, 'Oh shit! Why did we do that?' But they really didn't have anything else to go on at that time."

Retired judge Patrick T. Galligan would conclude as much in his official and exhaustive *Report to the Attorney General of Ontario on Certain Matters Relating to Karla Homolka,* released in March 1996.

Attached as an appendix to the report is "Compliant Victims of the Sexual Sadist," published in April 1993.

"I was very sceptical," wrote Galligan in the report, "about her statements that she was subjected to violence and threats to the point where she was in such fear of him that she would do his bidding, no matter how monstrous, yet she still loved him and would not rid herself of him."

Reading the Hazelwood-Warren-Dietz paper, however, "caused me to have an open mind on this issue, because it documents similar phenomena occurring to other women than Karla Homolka."

Galligan amplified the point in a telephone interview. "I still have made no conclusions about Karla Homolka," he said, "but that paper awakened me to a phenomenon of which I was totally unaware."

Crown psychiatrist Steve Hucker also tried to make sense of Homolka and what she'd done. Was Karla, as Bernardo's attorney's charged in court, every bit as culpable as her husband? Or was there some other dynamic at work, some way of explaining Karla's deadliness as a consequence of Paul's?

After consulting informally by telephone with Hazelwood, and spending twelve hours with Homolka, Hucker made up his mind.

"Basically, I saw her in the same light that I believed Roy would," he says. "There were some anomalies, but I don't dispute the general dynamic. That was there.

"All we were willing to say was that she was more likely to be the accomplice than the initiator. Of course, Bernardo's attorney was trying to show the exact opposite. That she was just as nasty a specimen, and just as capable of killing as he."

Hucker's still not entirely certain he understands Karla Homolka.

"I think she probably fit Hazelwood's idea," he says. "But no one has ever said she was a complete victim in this case. I think everyone has lingering doubts about Karla. Was this just a clever young woman, more clever than all of us? That's part of the enduring enigma."

There are two widely published images of Karla Homolka. One captures her as a luminous bride on her wedding day in June 1991. Sitting next to her smiling husband, Karla seems beatifically content in the photo.

The second picture was taken at St. Catharines General Hospital soon after she'd finally fled Bernardo in early January 1993.

According to records, Karla arrived in the emergency room with most of her body covered with bruises. Her battered legs were too painful for her to move them. There were huge contusions on her head, which the attending physician noted was soft to the touch. Doctors also found a puncture wound on her right thigh, which Homolka said Bernardo had inflicted with a screwdriver.

In the color picture taken that day, Homolka is clad in a hospital gown. She appears exhausted and disheveled. Circling her downcast eyes are huge black circles, known as "raccoon eyes," which are diagnostic of severe blows to the back of the head.

What occurs is a so-called contra coup. The victim's brain is slammed forward by the trauma—in this case a series of smashes from Bernardo's flashlight. As the organ collides violently with the front of the skull it produces raccoon-like circles of dark hemorrhages beneath the tissue surrounding the eyes.

Both images were fresh in Roy Hazelwood's mind as he and Ron Mackay pulled up in front of Kingston's aging stone-and-brick Prison for Women that August Tuesday in 1996. The rain was coming down more steadily now, and a knot of prison employees stood huddled near the front gate, taking a last few drags on their cigarettes before heading inside for work.

After showering that morning, Roy had carefully dressed in a conservative suit, white shirt, quiet tie, and expertly polished shoes, his standard uniform for prison interviews.

While lockups hardly are formal environments, Hazelwood always takes care with his wardrobe on interview trips. "The reason for the suit and tie is simple," he says. "People have an expectation of what an FBI agent should look like. Also—and this is very important—it differentiates you. They are the prisoner, and you are not."

That morning, Hazelwood and Ron Mackay would find Homolka had blurred that distinction. Inmates at the Prison for Women are responsible for their own wardrobes, and wear what they please. For her interview with the investigators, Karla asserted her individuality in an eye-pleasing sundress.

Neither Hazelwood nor Mackay had thought to bring an umbrella. So Roy hoisted his briefcase over his head and ran from the car to the gate, with Mackay chugging along beside him.

Inside the facility, Mackay was relieved of his side arm. He and Hazelwood then were escorted down narrow, high-walled corridors to a small, gray-painted interview room, where Karla soon materialized.

Although Steve Hucker and others had commented to Roy on Karla's exquisite softness, when she entered the interview room in her sundress, he remembers being forcefully struck by how feminine she really was, a trait he'd encountered with other subjects in his compliant victim study.

"I mean, fifties feminine," he says. "They project an aura of helplessness, and it's a weapon in their arsenal. A very effective weapon. You can be thrown off stride by it. You can forget what the person did, what they participated in."

Roy explained to Homolka his project and the seven-section, seventy-four-page, 448-question protocol that he'd brought with him. It was the same thick volume Debra Davis remembered from her long conversation with Hazelwood. Both he and Inspector Mackay would have questions, Roy said.

"I told her that we'd be asking some very, very personal questions. I conduct these interviews very clinically. There's no emotion. No sympathy given. I maintain the same tone of voice no matter what they say to me."

Then the dialogue began.

PROTOCOL QUESTION A-7: *Was she sexually abused as a child?*
No.
A-28: *What was her sexual experience prior to meeting Bernardo?*
One encounter.
A-35: *Had she been arrested prior to meeting him?*
No.
C-17: *Did Bernardo want her to dress in a particular way?*
Yes, as a schoolgirl. Sometimes in her sister Tammy's clothes.

Homolka sat up straight in a hard-backed chair throughout the interview, Hazelwood recalls. "She was very, very proper, and very forthright."

D-3: *Prior to sex, would he routinely ingest drugs or alcohol?*
Yes.
D-5: *Did Bernardo masturbate?*
Yes. Sometimes in the night he would tell Karla to go out into their yard and do a striptease for him. He stroked himself as he watched her.
D-11: *Did he have specific terms he used to describe body parts or sexual acts?*
Yes, Bernardo called his penis "Snuffles."
D-16: *Did he whip her?*
Yes.
D-17: *Did he engage in sexual bondage?*
Yes.
D-18: *Did he use foreign objects during sex?*
Yes. A bottle.
D-28: *Did he window-peep as an adult?*
Yes.

Because Karla's answers were so complete, the interview ran overtime, lasting until 7:30 that night, and continuing the next day. Although Roy told Karla they could stop for a rest whenever she wished, their only break was for lunch.

D-43: *Did he ever ask her to have sex with an animal?*
Yes, his dog. But she refused, telling Bernardo she'd rather be killed.
D-54: *Did he ever ask/force her to ingest urine or feces?*
Yes. Feces.

Although Homolka, like Debra and Michelle and the other interview subjects, was free to refuse any question she wished, she answered every one. In fact, all of the twenty women answered every question Hazelwood put to them.

E-13: *What was his attitude toward his mother?*
He hated her.
E-73: *Did he ever imprison Karla?*

Yes, she was made to spend a winter night in the same unheated root cellar where Bernardo had secreted the dead Leslie Mahaffy before dismembering the girl.

F-59: *Did he have an illegal occupation?*

Yes. Cigarette smuggling.

F-73: *Was he frequently depressed?*

Yes.

By the time the interview ground to an exhausted end the next day at noon, Hazelwood and Inspector Mackay were emotionally spent, which was usual for these encounters.

Karla presented Roy with her personal file of every psychological evaluation she'd ever been put through, plus copies of the famous raccoon-eyes photos. It was all very businesslike.

"She said she was very grateful for the opportunity to participate in the research," Hazelwood recalls, "because it helped her so much to know that other women had been through this.

"Then we thanked her, and talked a little bit about her situation. I said that right now the prison might not be so bad a place to be.

"She agreed."

TWENTY-TWO ✕

You Be the Analyst

At noon on Friday, September 5, 1986, Roy and a group of fellow agents were at lunch in the Academy cafeteria when Alan "Smoky" Burgess, chief of investigative support at the BSU, walked up to their table.

"What are you guys doing?" the boss asked.

"Being experienced FBI agents, and knowing it was a Friday, we asked him why he wanted to know," Hazelwood recalls.

The boss did not mince words. Burgess told the group that a young typist employed in the Bureau's San Antonio office had been raped and murdered in her apartment the previous night by an unknown intruder. FBI director William Webster wanted profilers flown to San Antonio to join in the search for Donna Lynn Vetter's killer.

The agents balked, arguing to Burgess that proper profiling required an autopsy, crime scene photos, and other forensic evidence for them to review. This kill was too fresh for the BSU.

"You didn't understand me," Burgess explained calmly. "I said the director said you *will* fly down there."

Within hours, Roy and fellow agent Jim Wright were aboard a helicopter bound from Quantico for Andrews Air Force Base near Washington. There they transferred to Judge Webster's Learjet and flew directly to San Antonio. They arrived at Donna Lynn Vetter's apartment by 5:00 P.M. Texas time.

Their instructions were to complete the UNSUB's profile overnight for presentation at 9:00 A.M. Saturday. One hundred or so investigators assigned to hunt for the killer would be gathered to benefit from their insights.

Roy knew this meeting could turn out to be the law enforcement equivalent of a Monday night audience at the end of the pier. A profiler can say little of value about an UNSUB unless he leaves *behavioral* evidence to be read and interpreted, and so far he and Wright had no idea what they'd find inside Donna Vetter's apartment.

The worst case would be a blank slate, something like a convenience-store robbery-murder, where the criminal leaves behind nothing but an empty cash drawer, a dead clerk, and perhaps a fuzzy black-and-white image on the store's security video.

"There's no interaction there," Roy explains. "No sexual assault. It is simply a cold, calculated, intentional murder."

Agencies nevertheless still submit such crimes for analysis.

A sheriff once contacted Hazelwood with a special request. "I would appreciate some priority service on a case we have here," said the lawman. "I'd like to send you the photographs."

A few days later, Roy received twenty-eight full-color eight-by-ten photos of the sheriff's battered car. Roy glanced through the photos, scene after scene of dents and smashed glass.

He reached for his phone and dialed up the sheriff.

"Sheriff," he said, "somebody's really pissed at you."

End of profile.

The Vetter murder scene, to Ray's relief, told a detailed story. It remains vivid in Roy's recollection for two reasons.

As he and Jim Wright stepped past the yellow police tape into the sealed-off apartment, the agents saw an enormous bloodstain where Donna Vetter had lain in her living-room rug. It was a detailed crimson impression of the dead woman; not just a vaguely suggestive blotch, but plain as a full-size photographic negative, done in her blood.

"It was like the Shroud of Turin," Roy recalls. "I've never ever seen anything like it."

Moments later, Hazelwood was struck with a sudden presentiment.

"Jim, a black guy did this," Roy said to Wright.

"You can't say that," the other agent replied. "You just got here."

Roy had made what is known to mental health workers as a threshold diagnosis. He could not say why he thought the UNSUB was black. He didn't know, and that annoyed him. A strict empiricist, Hazelwood does not believe in intuition.

When he returned to Quantico he thought perhaps Judd Ray, a black agent who had been with the Atlanta police before joining the FBI, could shed some light on the matter.

He couldn't.

Hazelwood showed Ray the Vetter crime-scene photos.

"Give me the race," he asked.

"Black," Ray answered without hesitation.

"How do you know that?"

Judd Ray shrugged. "You can just tell," he said. Ray was no better able than Hazelwood to articulate his certainty.

Donna Lynn Vetter's killer did leave a rich array of behavioral evidence behind him. In fact, as the Vetter investigation unfolded, her murder emerged as a classic instance of the applicability of behavioral analysis to criminal investigation. It also offered a broad range of features rarely seen all together in a single case, everything from clues that fell together under simple deductive reasoning to the development of an investigative strategy that dramatically narrowed and focused the hunt for Vetter's killer.

Today, when Hazelwood lectures on profiling to police and other professional audiences, he uses Donna Vetter's rape-murder as a case study and workshop problem for his students to analyze.

Readers who themselves are now familiar with some of profiling's rudiments are invited to draw their own step-by-step behavioral portrait of the UNSUB, as well.

Here are the facts.

Jerome and Virginia Vetter's daughter, Donna Lynn, twenty-four, was a 1982 high school honor graduate from New Braunfels, Texas, a small German American community and popular tourist destination a few miles northeast of San Antonio.

In February 1986, Donna moved to San Antonio, Texas's third-largest city, to be closer to her typist's job at the FBI office. Five nine and 165 pounds, Vetter was described by friends and family as a frugal, shy, naive, and deeply religious young woman with no sexual history, and almost no social life at all.

Her two passions were sewing and bubble gum.

She lived alone in a one-bedroom first-floor apartment fronting a heavily traveled walkway in an apartment complex located in a high-crime area of northeast San Antonio. The local population was 70 percent Hispanic, 20 percent black, and 10 percent white.

Vetter was anything but reckless in her views or habits. Yet perhaps because of her naïveté, she was not as cautious about her personal safety as prudence dictated.

Steve Harris, a security guard at the complex, later said that Donna almost always came home from work alone in the evening, and often spent her nights sewing. Despite his frequent admonitions, she would open her windows and curtains, offering any passerby a clear view of her as she worked.

Donna told Harris she disliked air-conditioning.

One other piece of victimology that would figure in the profile was her father's advice that Donna would resist wildly if any man attempted to hurt her. He advised that Donna would "fight to the death to defend her virginity."

Steve Harris last saw Donna Vetter alive as he walked past her apartment at 9:20 the previous evening. Her curtains were open.

The security officer returned to Vetter's apartment at 11:20, responding to a report that a screen was missing from her front window.

It was. Donna's curtains were drawn, as well, and her front door was ajar.

Harris pushed the door open, and immediately saw the lifeless woman, supine on the living-room rug. Her clothing had been ripped from her body.

"Her eyes were swollen shut," Harris later testified in court. "There were bruise marks on her face. She seemed covered in blood."

Besides the facial battering, Vetter was subjected to a furious knife assault. She had sustained defensive knife wounds to both hands, four superficial stab wounds in her chest, defense wounds to her left thigh, and two deep stab wounds to her chest.

She had been mortally wounded, her lungs filling with blood, when her attacker finally stopped stabbing her and violently raped the dying woman.

A schematic drawing of the crime scene is shown on the following page.

The killer climbed through the window by the chair shown at bottom, leaving telltale fingerprints as he did so. He also knocked over a potted plant, and then set it straight.

The telephone, shown at right, was unplugged from the wall.

Vetter's body was discovered as shown. Her assailant had dragged her by her knees onto the living-room rug—where she had been raped—from the kitchen, where the floor was slick with her blood. It was evident the shoeless UNSUB had slipped and lost his footing in the blood as he tried to move her. He left footprints in the kitchen.

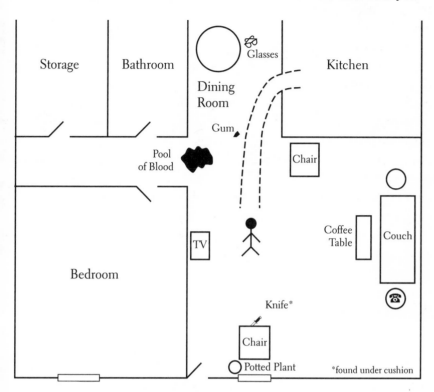

A fresh head of lettuce lay on the kitchen shelf. On the floor, investigators found a jar of salad dressing. On the kitchen wall were Vetter's carefully organized weeklong menus for breakfast, lunch, and dinner.

Lunch on Friday, had Donna Lynn Vetter lived to prepare it, was going to be a salad.

There was another small pool of her blood at the intersection of the apartment hallway and her living room.

A wad of chewing gum was found in the living room, as shown.

Her glasses were recovered from the floor near the dining-room table.

The bedroom was undisturbed, as was the storage area and the rest of the hallway. In the unflushed bathroom bowl, investigators discovered urine, but no tissue paper. The seat was down.

A butcher knife belonging to the victim was found beneath the cushion of the chair next to the front door.

Hazelwood and Wright's first step was to determine if this UNSUB was organized or disorganized. If the reader is analyzing, too, you may wish to cover

THE EVIL THAT MEN DO

the italicized text below as you consider which type of offender you believe attacked Donna Vetter, and why.

The bulk of the evidence suggests this was a spontaneous murder. The killer apparently had come completely unequipped for the crime, and committed the murder on an impulse. His means of entry was unsophisticated, and his failure to replace the window screen after gaining entrance reflected both his lack of planning and, probably, low-average level of intelligence.

He'd neglected even to wear shoes, meaning the killer quite literally had arrived on foot. He probably lived nearby, a conclusion buttressed by the fact he did not pause to wash up after the assault, but simply left as he came.

He used a weapon of opportunity (the kitchen knife) and made only a cursory effort to conceal it under a chair cushion as he left.

The UNSUB had trouble gaining control of his victim. To judge from her multiple defensive wounds, Donna Vetter put up a determined fight, as her father indicated she would.

This intruder was disorganized.

The second question was motive. Did the killer enter Vetter's apartment that night intent only on robbery or burglary? Was his primary motive murder? Or had this UNSUB originally come to rape?

Again, you may wish cover the italicized text below as you consider the evidence.

Theft was not on his mind. After killing Vetter and raping her, he left without taking anything from the apartment.

Had the UNSUB come with the intent to kill Vetter, rather than to rape her, he likely would have brought a weapon. Also, unplugging her telephone was inconsistent with a homicide motive. If he intended to kill her, whether the telephone worked or not would have been immaterial.

Finally, his behavior indicates he had no experience with killing.

So, if he was a rapist who murdered, and not a murderer who raped, which of Roy's four major classifications of stranger rapists did he fit?

Clearly he was not a power reassurance rapist, nor an anger excitation rapist. Both are highly ritualistic offenders, an element entirely missing from this crime.

Ripping Donna Vetter's clothing from her body was typical of a power as-sertive rapist. However, his impulsivity and use of excessive force suggested an anger retaliatory rapist. Also, Donna Vetter's facial battering attested to the blitz approach, commonly seen among anger retaliatory rapists.

He was an anger retaliatory rapist.

Now here's a list of questions that readers at this stage may begin to con-sider. Hazelwood and Wright's responses immediately follow the list.

1. What is his approximate age?
2. Is he single or married?
3. Has he ever served in the military?
4. How bright is he?
5. What is his level of education?
6. Does he work? If so, at what?
7. Does he have a criminal history, and what would it include?
8. Does he have a sense of humor?
9. What is his self-image?
10. How does he typically dress?
11. Is he athletic?
12. What is his attitude toward women?
13. Did he know Donna Vetter?
14. Does he own a car?
15. Is he a substance abuser?

Judging from his low level of sophistication, the type of rapist he apparently was, and his victim's age, Jim Wright believed the killer was twenty-two; Roy said twenty-six.

Both thought he was single, and probably lived with an older female relative.

Neither considered it likely the UNSUB had served in the military. He was too wild and violent, too quick to anger, too volatile to have survived boot camp. He would not do well around authority figures.

Both believed him of average intelligence at best. This was a high-risk crime for the perpetrator, and the means of entry reflected a lack of sophistication.

Both agents also thought it unlikely the UNSUB had made it through high school, and thought him a poor candidate to hold down any sort of job for long. Once again, he was too volatile, and would not take direction well.

He very likely had a criminal history, they agreed. He was apt to have an ar-

rest record for rape, attempted rape, assault and battery, and also breaking and entering.

He would have no sense of humor, certainly not when a joke was made at his expense. This UNSUB had a macho self-image, an attitude reflected in his cloth- ing, his choice of alcoholic beverage, and his attitude toward women, which would be derisive, hostile, and abusive. He probably used abusive language in their presence, as well.

He did not know Donna Vetter; otherwise he would not have entered her apartment through the window. But he was familiar enough with the apartment complex to be comfortable taking the risks that he did. He very likely had peeped Donna Vetter in the past, or otherwise had noticed her at home alone — her win- dows open.

He did not own a car. If he did, he'd drive farther away from home to commit his crimes.

And he did use alcohol and drugs, but did not abuse them. If he had an ex- pensive drug habit, he probably would have stolen something of value to help support it.

Finally, it is possible to attempt a re-creation of the crime itself, a recon- struction that takes into account all the known facts and physical evidence, while also consistent with the profile.

Hazelwood and Wright believed that when the intruder came through the window, Donna Vetter was in the bathroom. She heard him, and, consistent with what her father told police, she rose and rushed immediately to confront him, not concerned in this emergency with either wiping herself or flushing.

Victim and predator confronted one another where the hallway intersected the living room. There he struck her with several quick punches to the face. Her gum flew forward into the living room. Her glasses sailed next to the dining-room table.

As she collapsed to the floor, bleeding, the UNSUB returned to the window, pulled the drapes, and stopped to disconnect the telephone from the wall, leav- ing a partial palm print on the telephone table as he did. So far, he was being de- liberate, if careless, preparing to commit his intended crime, sexual assault.

Donna Vetter had a different script in mind.

In whatever few moments he spent in the living room, she jumped up and ran into the kitchen. Vetter knew her big knife lay on the counter, next to the lettuce and salad dressing for her Friday lunch.

She'd be ready for him.

The killer in all likelihood was not prepared to find his intended victim armed and ready to defend herself. Primarily motivated by anger toward women in the first place, he'd respond in rage to this challenge.

He took the knife from her and attacked. There was a ferocious, though probably brief, struggle.

First she tried to fend him off with her hands, and received several wounds to one hand. Then she tried to back away, sustaining four shallow chest wounds as he lunged at her with the blade.

Finally, Vetter fell to the floor of the kitchen. The stab wound to her leg probably occurred while she was on her back, kicking up at him as he tried to subdue her. The two deep stab wounds to her chest, his final blows, likely were inflicted as he straddled her on the kitchen floor, determined to stop Vetter's struggles.

Once she did go limp, he cut off her clothes, dragged her into the living room, slipping in her blood as he did so, and violently raped her as she expired. When he was through, he got up, slipped the bloody knife under the chair cushion, and walked out the front door, not even bothering to pull it completely shut.

After presenting their profile to the assembled investigators that Saturday morning, Hazelwood and Wright suggested he'd probably committed similar rapes in the past. Perhaps a linkage analysis could establish his pattern.

A careful review of all rapes and attempted rapes that had occurred within one mile of Donna Vetter's apartment in the previous year yielded thirty-two such incidents.

Hazelwood and Wright looked at the behavior in each crime, and selected out seventeen assaults in which a single white female was attacked in her apartment by a black male who punched her three or four times in the face, raped her, and then left. One such assault occurred September 15, just eleven days after the Vetter slaying. In another of the cases, coincidentally, a potted plant was knocked over and then set upright by the intruder.

On September 19, the police implemented a second investigative strategy at the FBI agents' suggestion. Hoping to convince anyone close to the UNSUB that the killer probably was a danger to them as well, Hazelwood and Wright advised the San Antonio police they might try releasing selected portions of the profile to the local press, emphasizing the UNSUB's violent nature.

"FBI: Secretary's killer has 'explosive temper'" read the headline over reporter Bill Hendricks's Saturday, September 20, story in the *San Antonio Express-News.*

"The rapist-killer of a young secretary at the FBI's San Antonio headquarters has an 'explosive temper,' and might vent his rage on anyone who suspected his guilt in the stabbing," wrote Hendricks.

> No suspect has been identified but police and FBI investigators say they are hoping their profile reveals new information in the case.
>
> Agents who drafted that profile believe the killer is in his early to mid-20s.
>
> "He works at convincing others that he is a macho male, and this will be reflected in his dress and lifestyle," the agents concluded, adding, "He has a poor work record and experiences difficulty with co-workers and/or bosses."
>
> The profile concluded, "Based upon the type of crime involved, we have reason to believe that someone close to the killer who may suspect his involvement in this crime may, in fact, be in danger."

One key conjecture that pointedly was not released to the media was Roy's belief that the UNSUB was black. This was standard operating procedure. If Roy was wrong in his conjecture, he did not want a reader with a strong reason to suspect a white male to ignore their misgivings in the belief the killer had to be African-American.

Hazelwood recalls that within hours of Bill Hendricks's story hitting the streets, the police received the payoff call.

"My partner killed the FBI woman," the caller said.

He explained that he and twenty-two-year-old Karl Hammond, a black male, robbed liquor stores together. Since the Vetter homicide, the caller continued, Hammond had turned trigger-happy, shooting store employees "for no reason," the caller reported, "and it's scaring the hell out of me."

The caller further reported Hammond had confessed Vetter's murder, claiming to have found her Bureau ID card while rifling Vetter's purse. "So I decided to murder her because she was an FBI bitch," the caller quoted Hammond.

Hazelwood knew that part of Hammond's story was a lie. FBI file clerks don't carry Bureau ID: The killer had learned of her employment in the papers.

The rest of the caller's information quickly was borne out by investigation.

Roy and Jim Wright happily congratulated each other on their strategem's success, until they learned the caller hadn't seen the paper at all. He was illiterate, and only contacted the police because he genuinely feared Hammond, who was arrested at his older sister's house, a short walk from Donna Lynn Vetter's apartment, on Wednesday evening, September 24, less than three weeks after the murder.

Hammond was identified by all seventeen rape victims, and was tied to the Vetter murder by DNA evidence, as well as his footprint in the kitchen, his fingerprint on the murder weapon, and a palm print taken from a telephone table.

How accurate was the FBI profile?

Roy had believed the UNSUB was twenty-six. Wright said twenty-two. Wright was right. The two also were correct that the killer was single, had never been in the military, and lived with an older sister. Hammond dropped out of high school in the ninth grade. His appeals attorneys would later argue he was mentally retarded.

One of Hammond's relatives told reporters that he worked intermittently as a construction laborer.

His rap sheet began when he was seventeen, in 1981, with a no-contest plea to a rape charge. Within three days of entering the plea, Hammond was arrested for burglary. In February 1982 he was sentenced to concurrent six- and eight-year prison terms on the two offenses.

He was paroled from prison in August 1985, a month after his twenty-first birthday, under a controversial mandatory release program designed to relieve prison crowding in Texas.

At the time he killed Donna Vetter he had been charged with armed robbery in connection with the liquor-store stickups, and was awaiting further armed robbery charges.

As far as can be determined, Hammond had never met Donna Vetter (and never confessed to her homicide). He was not known to be doing drugs in September 1986.

His capital murder trial lasted for three days in late March 1997.

On Monday the thirtieth, the jury required two hours to return a verdict of guilty. That night, after an hour-long meeting with his attorney, Hammond burst through an unlocked door in the county jail's second-floor visitation area, leaped over a counter, and raced barefoot down the staircase to freedom.

As an estimated thousand officers fanned out across San Antonio in search of him, the fugitive found a telephone and called the local FBI office to warn he would "off" an FBI agent, and a San Antonio policeman, before he was caught.

Nothing quite so dramatic occurred.

Tuesday evening, an off-duty San Antonio policeman spied the fugitive killer sneaking out a hospital door and into a Dumpster, where he was arrested. Roy later was told Hammond had been dallying upstairs with a nurse.

The following day in the interrupted penalty phase of his trial, the jury considered together for just ninety minutes before voting Hammond death by lethal injection. Donna Lynn Vetter's mother, Virginia, endorsed the decision, but told reporters the method of execution was too humane.

"I think he should be beaten to death slowly and left on the street for people to come by and kick him," Mrs. Vetter said as she left the courthouse. "He needs to feel what she felt."

Eight years later, on the evening of June 20, 1995, Karl Hammond ate his last meal: a double cheeseburger, French fries, chocolate milk, and dessert. Just after midnight, he was strapped onto a gurney to receive his sentence.

"I just wanna say I know it's so hard for people to lose someone they love so much," Hammond spoke into a microphone above him. "I think it's best for me to just say nothing at all."

Then the chemicals overtook him. The thirty-year-old killer snored loudly for a moment, and was dead.

AUTHOR'S NOTE AND ACKNOWLEDGMENTS

To undertake any serious book is an act both of hope and hubris — an invitation to make God laugh.

The Evil That Men Do was conceived in just that ambitious spirit, and gestated over several momentous years in my personal life; a period during which my wife, Susan, and I made a wrenching relocation from New York City to Texas; our wonderful twins, Alexandra and Spencer, made their surprise debut; and I toiled disconsolately at a woeful community daily covering grass fires and jackknifed 18-wheelers.

Evil was written mornings, evenings, and on weekends, time stolen from Susan and the twins, who all were patient if not wholly sympathetic with, or understanding of, Dad's obsessive project. I apologize once again to all three for those long absences at the computer.

I also wish to thank five colleagues for their generous assistance in helping research the book. They are Kay Melcher at the *Birmingham* (Alabama) *Post-Herald*; Ken Dilanian at the *Philadelphia Inquirer*; Jan Fennell at the *Fort Worth Star-Telegram*; Mike Dunne of the *Baton Rouge Advocate*; and Angie Mitchell of the *Walker County* (Georgia) *Messenger*.

Finally, a nod of appreciation to Charles Spicer, my editor at St. Martin's, for sticking by the project, and a warm embrace to Elizabeth Kaplan, my new agent, who is also the proud parent of twins.

SOURCES

Bruni, Frank. "Arguments and Tirades As Brawley Case Opens." *The New York Times*, December 4, 1997, p. A-23.

Burnside, Scott, and Alan Cairns. *Deadly Innocence*. New York: Warner Books, 1995.

Busch, Alva. *Roadside Prey*. New York: Kensington, 1996.

Callahan, Bill. "Beach Rapist Gets 96 years." *San Diego Union-Tribune*, May 26, 1995, p. A-1.

Dettlinger, Chet, and Jeff Prugh. *The List*. Atlanta: Philmay Enterprises, 1983.

Douglas, John, and Mark Olshaker. *Mind Hunter*. New York: Scribner's, 1995.

"Expert: Apartment Prints Match Suspect." *San Antonio Express-News*, March 24, 1987.

Foy, Nicole. "Woman's Killer Resigned As He Goes to Death." *San Antonio Express-News*, June 22, 1995, p. 1A.

Ganey, Terry. *St. Joseph's Children*. New York: Carol Publishing Group, 1989.

Groth, A. Nicholas. *Men Who Rape*. New York: Plenum, 1979.

Hill, Bob. *Double Jeopardy*. New York: William Morrow, 1995.

Jeffers, H. Paul. *Who Killed Precious?* New York: St. Martin's, 1992.

Lancaster, John. "Admiral Besmirched by Tailhook Scandal to Retire 2 Months Early." *Washington Post*, February 16, 1994, p. A-5.

McGuire, Christine, and Carla Norton. *Perfect Victim*. New York: Dell, 1989.

Newton, Michael: *Hunting Humans*. Port Townsend, Wash.: Loompanics, 1990.

Ressler, Robert K., and Tom Shachtman: *Whoever Fights Monsters*. New York: St. Martin's, 1992.

Report of the Grand Jury of the Supreme Court, State of New York, County of Dutchess. 1988.

Russakoff, Dale. "Decade After Tawana Brawley Episode, Trial Looms." *The Washington Post*, November 17, 1997, p. A1.

Scales, Joe. "Agents Followed Suspect for Days." *Baton Rouge Advocate*, December 1, 1981.

Scott, Steve. "Suspect in 12 Deaths Faces Trial; Defense Says Two Others Are Linked to Slayings." *Dallas Morning News*, March 17, 1996, p. 37A.

Von Krafft-Ebing, Richard. *Psychopathia Sexualis: A Medico-Forensic Study.* New York: Stein and Day, 1965.

SELECTED HAZELWOOD BIBLIOGRAPHY

ARTICLES

Hazelwood, Robert R., and John E. Douglas. "The Lust Murderer." *FBI Law Enforcement Bulletin*, April 1980.

Hazelwood, Robert R., Ann W. Burgess, and Park Elliott Dietz. "The Investigation of Autoerotic Fatalities." *Journal of Police Science and Administration*, vol. 9, no. 4 (1981).

Dietz, Park Elliott, and Robert R. Hazelwood. "Atypical Autoerotic Fatalities." *Medicine and Law*, vol. 1 (1982), pp. 307–319.

Hazelwood, Robert R., Park Elliott Dietz, and Ann W. Burgess. "Sexual Fatalities: Behavioral Reconstruction in Equivocal Cases." *Journal of Forensic Science*, vol. 27, no. 4 (October 1982).

Hazelwood, Robert R. "The Behavioral-Oriented Interview of Rape Victims: The Key to Profiling." *FBI Law Enforcement Bulletin*, September 1983.

LeDoux, John, and Robert R. Hazelwood. "Police Attitudes and Beliefs Toward Rape." *Journal of Police Science and Administration*, vol. 13, no. 3 (September 1985).

Dietz, Park Elliott, Harry Bruce, and Robert R. Hazelwood. "Detective Magazines: Pornography for Sexual Sadists?" *Journal of Forensic Science*, vol. 3, no. 1 (January 1986).

Hazelwood, Robert R., and Joseph A. Harpold. "Rape: The Dangers of Providing Confrontational Advice." *FBI Law Enforcement Bulletin*, June 1986.

Hazelwood, Robert R., and Ann W. Burgess. "An Introduction to the Serial Rapist: Research by the FBI." *FBI Law Enforcement Bulletin*, September 1987.

Burgess, Ann W., Robert R. Hazelwood, et al. "Serial Rapists and Their Victims: Reenactment and Repetition." *Current Perspectives in Human Sexual Aggression in Annals, New York Academy of Sciences*, vol. 528 (1987), pp. 277–295.

Hazelwood, Robert R., and Kenneth V. Lanning. "The Maligned Investigator of Criminal Sexuality." *FBI Law Enforcement Bulletin*, September 1988.

Hazelwood, Robert R., and Janet I. Warren. "The Serial Rapist: His Characteristic and Victims." Parts I and II. *FBI Law Enforcement Bulletin*, January and February 1989.

Hazelwood, Robert R., Roland Reboussin, and Janet I. Warren. "Correlates of Increased Aggression and the Relationship of Offender Pleasure to Victim Resistance." *Journal of Interpersonal Violence*, vol. 4, no. 1 (March 1989).

Dietz, Park Elliott, Robert R. Hazelwood, and Janet I. Warren. "The Sexually Sadistic Criminal and His Offenses." *The Bulletin of the American Academy of Psychiatry and the Law*, vol. 18, no. 2 (1990), pp. 163–178.

Hazelwood, Robert R., and Janet I. Warren. "The Criminal Behavior of the Serial Rapist." *FBI Law Enforcement Bulletin*, February 1990.

Hazelwood, Robert R., Park Elliott Dietz, and Janet I. Warren. "The Criminal Sexual Sadist." *FBI Law Enforcement Bulletin*, February 1992.

McCormack, Arlene, Frances E. Rokus, Robert R. Hazelwood, and Ann W. Burgess. "An Exploration of Incest in the Childhood Development of Serial Rapists." *Journal of Family Violence*, vol. 7, no. 3 (1992).

Hazelwood, Robert R., Janet I. Warren, and Park E. Dietz. "Compliant Victims of Sexual Sadists." *Australian Family Physician*, vol. 22, no. 4 (April. 1993).

Byard, Robert W., Stephen J. Hucker, and Robert R. Hazelwood. "Fatal and Near Fatal Autoerotic Asphyxial Episodes in Women." *The American Journal of Forensic Medicine and Pathology*, vol. 14, no. 1 (1993), pp. 70–73.

Ault, R. L., Robert R. Hazelwood, and R. Reboussin. "Epistemological Status of Equivocal Death Analysis." *American Psychologist*, January 1994.

Hazelwood, Robert R., and Carlos Schippers. "Behavioral Support in Criminal Cases: An Aide in Sexual Assault Cases." *Modus*, no. 5 (November 1995), pp 4–7.

Books

Hazelwood, Robert R., Park Elliott Dietz, and Ann Wolbert Burgess: *Autoerotic Fatalities*. Lexington, Mass.: Lexington Books, 1983.

Hazelwood, Robert R., and Ann Wolbert Burgess, eds. *Practical Aspects of Rape Investigation: A Multidisciplinary Approach*, 2d ed. Boca Raton, Fla.: CRC Press, 1995.

INDEX ✗

Aarau (Switzerland) child murders, 178–87
  Rebecca Bieri, 181–82, 187
  Benjamin Egli, 181–82
  Fabienne Imhof, 183–84, 187
  Loredana Mancini, 181, 187
  Sarah Oberson, 182–83, 186
  Peter Roth, 182, 186
  Ruth Steinmann, 180–81, 186, 187
  Daniel Suter, 182
  Edith Trittenbass, 183, 186
  Christian Widmer, 183
  See also Ferrari, Werner
Abel, Gene, 114
Abrams, Bob, 203, 207
Academy Group, 27
"Analysis of Materials Seized from James
  Mitchell DeBardeleben, An," 9–10
Armed Forces Institute of Pathology
  (AFIP), 38, 41–43
Aspin, Les, 160
Atlanta Child Murders (Wayne Williams),
  5, 26, 91–97
Ault, Dick, 27, 44, 149, 151–59
autoerotic asphyxia, 18, 44–47
  bondage and, 55
  fetishism and, 56
  Marquis de Sade and, 52
  See also hypoxia
Autoerotic Fatalities (Dietz/Hazelwood),
  52–54
Aynesworth, Hugh, 1

Baker, Ken, 27
Banda, Antonio, 36
Bass, John C., 167, 168
Behavioral Science Unit (BSU), 4–5, 6, 8,
  27, 43, 44, 85, 155
    VICAP (Violent Criminal Apprehen-
     sion Program), 155
Bell, Yusef, 91–92
Berkowitz, David (Son of Sam), 27, 43

Berman, Alan L., 157
Bernardo, Paul (Scarborough Rapist),
  224–38
Bernstein, Lester, 154
Bianchi, Kenneth (Hillside Strangler), 4
Bieri, Rebecca, 181–82, 187
Bogard, Kenneth (Pacific Beach Rapist),
  188–97
Bogard, Kenneth (victims)
  Kim Caldwell, 191–92, 197
  "Dana Holly," 189–90, 195, 196
  "Molly Iverson," 188–89, 195
  "Tina Mitchell," 191, 195
  "Jane Philips," 193, 194, 195, 196
  "Tammy Watkins," 190, 195
  "Marsha Wilson," 190–91, 195, 196
Borer, Leon, 178, 179
Brawley, Glenda, 200
Brawley, Tawana (Maryam Muhammad),
  11, 149, 198–208
Broderick, Betty, 48
Brooks, Pierce, 20
Brown, Lee, 92
Browning, Cliff, 79
Bruno, Gloria, 130–33
Brussel, James, 90
Bundy, Ted, 1–3, 16, 22, 23, 26, 27, 69–70
Buono, Angelo (Hillside Strangler), 4
Burgess, Alan "Smoky," 239
Burgess, Ann Wolbert, 7, 44, 52–53, 57
Buxton, Geneva, 198–99, 204
Buxton, Todd, 198

Caldwell, Kim, 191–92, 197
cannibalism, 48
"Carla" ("Andrew McIntyre death"), 138,
  139–40
Castillo, Jose, 34, 37
Cater, Nathaniel, 95
Chaves, Jesse, 34
Chaves, Juan "Johnny," 22, 27, 33–37